LAW, ETHICS, ANI

LAW, ETHICS, AND MEDICINE

Studies in Medical Law

By

P. D. G. SKEGG

CLARENDON PRESS · OXFORD

Oxford University Press, Walton Street, Oxford OX2 6DP

Oxford New York Toronto
Delhi Bombay Calcutta Madras Karachi
Petaling Jaya Singapore Hong Kong Tokyo
Nairobi Dar es Salaam Cape Town
Melbourne Auckland

and associated companies in
Berlin Ibadan

Oxford is a trade mark of Oxford University Press

Published in the United States
by Oxford University Press, New York

First published 1984
Reprinted 1985
Revised edition (New as Paperback) 1988
Reprinted 1990

British Library Cataloguing in Publication Data
Skegg, P. D. G.
Law, ethics and medicine.
1. Medical laws and legislation – England
I. Title
344.204'41   KD3395
ISBN 0-19-825365-6
ISBN 0-19-825642-6 (Pbk)

Library of Congress Cataloging in Publication Data
Skegg, P. D. G.
Law, ethics, and medicine.
Includes Index.
1. Medical laws and legislation – Great Britain.
2. Informed consent (Medical law) – Great Britain.
3. Medical ethics – Great Britain. I. Title.
[DNLM: 1. Ethics, Medical. 2. Legislation, Medical.
W50 S627L]
KD3395.S57   1984   344.41'041   344.10441   84-1175
ISBN 0-19-825365-6
ISBN 0-19-825642-6 (Pbk)

Printed in Great Britain by
Bookcraft Ltd
Midsomer Norton,
Avon

*To
my parents*

PREFACE

This book consists of studies of legal aspects of some issues that arise in medical practice. I have sought to give an account of English law as it now is, or as judges could develop it without statutory intervention. To do this it has been necessary to consider the case law of other common law jurisdictions within the Commonwealth, and also some United States authorities.

These studies have been prepared as a contribution to the academic legal discussion of these issues. Nevertheless I hope that some of the chapters will be of interest to persons without a legal training. Any such reader should skip chapters 1, 2, 6, and 8. Indeed, any reader without a special interest in the subject-matter of the first two chapters might well commence at chapter 3.

There will inevitably be some changes in the law before this book is published. One that can be foreseen is that a Mental Health Act 1983 will consolidate the surviving provisions of the Mental Health Act 1959, and the Mental Health (Amendment) Act 1982. But this will be a change of form, rather than substance, and does not warrant postponement of the completion of this book.

Many of the chapters of this book have their origin in articles that I wrote for legal and medico-legal journals in the 1970s. Some chapters, or parts of chapters, are expanded and updated versions of these articles; others deal with the same subject matter as earlier articles, but have been almost completely rewritten for inclusion here. A few deal with matters about which I have not written before. I am grateful to the editors of the *Cambridge Law Journal*, the *Criminal Law Review*, the *Law Quarterly Review*, *Medicine, Science and the Law*, and the *Modern Law Review*, for permitting me to incorporate material which first appeared in their journals.

In preparing these studies I have benefited from the advice of many doctors and lawyers. In the earlier stages Sir Rupert Cross, Donald Harris, and my brother David Skegg, were especially helpful. More recently John Finnis and Peter Glazebrook have both read two chapters and made very helpful comments, and I have also benefited from the advice of other friends and colleagues, including John Eekelaar, Tony Honoré, and Martin Matthews. I learnt much from discussions with fellow members of a working party that was appointed by the United Kingdom Health Departments to prepare a code of practice for the removal of cadaveric organs for transplantation. I also owe a debt to Professor Glanville Williams, whose writings have been a constant source of illumination and stimulation.

I am grateful to the Warden and Fellows of New College for granting me the periods of sabbatical leave during which much of this book was written.

New College, Oxford   P.D.G.S.
May 1983

Note to Paperback Edition

For this paperback edition I have provided a Postscript to alert readers to recent developments in areas of law discussed in the book. The tables of statutes and cases and the index have been updated, and a few minor typographical errors eliminated.

University of Otago,   P.D.G.S.
February 1988.

CONTENTS

SELECTED ABBREVIATIONS

Ann. N.Y. Acad. Sci.	*Annals of the New York Academy of Sciences*
Br. Med. J.	*British Medical Journal*
C.L.J.	*Cambridge Law Journal*
Code of Practice	*The Removal of Cadaveric Organs for Transplantation: A Code of Practice* (H.M.S.O., 1979)
Crim. L.R.	*Criminal Law Review*
Devlin, *Samples*	Lord Devlin, *Samples of Lawmaking* (1962)
Dict. Med. Ethics	*Dictionary of Medical Ethics* (2nd edn., 1981, edd. A. S. Duncan, G. R. Dunstan, and R. B. Welbourn)
Edmund Davies, 'Transplants'	Edmund Davies L.J., 'A Legal Look at Transplants' (1969) 62 *Proc. Roy. Soc. Med.* 633–8
Halsbury	*Halsbury's Laws of England* (4th edn., gen. ed. Lord Hailsham of St. Marylebone)
J.A.M.A.	*Journal of the American Medical Association*
J. Roy. Soc. Med.	*Journal of the Royal Society of Medicine*
L.Q.R.	*Law Quarterly Review*
Linacre Papers	*Linacre Centre Papers* (Prolongation of Life Series)
Linacre Report	*Euthanasia and Clinical Practice: trends, principles and alternatives* (1982)
M.L.R.	*Modern Law Review*
Med.-Leg. J.	*Medico-Legal Journal*
Med. Sci. Law	*Medicine, Science and the Law*
New L.J.	*New Law Journal*
Ormrod, 'Ethics'	Ormrod L.J., 'A Lawyer Looks at Medical Ethics' (1978) 46 *Med.-Leg. J.* 18–30
Parl. Deb. H.C.	Parliamentary Debates, House of Commons (Fifth Series, unless otherwise specified)
Parl. Deb. H.L.	Parliamentary Debates, House of Lords (Fifth Series)

President's Commission	President's Commission for the Study of Ethical Problems in Medicine and Biomedical and Behavioral Research, *Defining Death: A Report on the Medical, Legal and Ethical Issues in the Determination of Death* (1981)
Proc. Roy. Soc. Med.	*Proceedings of the Royal Society of Medicine*
Smith and Hogan	J. C. Smith and B. Hogan, *Criminal Law* (4th edn., 1978)
Sol. J.	*Solicitors' Journal*
Speller, *Hospitals*	*Speller's Law relating to Hospitals* (6th edn., 1978, by Joe Jacob)
Stephen, *Digest*	J. F. Stephen, *Digest of the Criminal Law* (4th edn., 1887)
Williams, *Sanctity*	Glanville Williams, *The Sanctity of Life and the Criminal Law* (1958)
Williams, *Textbook*	Glanville Williams, *Textbook of Criminal Law* (1978)

For other abbreviations, see Donald Raistrick's *Index to Legal Citations and Abbreviations* (1981).

PART I
THE BEGINNING OF LIFE

LAWFUL ABORTION AND THE PROTECTION OF LIFE

> I will maintain the utmost respect for human life from
> the time of conception . . .
>
> World Medical Association's
> Declaration of Geneva, 1948

Under the Abortion Act 1967 a doctor is often free to terminate a pregnancy, with the intention of killing the fetus,[1] without committing an offence under 'the law relating to abortion'.[2] The Act provides that a registered medical practitioner who terminates a pregnancy is not guilty of an offence under the law relating to abortion if two registered medical practitioners are of the opinion, formed in good faith,[3]

(a) that the continuance of the pregnancy would involve risk to the life of the pregnant woman, or of injury to the physical or mental health of the pregnant woman or any existing children of her family, greater than if the pregnancy were terminated; or

(b) that there is a substantial risk that if the child were born it would suffer from such physical or mental abnormalities as to be seriously handicapped.

Where these conditions are fulfilled the termination of pregnancy (in an authorized place) does not amount to any offence of abortion, however far the pregnancy has progressed.

[1] In this chapter 'fetus' will be used to refer to the human embryo from conception to delivery. (This is the sense in which the word was used by the Advisory Group which produced the report on *The Use of Fetuses and Fetal Material for Research* (H.M.S.O. 1972): see para. 6.)

[2] S. 6 of the Abortion Act 1967 provides that 'In this Act . . . "the law relating to abortion" means sections 58 and 59 of the Offences against the Person Act 1861, and any rule of law relating to the procurement of abortion'.

[3] Abortion Act 1967, s. 1(1). There are restrictions on the places where abortions may be performed: see s. 1(3). For a helpful discussion of the Abortion Act 1967, and the law relating to abortion generally, see Williams, *Textbook*, 252–65. See also, now, *Royal College of Nursing* v. *Department of Health and Social Security* [1981] A.C. 800.

But there are circumstances in which an 'abortion'[4] which is lawful for the purpose of the law relating to abortion may nevertheless amount to the offence of child destruction, or even to murder. This chapter discusses these circumstances.

I CHILD DESTRUCTION

The offence of child destruction[5] was created by the Infant Life (Preservation) Act 1929, and the continuing effect of that enactment is specifically preserved by the Abortion Act 1967.[6] There are undoubtedly some circumstances in which an abortion would be lawful for the purpose of the law relating to abortion, yet nevertheless amount to the offence of child destruction. The difficulty lies in determining the extent of the protection afforded fetal life by the Infant Life (Preservation) Act.

Before the enactment of the Infant Life (Preservation) Act, it was widely accepted that it was possible to avoid criminal liability by killing a child in the course of normal birth, but before it was fully born.[7] As such conduct did not involve an attempt to procure a miscarriage, it did not amount to an offence of abortion. As the child was not fully born, it was not murder.[8] Earlier attempts to plug the gap had not

---

[4] For legal purposes 'abortion' means 'the intentional destruction of the fetus in the womb, or any untimely delivery brought about with intent to cause the death of the fetus' (Williams, *Textbook*, 252), and the term will be used in this sense in this chapter. In medical circles 'abortion' is commonly used to refer to the removal or expulsion of the products of conception before, but not after, the fetus is viable. See e.g. *Butterworths Medical Dictionary* (2nd edn., 1978), 4 ('before the 28th week'). Cf. the American publication, *Obstetric-Gynecologic Terminology* (1972), 414–15 ('before the 20th completed week of gestation').

[5] The offence is named 'child destruction' in s. 1(1) of the Act. (The side-note to s. 1 is 'Punishment for child destruction'.)

[6] S. 5(1) of the Abortion Act 1967 provides that 'Nothing in this Act shall affect the provisions of the Infant Life (Preservation) Act 1929 (protecting the life of the viable foetus).'

[7] See e.g. *Report of the Royal Commission appointed to consider the Law relating to Indictable Offences* (C. 2345; 1879), 25. Sir James Fitzjames Stephen was one of the four Commissioners. But see *Report of the Capital Punishment Commission* (10438; 1866), Minutes of Evidence, 23 (Sir George Bramwell's answer to Q. 144); cf. ibid., 275 (The Hon. Sir J. S. Willes's answer to Q. 2092).

[8] See n. 57, below.

met with success,[9] and in June 1928 Talbot J. said 'It is a felony to procure abortion and it is murder to take the life of a child when it is fully born, but to take the life of a child while it is being born and before it is fully born is no offence whatever.'[10] The following week there was introduced into the House of Lords a Bill which led to the enactment, in the following session, of the Infant Life (Preservation) Act.[11]

Although the Bill was introduced to plug the gap between abortion and murder, the Act does more than that. It imposes some restrictions on the killing of unborn children before, as well as during, birth. The Long Title of the Act describes it as 'An Act to amend the law with regard to the destruction of children at or before birth', and section 1(1) states:[12]

Subject as hereinafter in this subsection provided, any person who, with intent to destroy the life of a child capable of being born alive, by any wilful act causes a child to die before it has an existence independent of its mother, shall be guilty of [an offence], to wit, of child destruction, and shall be liable on conviction thereof on indictment to [imprisonment] for life:

Provided that no person shall be found guilty of an offence under this section unless it is proved that the act which caused the death of the child was not done in good faith for the purpose only of preserving the life of the mother.

[9] Criminal Code (Indictable Offences) Bill 1878, s. 168; Criminal Code (Indictable Offences) Bill 1879, s. 212; Criminal Code Bill 1880, s. 205; Infant Life Protection Bill 1909, s. 1. See also Law of Capital Punishment Amendment Bill 1866, ss. 8–12; Law of Murder Amendment Bill 1867, ss. 8–12; Infanticide Law Amendment Bill 1873, ss. 3–6, as amended by Committee, ss. 3–6; Infanticide Law Amendment Bill 1874, s. 3.

[10] The statement occurred in the course of Talbot J.'s charge to the Grand Jury at Liverpool Assizes, extracts from which (including the sentence quoted above) were quoted by Lord Darling in his speech introducing the Infanticide Bill in the House of Lords on 21 June 1928: see (1928) 71 Parl. Deb. H.L. 617–18.

[11] The Bill was referred to a Select Committee of the House of Lords, and emerged as the Child Destruction Bill 1928, in terms similar to those eventually enacted as the Infant Life (Preservation) Act 1929.

[12] The words in square brackets have been inserted in place of 'felony' and 'penal servitude', to give effect to s. 1 and s. 12(5) of the Criminal Law Act 1967 and s. 1(1) of the Criminal Justice Act 1948, respectively.

The external elements[13] of the offence are very broad indeed. They are present whenever 'any person . . . by any . . . act causes a child to die before it has an existence independent of its mother'. Many induced abortions could be regarded as having this effect—although some do not cause the child to die until after it has an existence independent of its mother,[14] and therefore could not amount to the completed offence of child destruction.[15] But a doctor does not contravene the criminal law whenever his act[16] causes a child to die before it has an existence independent of its mother. He would be guilty of the offence of child destruction only if he acted 'with intent to destroy the life of a child capable

[13] The term 'external elements' is used in this chapter, and elsewhere in this book, to refer to all the elements of the offence other than the mental, or other fault, element. See generally C. Howard, *Criminal Law* (4th edn., 1982), 9-12; Williams, *Textbook*, 30-3. See also *Codification of the Criminal Law: General Principles: The Mental Element in Crime* (Law Commission Published Working Paper No. 31, 1970), esp. 1, n. 1; *Report on the Mental Element in Crime* (Law Com. No. 89, 1978), esp. 37, n. 198.

[14] A statement in one case (decided in apparent ignorance of many earlier authorities: see n. 57) supports the view that a child can have a 'separate existence', and its death be the concern of the law of homicide, even though it is not 'fully born' (*R.* v. *Pritchard* (1901) 17 T.L.R. 310, 311). But the better view is that 'separate existence' is a synonym for 'born alive' or 'fully born' (although see (1928) 72 Parl. Deb. H.L. 270 (Lord Atkin), 276 (Lord Hailsham L.C.)). It appears to have been used in such a sense in *R.* v. *Izod* (1904) 20 Cox C.C. 690, 691 (and in *R.* v. *Woodgate* (1877) 2 J.R.N.S. (C.A.) 5, 3 C.A. 320 (N.Z.)). See also *R.* v. *Moore* (1910) 5 Cr. App. R. 191, 192 (where the judgment of the Court of Criminal Appeal supports the view that a child becomes the subject of the law of homicide when it is 'born alive'); *Paton* v. *British Pregnancy Advisory Service Trustees* [1979] Q.B. 276, 279; and the Congenital Disabilities (Civil Liability) Act 1976, s. 4(2). A child should not be regarded as having 'an existence independent of its mother' before it is 'born alive', for there would then be a stage at which it was possible to kill a viable child without infringing the criminal law.

[15] The applicability of the law of murder to such abortions is discussed in pt. II of this chapter. In some circumstances such abortions could amount to an attempt to commit the offence of child destruction.

[16] S. 1(1) speaks of any wilful 'act', and there is a further reference to 'act' in the proviso. Although judges have sometimes spoken of 'an act of commission' and 'an act of omission' (see e.g. *R.* v. *Lowe* [1973] Q.B. 702, 709), a bare reference to 'act' in a criminal statute would not normally be interpreted as comprehending any omissions. Cf. Infanticide Act 1922, s. 1, and its successor, Infanticide Act 1938, s. 1(1) ('act or omission'); Homicide Act 1957, s. 2(1) ('acts and omissions'). S. 168 (a) (iii) of the Criminal Code (Indictable Offences) Bill 1878 would have made it an offence—subject to a defence concerning the preservation of the mother's life—to cause the death of a child 'which has not proceeded in a living state from the body of its mother' (cf. Bill, s. 131), by '*any act or omission* which would have amounted to murder if such child had been fully born' (emphasis added).

of being born alive',[17] his act was 'wilful',[18] and it was 'not done in good faith for the purpose only of preserving the life of the mother'.

It has been argued that a great many abortions are performed 'with intent to destroy the life of a child capable of being born alive', and that very few of these are 'for the purpose only of preserving the life of the mother'. If this is so, some doctors are frequently committing the offence of child destruction. The controversy about the scope of the offence depends in large measure on the interpretation of the terms 'a child capable of being born alive', and 'preserving the life of the mother', so it is necessary to examine them in some detail.

'a child capable of being born alive'

An unborn child which (with appropriate care and nourishment) is capable of surviving indefinitely outside its mother's body is 'viable', and is undoubtedly 'a child capable of being born alive' for the purpose of the Infant Life (Preservation) Act. Hence it is agreed on all sides that if a doctor intended to destroy the life of a viable[19] fetus, and his act did in fact do so, he would commit the offence of child destruction—unless he acted 'in good faith for the purpose only of preserving the life of the mother'. Except in the circumstances specified in the proviso, the effect of the Act is to prohibit the killing of an unborn but viable child, as well as the killing of such a child in the course of birth. It is irrelevant that the doctor complied with the provisions of the Abortion Act 1967, and is therefore not guilty of any offence under the law relating to abortion.

The disagreement arises over whether an unborn child which is not capable of surviving indefinitely outside its

---

[17] On 'intent', see generally *R.* v. *Belfon* [1976] 1 W.L.R. 741 (Offences against the Person Act 1861, s. 18).

[18] On 'wilful', see generally *R.* v. *Sheppard* [1981] A.C. 394 ('wilfully' in s. 1 of the Children and Young Persons Act 1933).

[19] In *Planned Parenthood of Central Missouri* v. *Danforth* (1976) 428 U.S. 52, 63 Blackmun J. quoted a helpful statutory definition of 'viable'. It is 'that stage of fetal development when the life of the unborn child may be continued indefinitely outside the womb by natural or artificial life-supportive systems'. See also e.g. *Butterworths Medical Dictionary* (2nd edn., 1978), 1814, and see generally P. A. King, 'The Juridical Status of the Fetus: A Proposal for Legal Protection of the Unborn' (1979) 77 *Michigan Law Review* 1647, 1653-6, 1678-82.

mother's body is 'a child capable of being born alive', for the purpose of the offence of child destruction.[20] On the face of it, at least some non-viable fetuses do come within the scope of the phrase 'a child capable of being born alive', for it is well established that a child can be 'born alive', for the purpose of the law of homicide, even though it is not viable.[21] Furthermore the Act does not contain any express reference to viability. It speaks of capacity to be born alive, not of capacity to survive after birth.[22] On this interpretation, many abortions which are performed in circumstances specified in section 1 of the Abortion Act 1967 contravene the Infant Life (Preservation) Act. It would often be possible to perform an abortion in such a way that the child showed signs of life ('alive') after it was clear of the mother's body ('born'). Many fetuses which are not yet viable could be regarded as being, in this sense, 'capable of being born alive'.[23]

However, judges would be very reluctant to adopt an interpretation of the Infant Life (Preservation) Act which outlawed the abortion of non-viable fetuses, if the abortions were performed on grounds specified in section 1 of the Abortion Act. To avoid this consequence they might be willing to

[20] Compare the views expressed in the publication of the Association of Lawyers in Defence of the Unborn (*News and Comment*, No. 1, Spring 1979, [p. 3]; No. 4, Winter 1979-80, [p. 2]) with those of a Law Officer (Sir Ian Percival S.-G., Parl. Deb. H.C., Standing Committee C, 4 December 1979, col. 369). See also e.g. *Report of the Committee on the Working of the Abortion Act* (Cmnd. 5579; 1974), para. 278(vi) (but see para. 278(ii), which contains a reference to 'viability'); *McKay* v. *Essex Area Health Authority* [1982] Q.B. 1166, 1180A per Stephenson L.J.

[21] See e.g. *R.* v. *West* (1848) 2 C. & K. 784. See also *R.* v. *Woodger and Lyall* (1812) 54 *Annual Register*, Chronicle, 96-7; *R.* v. *Castles* [1969] Q.W.N. 36 (pp. 77-80); Williams, *Textbook*, 249, 263 n. 8, 264.

[22] Victor Tunkel, 'Abortion: How Early, How Late, and How Legal?' [1979] 2 *Br. Med. J.* 253, 254 stresses this point, when speaking of the 'misunderstanding' whereby the Act 'is treated as if it made it an offence to destroy only a viable fetus'. But his later statement that 'with modern techniques of antenatal investigation, delivery, *and intensive care* the fetus must be regarded as becoming ever-earlier "capable of being born alive" ' (emphasis added) (ibid. 254) appears to concede that viability is crucial.

[23] Cf. Official Record, World Health Organisation 1950/28/17, 1967/160/11, 1976/223/18: 'Live birth is the complete expulsion or extraction from its mother of a product of conception *irrespective of the duration of the pregnancy*, which after such separation breathes *or shows any other evidence of life*, such as beating of the heart, pulsation of the umbilical cord or definite movement of voluntary muscle whether or not the umbilical cord has been cut or the placenta is attached.' (Emphasis added.)

develop more stringent criteria for 'live birth', or to adopt a restrictive concept of 'child'.[24] But they would not need to do this, for there is an indication in the Act itself that it should not be interpreted as protecting the lives of all those who are capable of being 'born alive', for the purpose of the law of homicide.

Section 1(2) of the Infant Life (Preservation) Act provides that:[25]

> For the purposes of this Act, evidence that a woman had at any material time been pregnant for a period of twenty-eight weeks or more shall be primâ facie proof that she was at that time pregnant of a child capable of being born alive.

In 1929 it would have been possible to remove, or cause to be expelled, from the mother's womb, a child which had been conceived much less than twenty-eight weeks earlier, yet which would have shown signs of life—even breathed[26] —after it was clear of its mother's body. But by the time a woman had been pregnant for twenty-eight weeks there would have been the possibility, not simply of the child being 'born alive', but also of its life being sustained indefinitely. In other words, by this time the child could quite possibly be viable. Thus section 1(2) implies that the concern of the Infant

[24] It would, for example, be possible to develop a concept of 'child' in this context, so as to exclude the 'product of conception' which had not developed to a stage when it had the outward appearance of a child. (A newly-pregnant woman would almost certainly be regarded as 'with child' for the purpose of s. 58 of the Offences against the Person Act 1861, but if such an embryo miscarried it would not be regarded as a 'child' for the purpose of s. 60 of that Act: see *R.* v. *Colmer* (1864) 9 Cox C.C. 506; *R.* v. *Hewitt* (1866) 4 F. & F. 1101; and see also *R.* v. *Berriman* (1854) 6 Cox C.C. 388; *R.* v. *Holt* (1937) 2 *Journal of Criminal Law* 69; *R.* v. *Matthews* [1943] C.P.D. 8.)

[25] The Act does not provide a countervailing presumption that if a woman has not been pregnant for twenty-eight weeks she is not 'pregnant of a child capable of being born alive'. On the interpretation of s. 1(2), see Williams, *Textbook*, 251, n. 1.

[26] If a child 'has been wholly born, and is alive, it is not essential that it should have breathed at the time it was killed; as many children are born alive, and yet do not breathe for some time after their birth': *R.* v. *Brain* (1834) 6 C. & P. 349, 350 per Park J. See also Births and Deaths Registration Act 1953, s. 41 (definition of 'still-born child'); *Report of the Committee on Death Certification and Coroners* (Cmnd. 4810; 1971), para. 8. 10; J. P. M. Tizard, 'Birth Injury', *Report of the Royal Commission on Civil Liability and Compensation for Personal Injury* (Cmnd. 7054-I; 1978), Annex 12, paras. 18, 20.

Life (Preservation) Act is to protect the lives of viable fetuses, rather than of fetuses which could not survive outside their mothers' bodies.[27]

It would be wrong to interpret the phrase 'a child capable of being born alive' in section 1(1), without taking account of section 1(2).[28] Therefore section 1(1) should be construed as protecting the lives of viable, but not of non-viable, fetuses. This interpretation avoids thwarting the clear intent of the Abortion Act 1967 to enlarge the circumstances in which it is lawful to kill a non-viable fetus. But it does have the disadvantage that, on this view, the Infant Life (Preservation) Act fails to close completely the gap between abortion and murder. If a non-viable fetus miscarries spontaneously, or is being born prematurely, it would not be an offence to kill it intentionally during the course of birth, even though it would be murder to kill it intentionally once it was fully extruded

[27] Professor Glanville Williams (*Textbook*, 263) also argues that the presumption shows that 'capable of being born alive' means 'viable', and he favours this way of limiting the application of the Act. But as an alternative he suggests that 'born' could be interpreted as 'natural birth', so that if a child could not be born without medical intervention it should not be regarded, in this context, as capable of being 'born' (ibid. 264). However, viable children delivered by Caesarean section are invariably regarded as having been 'born', and there is nothing in the Act which suggests that it does not apply to protect the lives of unborn children who, although viable, could not be 'born alive' without medical intervention.

[28] S. 1(2) is not mentioned in an article by a Queen's Counsel which seeks to demonstrate that the Infant Life (Preservation) Act protects the lives of all those who, for the purpose of the law of homicide, are capable of being 'born alive', even though they are not viable. See Gerard Wright, 'Capable of Being Born Alive?' (1981) 131 *New L. J.* 188–9. The writer appears to hold the view that some fetuses are not capable of being 'born alive', but does not indicate on what basis he would distinguish between those non-viable fetuses which can be born alive, and those which cannot. (He does not argue that even those children who, in his view, could not at present be 'born alive' are 'capable of being born alive', in that they could in due course be born alive if they are not killed first.) The Association of Lawyers in Defence of the Unborn has stated that 'from the time that a child is capable of being born (which we understand to be around 12 weeks or so) the offence is committed if the child is destroyed in the womb' (*News and Comment*, No. 6, Summer 1980, [p. 3]; see also ibid. No. 1, Spring 1979, [p. 3]). The stress appears to be, not on 'child' or 'alive', but on 'born'. Judges would be very reluctant to accept that the Infant Life (Preservation) Act prohibits most abortions in the second trimester of pregnancy. Abortions performed on the ground that there is a substantial risk that the child would be seriously handicapped (see Abortion Act 1967, s. 1(1) (b)) are normally performed at this stage, and there is widespread support for abortion on this ground, even among many who are opposed to abortion in most other circumstances.

from its mother's body.[29] However, this gap is of little practical importance. Even if a non-viable child was alive during the course of birth, there would rarely be any reason for anyone to seek to kill it. Its death would already be imminent and inevitable. The serious gap in English law, prior to the enactment of the Infant Life (Preservation) Act, was that it was not an offence to kill a viable child during the course of birth. There are reasons why people might wish to kill a child which would not die within a short time in any event. The Infant Life (Preservation) Act supplements the protection afforded by the law of murder by making it an offence to act to kill such a child before it has an existence independent of its mother, unless the act is performed 'in good faith for the purpose only of preserving the life of the mother'. Section 1(2) was included to assist in problems of proof, as it would sometimes be difficult to establish whether the child was or was not viable.

An interpretation of the Infant Life (Preservation) Act 1929 that leaves a small but, in practice, unimportant gap in the protection afforded non-viable children during the course of birth is preferable to one that ignores section 1(2) and has the effect of frustrating the clear intent of the Abortion Act 1967.[30] That Act was enacted on the assumption that the Infant Life (Preservation) Act would provide continuing protection for viable, but not for non-viable, fetuses. Section 5(1) of the Abortion Act provides that 'Nothing in this Act shall affect the provisions of the Infant Life (Preservation) Act 1929 (protecting the life of the viable foetus).' Although the words in brackets cannot be taken to provide an authoritative gloss on the earlier Act,[31] they do make it still more

[29] If the doctor terminated the pregnancy, with the intention that the non-viable fetus should die in consequence, the law of abortion would apply.

[30] For a different view, see Gerard Wright, op. cit., 189. In *Royal College of Nursing* v. *Department of Health and Social Security* [1981] A.C. 800, 824 Lord Diplock said that the Abortion Act 1967 'started its parliamentary life as a private member's bill and, maybe for that reason, it lacks the style and consistency of draftsmanship . . . which one would expect to find in legislation that had its origin in the office of parliamentary counsel'. The parliamentary history of what became the Infant Life (Preservation) Act 1929 may explain some of the inadequacies of that Act. *Quaere* whether it was drafted on the mistaken assumption that only viable fetuses are capable of being born alive, for the purpose of the law of homicide.

[31] S. 5(1) does, after all, provide that nothing in the Abortion Act is to affect the provisions of the Infant Life (Preservation) Act.

likely that a judge would adopt the view that the Infant Life (Preservation) Act protects the lives of only those fetuses that are viable.[32]

'preserving the life of the mother'

Before someone can be convicted of child destruction, it is not enough for the prosecution to prove that that person has 'with intent to destroy the life of a child capable of being born alive' by 'any wilful act' caused a child to die 'before it has an existence independent of its mother'. It must also be proved that the act which caused the death 'was not done in good faith for the purpose only of preserving the life of the mother'.[33]

It would be reasonable to assume that 'preserving the life of the mother' is the same as 'preventing the death of the mother'. Had it been intended that a viable child could be killed intentionally for any other purpose, this could easily have been spelt out. For example, section 1(4) of the Abortion Act provides that the usual requirement concerning the opinion of two registered medical practitioners, and the restrictions as to place, do not apply where the doctor believes that the abortion is immediately necessary 'to save the life or to prevent grave permanent injury to the physical or mental health of the pregnant woman'. This provision does not affect the offence of child destruction, but its reference to 'grave permanent injury' to the mother's health contrasts with the proviso to section 1(1) of the Infant Life (Preservation) Act, which refers solely to 'preserving the life of the mother'.[34]

[32] Judges might also be influenced by the fact that the distinction between viable and non-viable fetuses is widely, if irrationally, believed to be of moral significance. In *McKay* v. *Essex Area Health Authority* [1982] Q.B. 1166, 1180A, Stephenson L.J. said that the inroad made by the Abortion Act 1967 on the sanctity of human life seemed to stop short of a child capable of being born alive, 'because the sanctity of the life of a viable foetus is preserved by the enactment of section 5(1)'.

[33] Infant Life (Preservation) Act 1929, s. 1(1). This absence of the specified purpose must be proved, whether or not the act was that of a registered medical practitioner. Cf. Abortion Act 1967, s. 1(1) and (4), s. 5(2). On the question of good faith, see *R.* v. *Smith* [1973] 1 W.L.R. 1510, 1515–16 (Abortion Act 1967).

[34] See also the contrast between 'life' and 'health' in other provisions of Abortion Act 1967: s. 1(1) (a) ('risk to the life of the pregnant woman, or of injury to . . . health . . . greater than . . .'); s. 4(2) ('necessary to save the life or to prevent grave permanent injury to the . . . health of a pregnant woman').

However, there is one important case that lends support to the view that, for the purpose of the offence of child destruction, a person could be regarded as acting to preserve 'the life of the mother' even though he did not believe that there was any risk of her dying if he did not act. The case is *R*. v. *Bourne*.[35] Mr Bourne was an obstetrician who was prosecuted under section 58 of the Offences against the Person Act 1861. That section makes it an offence to 'unlawfully use any instrument' with intent to procure a miscarriage. Although at the time when Mr Bourne operated there was no statutory provision which set out the grounds on which it was lawful to perform an abortion,[36] it was accepted that the presence of the word 'unlawfully' in section 58 implied that there were circumstances in which it was lawful to procure an abortion.[37] Counsel disagreed, not as to whether it was lawful to perform an abortion where there was a danger of the mother dying,[38] but whether it was lawful to perform an abortion for some other therapeutic purpose.

The trial judge, Macnaghten J., could have adopted the view expressed in the then current edition of a leading textbook on criminal law. This stated that the word 'unlawfully',

---

[35] [1939] 1 K.B. 687, [1938] 3 All E.R. 615. There are two versions of Macnaghten J.'s summing-up. The one reported in the *All England Reports* appears to be the one actually delivered; it was extensively revised for the *Law Reports*. The main alterations were the expansion of the passage which appeared at 616H–617B (see [1939] 1 K.B. 690-1), and the omission of the lengthy passage which appeared at 619H–620H. Two briefer passages were also deleted (616 E-G, 617 G-H). There were several dozen other alterations, most of them of little or no significance. The account of the case which is given in this chapter is consistent with both versions.

[36] See now Abortion Act 1967.

[37] *R*. v. *Bourne* was the first English case in which this view was adopted. But the same view had been adopted by Lamont J. in *Re McGready* (1909) 14 C.C.C. 481, 485, when discussing s. 303 of the Canadian Criminal Code 1906. See also the extrajudicial statement of Salter J., reported in 'Abortion: Medico-Legal and Ethical Aspects' [1927] 1 *Br. Med. J.* 188, 190.

[38] In *R*. v. *Bourne* the Attorney-General accepted that abortion was lawful where the mother's life was endangered: see D. Seaborne Davies, 'The Law of Abortion and Necessity' (1938) 2 *M.L.R.* 126, 127, 128. More than forty years earlier counsel had advised the Royal College of Physicians that it was lawful to procure an abortion to save the life of the mother: see *Taylor's Principles and Practice of Medical Jurisprudence* (5th edn., 1905, ed. F. J. Smith), vol. ii, p. 154. See also *Cull* v. *Royal Surrey County Hospital and Butler* [1932] 1 *Br. Med. J.* 1195, [1932] 1 *Lancet* 1377; *Royal College of Nursing* v. *Department of Health and Social Security* [1981] A.C. 800, 825F.

in section 58, 'excludes from the section acts done in the course of proper treatment in the interests of the life or health of the mother'.[39] In the event, he held that the proviso to section 1(1) of the Infant Life (Preservation) Act expressed what had always been the law with regard to abortion.[40] But in part of his judgment he gave the words 'preserving the life of the mother' a much broader interpretation than they would appear on the face of it to bear. It is this aspect of his summing-up which is of continuing importance in the context of the offence of child destruction.

Macnaghten J. said that he found difficulty in understanding the difference between danger to life and danger to health, since 'life depends upon health, and it may be that health is so gravely impaired that death results'.[41] He went on to quote from Mr Bourne's response to the suggestion that there was a clear line of distinction between danger to health and danger to life. Mr Bourne had said that although there was a large group 'whose health may be damaged, but whose life almost certainly will not be sacrificed' there was another group 'whose life will be definitely in very grave danger'. Mr Bourne had then added:

There is a large body of material between those two extremes in which it is not really possible to say how far life will be in danger, but we find, of course, that health is depressed to such an extent that life is shortened, such as in cardiac cases, so that you may say that their life is in danger, because death might occur within measurable distance of the time of their labour.

Macnaghten J. said that if that view commended itself to the jury they would not accept the suggestion that there was a clear line of distinction between danger to health and danger to life.[42]

[39] *Russell on Crime* (9th edn., 1936, ed. R. E. Ross), vol. i, p. 517.

[40] [1938] 3 All E.R. 617A; re-expressed at [1939] 1 K.B. 691.

[41] [1939] 1 K.B. 692, [1938] 3 All E.R. 617 E-F. In the version of his summing-up which was reported in the *All England Reports*, Macnaghten J. went on to say 'Of course there are maladies that are a danger to health without being a danger to life.' (Ibid. 617G.) But this passage—which might be thought to undermine other aspects of the summing-up—was deleted before it was reported in the *Law Reports*.

[42] Macnaghten J. went on to tell the jury that they should take a 'reasonable' view of the words 'for the preservation of the life of the mother' (or, as he put it in the revised version 'for the purpose of preserving the life of the mother'):

The fact that impairment to health can reach a stage where it is a danger to life means it would sometimes be difficult for the prosecution to establish that a doctor was not acting to preserve the life of the mother, if he took action which averted an acknowledged and serious risk to her health. But it does not provide a reason for holding that a doctor can be said to be acting for the purpose of preserving the life of the mother when he does not believe that her life is endangered. However, this was the effect of Macnaghten J.'s subsequent statement that:[43]

if the doctor is of opinion, on reasonable grounds and with adequate knowledge, that the probable consequence of the continuance of the pregnancy will be to make the woman a physical or mental wreck, the jury are quite entitled to take the view that the doctor who, under those circumstances and in that honest belief, operates, is operating for the purpose of preserving the life of the mother.

This did not follow from what had been said earlier. It was also inconsistent, in several respects, with the proviso to section 1(1) of the Infant Life (Preservation) Act,[44] which the judge had earlier said expressed the common law on abortion.

It is possible to welcome Macnaghten J.'s ruling that abortion was legally justified where the doctor reasonably believed that the continuance of the pregnancy would make the

[1938] 3 All E.R. 618B–C; [1938] 1 K.B. 692. Later in his summing-up he again told them to construe the words 'in a reasonable sense' (ibid. 619B and 693–4, respectively). In context, it was apparent that in his opinion a reasonable interpretation was one that did not equate 'preserving the life of the mother' with 'preventing the death of the mother'.

[43] [1939] 1 K.B. 694. The passage at [1938] 3 All E.R. 619B–C is almost identical to the one quoted here.

[44] A person could act 'for the purpose only of preserving the life of the mother' even though his opinion was not formed 'on reasonable grounds and with adequate knowledge'. He could also do so even if he did not believe that, if he did not act, the 'probable consequence' of the continuance of the pregnancy would be that the mother would die or become a physical or mental wreck. Whereas the proviso to s. 1(1) refers to cases where the person acts 'for the purpose only of preserving the life of the mother', Macnaghten J.'s formulation omits any reference to 'only'. (Earlier in the summing-up, Macnaghten J. had said that the Infant Life (Preservation) Act was simply dealing with a case 'where the child is killed while it is being delivered from the body of the mother': [1938] 3 All E.R. 616–17. Cf. the revised version, where the reference to the child 'being delivered in the ordinary course of nature', [1939] 1 K.B. 691, could be cited in support of the interpretation of 'born' discussed in n. 27, above.)

woman a physical or mental wreck,[45] yet take the view that it
is misleading to describe this as an instance of the doctor
acting 'for the purpose of preserving the life of the mother'.
Macnaghten J.'s reasons for holding that a doctor could be
said to be acting 'for the purpose of preserving the life of the
mother', even though he was not acting to prevent a risk of
death, were not convincing. Furthermore, nothing said in
that case would be binding on a later court, dealing with the
offence of child destruction.[46] Nevertheless Macnaghten J.'s
judgment would undoubtedly prove helpful to a judge who
wished to adopt a broad interpretation of the proviso to section 1(1), so as to avoid the conviction of a doctor who
intentionally killed a child 'capable of being born alive',
although he believed that there was no risk of the mother
dying if he did not act.

There is another consideration that might encourage a judge
to adopt the view that 'preserving the life of the mother'
should not be treated as synonymous with 'preventing the
death of the mother'. By virtue of the proviso to section 1(1)
of the Infant Life (Preservation) Act a person cannot be convicted of child destruction unless it is proved that he did not

[45] On the facts there was no need for Macnaghten J. to consider whether
abortion was legally justifiable to avoid lesser injuries to health. Mr Bourne had
said (and there was no reason to doubt) that he believed that the continuance of
the pregnancy would probably cause serious injury to the girl, and an expert
witness had said that if the girl gave birth she was likely to become a mental
wreck. For a more restrictive interpretation of *R.* v. *Bourne* than that favoured
here, see Williams, *Sanctity*, 153.

[46] In *R.* v. *Bergmann and Ferguson* [1948] 1 *Br. Med. J.* 1008 Morris J.
adopted the test formulated by Macnaghten J., and quoted on p. 15 above. However in *Bravery* v. *Bravery* [1954] 1 W.L.R. 1169, 1180 Denning L.J. did not state
the law in terms of 'preserving the life of the mother'. He said, *obiter*, that abortion is unlawful 'unless it is necessary to prevent serious injury to health'. Similarly, in *R.* v. *Newton and Stungo* [1958] *Crim. L.R.* 469, [1958] 1 *Br. Med. J.*
1242-8 (see also J. D. J. Havard, 'Therapeutic Abortion' [1958] *Crim. L.R.* 600-
13) Ashworth J. directed the jury that it was unlawful to use an instrument to
procure a miscarriage 'unless the use is made in good faith for the purpose of
preserving the life or health of the woman'. His statement implied that to act to
preserve health was not necessarily the same as to act to preserve life. (*Pace*,
Smith and Hogan, 341, the reports do not indicate that the directions of Morris J.
and Ashworth J. 'purport to be an interpretation of the proviso in the 1929 Act').
(Newton's appeal against sentence is reported in *The Times*, 14 October 1958.)
For an account of cases elsewhere in the Commonwealth in which the decision in
R. v. *Bourne* has been discussed, see B. M. Dickens and R. J. Cook, 'Development
of Commonwealth Abortion Laws' (1979) 28 *International and Comparative Law
Quarterly* 424, 432-9.

act 'in good faith for the purpose only of preserving the life of the mother'. A doctor who gives a tetanus innoculation could usually be said to have acted 'for the purpose only' of preventing his patient contracting tetanus, even though he thought there was only a tiny risk of the patient doing so. Similarly, a doctor whose purpose was to avert a risk of death could be said to have acted 'for the purpose only' of preventing the death of the mother, even though he thought there was only a very remote risk of death.[47] As the Act countenances the intentional killing of a child late in pregnancy, or in the course of birth, to avert a tiny risk of the mother dying, it could be argued that it would be extraordinary if it did not permit the killing of an unborn child if there was a considerable risk of serious injury to the mother's health, even though her life was not endangered. In response to such an argument, it could be stressed that the proviso refers to preservation of 'life', not 'health', and that although it is sometimes difficult to distinguish between risk to life and risk to health, it is often more difficult to distinguish between different degrees of injury to health.

If the purpose of preventing the slightest injury to health is encompassed by the proviso to section 1(1), with its reference to 'preserving the life of the mother', it is difficult to explain why the proviso does not speak of 'preserving the health of the mother'. But if 'preserving the life of the mother' is taken to include the prevention of serious, but not less-than-serious, injury to health, there is the difficulty of deciding whether a threatened injury to health, not involving

---

[47] But if the person could have achieved the same end without intentionally killing the child, it might be apparent that he had not acted 'for the purpose only' of preserving the life of the mother. Cf. M. A. Somerville, 'Reflections on Canadian Abortion Law: Evacuation and Destruction—Two Separate Issues' (1981) 31 *University of Toronto Law Journal* 1–26. 'Purpose' has sometimes been equated with intention, or foresight of consequences (see e.g. *Chandler* v. *Director of Public Prosecutions* [1964] A.C. 763). In the context of s. 1(1), the question whether the doctor may have acted 'for the purpose only of preserving the life of the mother' will not arise unless it is apparent that he acted 'with intent to destroy the life of a child capable of being born alive'. A doctor should be regarded as acting 'for the purpose only of preserving the life of the mother' if this was his sole reason for acting. The fact that he knew of, or even welcomed, other consequences of his action should not lead a court to conclude that the doctor was not acting 'for the purpose only' of preserving the life of the mother if, but for that consideration, he would not have so acted.

a risk of death, is sufficiently serious to justify what would otherwise amount to the offence of child destruction. It is entirely possible that those responsible for the Infant Life (Preservation) Act had no intention of permitting such questions to be raised in the context of deliberate killings of the sort primarily envisaged by the Act.

In relation to a viable or nearly viable fetus, it would not make a great difference if a court adopted an extensive interpretation of 'preserving the life of the mother', rather than the more obvious interpretation. To avert a risk to the mother's life, or health, a doctor will sometimes take action which will put the unborn child at some degree of risk. He may perform a Caesarean section, or induce birth, before the child has grown to a stage when it is reasonably certain that it can survive outside its mother's body. Although the child may sometimes die in consequence, the doctor will not have acted 'with intent to destroy the life of a child capable of being born alive'. There are extremely few circumstances in which the preservation of the health—much less the life—of the mother would nowadays[48] require the doctor intentionally to kill a viable fetus.[49] But in relation to fetuses which are not

[48] At the time the Infant Life (Preservation) Act was enacted 'antenatal care was in its infancy, obstructed labour was common, and so great was the danger of fatal infection to the mother if a Caesarian section was carried out after obstructed labour, or prolonged labour with ruptured membranes, that the only course was to destroy the child in the uterus by means of those terrible instruments the cranioclast and cephalotribe, now happily consigned to the medical museums and rarely ever used': J. D. J. Havard, 'Legal Regulation of Medical Practice—Decisions of Life and Death: A Discussion Paper' (1982) 75 *J. Roy. Soc. Med.* 351.

[49] There is, however, one situation where it would appear to make a difference whether the court interpreted 'preserving . . . life' as synonymous with preventing death, or as extending to the prevention of serious—or even any—injury to health. This is where a doctor kills a viable fetus in the belief that there is a substantial risk that if the child were born it would suffer from such physical or mental abnormalities as to be seriously handicapped. The strain of bringing up a seriously handicapped child can have a detrimental effect on a mother's health. Hence, prior to the enactment of the Abortion Act 1967, it was sometimes argued that a doctor could be said to be acting for the purpose of preserving the mother's health in procuring an abortion in such a case. If the courts accepted a very broad interpretation of 'preserving the life of the mother' this would certainly raise the possibility of a doctor being permitted to kill a viable fetus if he believed that there was a substantial risk that the child would be seriously handicapped. However, unless the doctor would kill a normal fetus to avert an equivalent risk to a mother's health, it could be questioned whether he had acted 'for the purpose only' of preserving the health of the mother.

yet viable, the adoption of a broad interpretation of 'preserving life' would have very different consequences from one which took the words at face value.

If a court did feel obliged to hold that a pre-viable fetus was a 'child capable of being born alive' for the purpose of the Infant Life (Preservation) Act, it might well adopt an extensive interpretation of the phrase 'preserving the life of the mother', in order to mitigate the extent to which its interpretation of the Act would outlaw the abortion of pre-viable fetuses, in circumstances specified in section 1(1) of the Abortion Act 1967. Otherwise there is a greater likelihood of a court adopting the view that in this context 'for the purpose only of preserving the life of the mother' means 'for the purpose only of preventing the death of the mother'.

II MURDER

It has long been accepted that if something is done to a child before it is born which causes the child to die after it has been born, the person responsible may be guilty of murder.[50] Hence in *R. v. West*[51] Maule J. said that:[52]

if a person intending to procure abortion does an act which causes a child to be born so much earlier than the natural time, that it is born in a state much less capable of living, and afterwards dies in consequence of its exposure to the external world, the person who by her misconduct so brings the child into the world, and puts it thereby in a situation in which it cannot live, is guilty of murder.

In the past most methods of procuring an abortion usually led to the death of the fetus while it was still within its mother's body. But methods now used for abortions after the first trimester of pregnancy can result in death occurring after the child has been removed, or expelled, from its mother's body.[53] One such method involves the use of

[50] For the relevant authorities, see *Russell on Crime* (12th edn., 1964, ed. J. W. C. Turner), 401, n. 14. See also D. Seaborne Davies, 'Child-Killing in English Law' (1937) 1 *M.L.R.* 203, 208–11; R. W. Cannon, ' "Born Alive" ' [1963] *Crim. L.R.* 748, 750–1. [51] (1848) 2 C. & K. 784, 2 Cox C.C. 500.

[52] Ibid. 788 and 503, respectively.

[53] Two major gynaecological procedures which can result in the removal of a living fetus are hysterotomy and hysterectomy. A hysterotomy is usually performed by making an incision in the lower abdomen. The pregnant uterus is then opened, and the fetus removed. In a hysterectomy the uterus itself is removed.

prostaglandins,[54] which stimulate powerful contractions of the uterine muscles of the pregnant woman, eventually causing expulsion of the fetus.[55]

If the defendant in *R.* v. *West* had used an instrument with intent to procure a miscarriage, she would have committed an offence of abortion.[56] Nowadays a doctor who complies with the terms of the Abortion Act 1967 will not commit an offence of abortion in intentionally procuring a miscarriage. As has already been stressed, a doctor who aborts a woman in circumstances permitted by section 1 of the Abortion Act might sometimes commit the offence of child destruction if the child is viable and dies before it is fully born. However, the offence of child destruction does not apply if a child dies after it has an existence independent of its mother. The issue to be discussed here is whether a doctor who procures an abortion in circumstances permitted by section 1 of the Abortion Act 1967 could ever be guilty of murder if the child does not die until after it is fully born. It is proposed to consider first the external elements of murder and then the fault element. The possibility of the Abortion Act providing a defence to a charge of murder will then be considered.

External elements

A child's death is no concern of the law of homicide if it occurs before or during birth.[57] But if a person does something

[54] See generally M. P. Embrey, 'Prostaglandins in Human Reproduction' (1981) 283 *Br. Med. J.* 1563-6.

[55] One legal issue to which this method of abortion gave rise was considered in *Royal College of Nursing* v. *Department of Health and Social Security* [1981] A.C. 800. However, although one judge recognized that the children were not always dead before they were expelled from their mothers' bodies (ibid. 803G), none of the judges considered the application of the law of homicide to this method of procuring abortions.

[56] Such conduct was prohibited by s. 6 of the Offences against the Person Act 1837.

[57] On the inapplicability of the law of homicide where death occurs before the child is fully extruded from its mother's body, see e.g. *R.* v. *Poulton* (1832) 5 C. & P. 329, 330; *R.* v. *Brain* (1834) 6 C. & P. 349, 349-50; *R.* v. *Sellis* (1837) 7 C. & P. 850, 851; *R.* v. *Trilloe* (1842) Car. & M. 650, 651, 2 Mood. C.C. 260; *R.* v. *Izod* (1904) 20 Cox C.C. 690, 691. *Contra R.* v. *Pritchard* (1901) 17 T.L.R. 310, 311; but see *R.* v. *Moore* (1910) 5 Cr. App. R. 191, 192 ('born alive'); and also *R.* v. *Shephard* [1919] 2 K.B. 125, 126 (reference to 'born alive', in appeal from conviction under Offences against the Person Act 1861, s. 4). The umbilical

to a child before it is fully born, which causes the child to die after it is fully born, that person may be held responsible for the death, for the purpose of the law of homicide. This proposition was accepted by the judges in *R.* v. *Senior*,[58] and was an element in Maule J.'s direction to the jury in *R.* v. *West.*[59] It has been reaffirmed this century by the Court of Criminal Appeal.[60]

There are good reasons for retaining the rule that something done to a child before or during birth can be regarded as a cause of death, for the purpose of the law of homicide, if it causes the child to die after it has been fully born. As the killing of a child before it is fully born sometimes amounts to the offence of child destruction, it should not be possible to avoid criminal liability by ensuring that the child does not die until after it has an existence independent of its mother.[61] If the law of homicide could not take cognizance of things done to a child before or during birth which could cause a child to die after it was fully born, there would be a significant and undesirable gap in the law.

Fault element

At the time of the decision in *R.* v. *West*, an intention to procure an abortion sufficed for conviction of murder if, in

cord need not be severed: see *R.* v. *Trilloe*, above, and also *R.* v. *Hutty* [1953] V.L.R. 338, 339.

[58] *R.* v. *Senior* (1832) 1 Mood. C.C. 346.

[59] (1848) 2 C. & K. 784, 2 Cox C.C. 500.

[60] Lord Darling, in his speech when introducing the Infanticide Bill 1928 (see nn. 10, 11), referred to Coke's view that to injure a child before it is fully born, and thereby to cause it to die after it is fully born, may amount to murder. He went on to say that 'in consequence of a case decided a few years ago in the Court of Criminal Appeal, it becomes plain that the view taken by Sir Edward Coke was a true one' ((1928) 71 Parl. Deb. H.L. 617). The view that prenatal wounds that result in a child dying after it has been born alive can lead to liability in homicide, was accepted by the Hong Kong courts in *R.* v. *Kwok Chak Ming* [1963] H.K.L.R. 226, 349 (discussed by R. W. Cannon, ' "Born Alive" ', [1963] *Crim. L.R.* 748, esp. 748-54). See also *R.* v. *Brown, ex p. Mayor of Wigan* (1898) 62 J.P. 521; *R.* v. *Castles* [1969] Q.W.N. 36 (pp. 77-80).

[61] As has been seen, the offence of child destruction does not apply if the child dies after it has an existence independent of its mother. Something done to a child before it is fully born, which leads to its death after it is fully born, would only sometimes come within the scope of an offence of abortion; it would not do so if the act which caused death took place during birth, or did not have the effect of terminating the pregnancy.

consequence of the abortion, the child was born alive but
subsequently died.[62] Abortion was a felony, and an intention
to commit a felony was a sufficient fault element for murder.
But the 'felony-murder' rule has been abolished,[63] so even in
those circumstances in which an attempt to procure an abortion is still an offence, the intention to do so is not of itself a
sufficient fault element for murder.

Nevertheless, there are circumstances in which a doctor
who performed an abortion would have a sufficient fault
element for murder.[64] A doctor would have the fault element
for murder if he acted with the intention of causing the child
to die after it was fully born,[65] or if he was substantially

[62] Hence Maule J. directed the jury that 'If the child, by the *felonious* act of
the prisoner, was brought into the world in a state in which it was more likely to
die than it would have been if born in due time, and did die in consequence, the
offence is murder', and said that 'If, therefore, you are satisfied . . . that the
prisoner, by a *felonious* attempt to procure abortion, caused the child to be
brought into the world, for which it was not then fitted, and that the child did die
in consequence of its exposure to the external world, you will find her guilty [of
murder]' (emphasis added): *R.* v. *West* (1848) 2 C. & K. at 788-9, 2 Cox C.C.
at 503.

[63] The rule was restricted by judicial decisions, and was abolished by the
Homicide Act 1957, s. 1. (In consequence of the Criminal Law Act 1967, s. 1,
there is no longer a separate category of felonies in English law.) But an intention
to cause grievous bodily harm (to a fully-born human being) is still a sufficient
fault element for murder: see *R.* v. *Cunningham* [1982] A.C. 566. By virtue of
the doctrine of 'transferred malice', an intention to cause grievous bodily harm to
the mother would normally be a sufficient fault element for murder if, in consequence of the defendant's conduct, the child died after it was born alive (see
e.g. *R.* v. *Kwok Chak Ming* [1963] H.K.L.R. 226, 349). But a doctor who performs
an abortion should not be regarded as intending to cause grievous bodily harm to
the mother if the abortion is performed to benefit the mother's health (see
pp. 30-1)—or at a stage of pregnancy, or in a way, which does not involve
really serious injury to the mother's health. Even where it could be said that the
doctor did intend to cause grievous bodily harm to the mother, he should not be
guilty of murder if it is accepted that he would have a lawful excuse, for the
purpose of s. 18 of the Offences against the Person Act 1861 (see pp. 40-3). If
death did result from a lawful operation performed without negligence, the
doctor should not be guilty of manslaughter, much less of murder.

[64] On the fault element of murder, see generally Smith and Hogan, 285-91;
Williams, *Textbook*, 208-18. See also pp. 122-6, below.

[65] B. M. Dickens, *Abortion and the Law* (1966), 53 suggests that an intention
to kill the fetus, implicit in an attempt to procure an abortion, is of itself a sufficient intent to kill for the purpose of the law of murder. But the cases do not
support the view that the intention to prevent a child being born alive is of itself
a sufficient fault element for murder if the child does not die until after it is fully
born. *R.* v. *West* is explicable in terms of the old 'felony-murder' rule (see n. 62,
above).

certain that his action would have this consequence. There could therefore be the possibility of a doctor being guilty of murder if he performed the abortion in the hope of providing a living subject for 'fetal' experimentation *ex utero*, or if he performed an abortion by hysterotomy, knowing that the child would not die until after it was removed from its mother's body. However, if the doctor was simply aware that there was a slight risk that death would not occur until after the child was fully born, he would probably not have a sufficient fault element for murder.[66]

Defence?

Unless the Abortion Act 1967 can be regarded as providing him with a defence, a doctor is guilty of murder if he performs an abortion with the knowledge that the child will not die until after it has been removed or expelled from its mother's body.[67]

Section 1(1) of the Abortion Act states that a registered medical practitioner shall not be guilty of an offence under 'the law relating to abortion' if he terminates a pregnancy in accordance with the conditions specified in that section, and section 6(1) provides that in the Act ' "the law relating to abortion" means sections 58 and 59 of the Offences against the Person Act 1861, and any rule of law relating to the procurement of abortion'.

The phrase 'any rule of law relating to the procurement of abortion' is of crucial importance in this context. If a literal

[66] A person may also have the fault element for murder if he realizes that death or really serious bodily harm is the 'probable' or 'likely' consequence of his conduct—unless, it seems, there is a 'lawful excuse' for taking that risk (see ch. 6, esp. pp. 125-6 and 132-3, where the leading case of *R.* v. *Hyam* [1975] A.C. 55 is discussed). If a doctor removes a living child from its mother's body, in an attempt to save the life of the child, he should certainly not be regarded as having the fault element of murder simply because he realizes that it is probable, or even highly probable, that the child will die in consequence. It is possible that a court would adopt the view that there was a 'lawful excuse' for using a method of abortion which would probably result in death occurring after live birth if the abortion was performed in accordance with the Abortion Act 1967, it would not have amounted to the offence of child destruction if the doctor had intentionally caused the child to die before it had an existence independent of the mother, and the method of abortion was adopted because it was in the best interests of the mother's health.

[67] It is assumed that the fetus in question could be regarded as a 'child', and that after it was 'fully born' it exhibited any necessary sign of life.

interpretation is adopted, the Abortion Act has the effect of providing a doctor with a defence in the law of murder, if he performs the abortion (in accordance with the provisions of section 1 of the Abortion Act) by a means which ensures that the child will not die until after it is removed or expelled from its mother's body. For it can be argued that the rule in *R. v. West*[68] is not simply a rule of law relating to murder, but is also a 'rule of law relating to the procurement of abortion'. This interpretation is supported by two other considerations. One is that although there is a specific provision in the Abortion Act, by virtue of which the Act cannot be taken to provide a defence to a charge of child destruction,[69] there is no equivalent provision concerning the law of murder. The other consideration is that it would be remarkable if a doctor could act lawfully in terminating a pregnancy, and thereby killing a pre-viable fetus before it was born alive, but would risk liability in murder if he performed the abortion in a way that would not result in the child dying until after it was fully born.

But, were it to be adopted, the literal interpretation would itself have a remarkable consequence. Despite the clear intention of the framers of the Abortion Act that it should not affect the protection afforded viable fetuses by the Infant Life (Preservation) Act, a doctor could now avoid criminal liability by aborting a viable fetus by a method which ensured that the child did not die until after it had an existence independent of its mother.

It is in fact most unlikely that the words 'or any rule of law relating to the procurement of abortion' were included for the purpose of providing a doctor who acted in this way with a defence to the law of murder. If 'the law relating to abortion' had been defined solely in terms of the statutory offences of abortion, it could have been argued that doctors would still have been infringing some common law offence of abortion[70] if they performed abortions in accordance with

---

[68] (1848) 2 C. & K. 784, 2 Cox C.C. 500.

[69] Abortion Act 1967, s. 5(1).

[70] See generally D. Seaborne Davies, 'The Law of Abortion and Necessity' (1938) 2 *M.L.R.* 126, 133–4; C. C. Means, 'The Phoenix of Abortional Freedom: Is a Penumbral or Ninth-Amendment Right about to arise from the Nineteenth-Century Legislative Ashes of a Fourteenth-Century Common-Law Liberty?' (1971)

the provisions of section 1 of the Abortion Act. It was probably for this reason that section 6(1) was drafted so as to
provide that in the Abortion Act ' "the law relating to abortion" means sections 58 and 59 of the Offences against the
Person Act 1861, and any rule of law relating to the procurement of abortion'.

The rule of the law of homicide, whereby something done
to a child before it is fully born can sometimes result in liability
for murder if the child dies after it is fully born, is not simply
a 'rule of law relating to the procurement of abortion'. For
example, the rule would apply if parents wanted a child to
be born alive (so that the child would inherit a large sum of
money) but then die (so that the money would pass to them),
and they therefore arranged for a substance to be implanted
into the child before it was born which would cause it to die
soon after it was born.[71] It can be argued that the phrase 'any
rule of law relating to the procurement of abortion' should
not be interpreted as affecting this rule of the law of homicide,
whether or not the death results from the procurement of an
abortion.

The Abortion Act evinces a clear intention to maintain the
prohibition on the killing of viable fetuses before they are
fully born, except in the circumstances specified in the proviso
to section 1 of the Infant Life (Preservation) Act. Section 5(1)
could not be more explicit: 'Nothing in this Act shall affect
the provisions of the Infant Life (Preservation) Act 1929
(protecting the life of the viable foetus).' But if the phrase
'any rule of law relating to the procurement of abortion' is
interpreted literally, the Abortion Act enables viable fetuses
to be killed wherever the conditions of section 1 of the Abortion Act are met, provided the 'abortion'[72] is carried out by a
means which ensures that the child does not die until after it

17 *New York Law Forum* 335, 336–75; R. M. Byrn, 'An American Tragedy: The
Supreme Court on Abortion' (1973) 41 *Fordham Law Review* 807, 815–27; J. W.
Dellapenna, 'The History of Abortion: Technology, Morality and Law' (1979) 40
University of Pittsburgh Law Review 359, 366–407. See also Victor Tunkel,
Letter to the Editor, 'The Law on Abortion', *The Times*, 28 June 1978; Gerard
Wright Q.C., Letter to the Editor, 'Post-coital Pill', *The Times*, 15 April 1983.

[71] This example is adapted from one used by Paul Ramsey, *Ethics at the Edges
of Life* (1978), 128.

[72] See n. 4.

has an existence independent of its mother.[73] Hence it can be argued that the phrase 'any rule of law relating to the procurement of abortion' should not be interpreted literally, but in the light of its original purpose, and in a way which is consistent with the policy reflected in section 5(1) of the Abortion Act. On this approach 'any rule of law relating to the procurement of abortion' would be taken to refer to any common law offence of abortion, but not to the rule of the law of homicide discussed above.

Were a doctor to seek to avoid committing the offence of child destruction by performing the abortion in such a way that the child did not die until after it had an existence independent of its mother, most judges would probably be reluctant to hold that the Abortion Act provided the doctor with a defence to the law of murder. But if the issue first came before a court in a case involving the abortion of a pre-viable fetus, and the abortion was performed in a way that was in the best interests of the mother's health, judges would be more likely to take the view that on these facts the doctor was not guilty of murder, even if he knew that the child would not die until after it was removed from its mother's body. As the doctor would not have been guilty of any offence if the fetus had died before it was removed or expelled from its mother's body, judges would be very reluctant to accept that the doctor could be guilty of murder because the death occurred a little later. But it is only by ensuring that the child is not born alive, following an abortion, that a doctor can be certain that his conduct could not under any circumstances amount to the offence of murder.

[73] See n. 53.

PART II
DURING LIFE

GENERAL CAPACITY TO CONSENT
TO MEDICAL PROCEDURES

> In strict legal terminology I doubt if doctors ever
> assault; they batter.
>
> Devlin J., 1960[1]

In the absence of legally effective consent or some other legal justification, a doctor will normally incur criminal and civil liability if he carries out any medical procedure involving a bodily touching. In this and the next chapter it is proposed to consider capacity to give legally effective consent. In the following chapters there will be an examination of what constitutes legally effective consent, and of the circumstances in which a doctor may be justified in performing medical procedures in the absence of consent.

The question of capacity to give a legally effective consent has two aspects: first, whether anyone may give a legally effective consent, for the purpose of the crime or tort in question; and secondly, whether the person in question can give a legally effective consent. For the present purpose it is convenient to refer to the first issue as one of 'general capacity' and the second as one of 'individual capacity'.

With the overwhelming majority of medical procedures there is no need to pause to consider the question of 'general capacity', for it is clear that some people can give a legally effective consent to the procedures in question.[2] However doubts have sometimes been expressed as to whether it is possible to give a legally effective consent to some medical

---

[1] Devlin, *Samples*, 84. However, the judge went on to say that 'in popular usage assault has come to include battery'. A 'battery' is often preceded by an 'assault'. If a doctor caused a patient to apprehend that a battery was about to be committed upon him, the doctor would commit a common law assault—if he had the required fault element.

[2] Consent, whether of the mother or anyone else, does not provide a defence to the offences of abortion and child destruction.

procedures. Most recently concern has focused on those operations in which a kidney is removed from a healthy living donor for transplantation into a patient with kidney failure. This practice will therefore receive particular attention in the discussion which follows.

The crime and the tort of battery will be examined first, and then two other crimes which have been thought to give rise to difficulties in this context. The accounts of these crimes will include some consideration of the extent to which, in the absence of consent, they would apply to medical procedures. It is only where an offence appears likely to apply to the conduct in question that it becomes important to determine whether or not consent will prevent liability being incurred.

There is one matter which arises in relation to more than one offence, and which it is convenient to deal with at this stage. This is whether a medical procedure which benefits bodily health can be regarded as causing bodily harm. The answer might be thought to be obvious. But some lawyers have assumed that operations which are performed to benefit the health of the patient, and which do in fact do so, nevertheless constitute 'bodily harm'. One reason for this may be that 'bodily harm' has been said to include 'any hurt or injury calculated to interfere with . . . health or comfort'.[3] Many therapeutic medical procedures can be said to 'interfere with health or comfort', and to do so in a manner which is 'more than merely transient and trifling'.[4]

But when, in *R.* v. *Donovan*,[5] the Court of Criminal Appeal said that bodily harm includes any hurt or injury calculated to interfere with health or comfort, the court was not concerned with medical procedures. In the later case of *Director of Public Prosecutions* v. *Smith*,[6] Viscount Kilmuir L.C. said that he could find no warrant for giving the words 'grievous bodily harm' a meaning 'other than that which the

---

[3] *R.* v. *Donovan* [1934] 2 K.B. 498, 509. But see also Stephen, *Digest*, 148 ('bodily injury').

[4] *R.* v. *Donovan* [1934] 2 K.B. 498, 509.

[5] Ibid. 509. (The court said that, for the purpose of the relevant principle, 'we think that "bodily harm" has its ordinary meaning and includes any hurt or injury calculated to interfere with . . . health or comfort . . .'.)

[6] [1961] A.C. 290.

words convey in their ordinary and natural meaning'.[7] The ordinary and natural meaning of bodily harm scarcely includes medical procedures which benefit the bodily health of the person on whom they are performed. Benefit is, after all, the converse of harm. In determining what constitutes bodily harm, a commonsense approach is preferable to one which involves the mechanical application of a definition which was propounded in a context in which medical procedures were not under consideration.[8]

In deciding whether a doctor's conduct is intended to cause, or does cause, bodily harm, it is desirable that the treatment of the patient be considered as a whole. If skin is removed from one part of a person's body, for transplantation to a part which has been burnt, it would be unrealistic to consider the removal of skin on its own. However, there may be a small category of procedures which benefit the patient's health, yet do involve bodily harm. These are procedures which could be regarded as involving physical detriment, but where such detriment is thought to be outweighed by psychological benefit. Examples include some 'sex-change' operations. Whether such procedures amount to bodily harm could depend upon whether 'bodily harm' is taken to include psychological harm which does not have any apparent physical effects. In R. v. Miller[9] Lynskey J. said that an injury to a person's 'state of mind for the time being' now comes within the definition of actual bodily harm. This interpretation involves a very liberal interpretation of a penal provision. But if it is accepted that bodily harm includes purely psychological harm as well as physical harm, it could be argued that a medical procedure should not be regarded as causing bodily harm if physical detriment is outweighed by psychological benefit.

Fortunately, even if therapeutic medical operations were held to cause bodily harm, this would very rarely have important legal consequences.[10] The classification will normally

----

[7] Ibid. 334.

[8] In R. v. Hyam [1975] A.C. 55, 77C Lord Hailsham said 'It is the absence of intention to kill or *cause grievous bodily harm* which absolves the heart surgeon in the case of the transplant . . .' (emphasis added). Cf. Stephen, *Digest*, 148.

[9] [1954] 2 Q.B. 282, 292.

[10] Very occasionally the classification may be of some importance. If a doctor

affect the way in which the conduct is analysed, rather than the result. As will be seen later, where an operation is performed for the benefit of the patient's health, and consent has been given, there is no question of its being unlawful. In these cases the reason for distinguishing between bodily harm and bodily good is simply that it is unrealistic and offensive to regard all operations as causing bodily harm.[11]

I CRIME OF BATTERY

Medical procedures which involve bodily touchings come within the potential scope of the crime of battery[12] (known more popularly as assault).[13] But the absence of legally effective consent is an essential element of the offence.[14] If

operates without consent on an unconscious accident victim, in circumstances in which he is not legally justified in proceeding without consent, he commits a battery. Whether he is also guilty of assault occasioning actual bodily harm, of 'maliciously' inflicting grievous bodily harm, and of causing grievous bodily harm with intent (see Offences against the Person Act 1861, ss. 47, 20, and 18, respectively) will at least sometimes depend upon the way in which the operation is classified.

[11] *Quaere* whether a surgical incision which benefits bodily health is a wound, for the purpose of the offences of wounding in the Offences against the Person Act 1861, ss. 18, 20. It has often been said that there is a wound when the continuity of the skin is broken. See e.g. *R. v. Payne* (1831) 4 C. & P. 558; *Moriarty v. Brooks* (1834) 6 C. & P. 684, 686; *R. v. Beckett* (1836) 1 Mood. & R. 526, 527; *R. v. Smith* (1837) 8 C. & P. 173, 175; *R. v. M'Loughlin* (1838) 8 C. & P. 635, 638; *R. v. Waltham* (1849) 13 J.P. 183. See also *R. v. Newman* [1948] V.L.R. 61, 64. However, the cases were not concerned with medical procedures, and it is desirable that the courts take the view that a wound involves an element of injuriousness. Note the reference to 'injury' in *Moriarty v. Brooks*, above, 686, and *R. v. Newman*, above, 64.

[12] The touching need not be 'hostile' or 'aggressive' for it to amount to the offence of battery: see *Faulkner v. Talbot* [1981] 1 W.L.R. 1528, 1534.

[13] In the context of the criminal law, the term 'assault' has long been used to encompass battery, or as a synonym for battery, even though assault and battery are distinct crimes at common law. The reason why this sensible usage has not been adopted in this book is that writers on the law of torts often distinguish between the tort of assault and the tort of battery. This and subsequent chapters of Part II deal with the law of torts, as well as the criminal law. It is therefore simpler to refer to the crime and the tort of battery, rather than to speak of the crime of assault and the tort of battery (or trespass to the person—which includes both the tort of assault and the tort of battery).

[14] *Fagan v. Commissioner of Metropolitan Police* [1969] 1 Q.B. 439, 444E; *A.-G.'s Reference (No. 6 of 1980)* [1981] Q.B. 715, 718D-E. There is therefore no need to regard medical touchings as batteries (or assaults) licensed by consent. Such an approach is comparable to one which regards consensual sexual intercourse as rape licensed by consent. Although the absence of consent has long

legally effective consent has been given, the medical touching will not constitute the offence of battery. If legally effective consent has not been given, and the doctor is aware of that fact, then even a therapeutic medical touching will amount to the offence of battery, except where a statutory or common law justification is available to the doctor.

Although the absence of consent has been said to be an essential element of the offence of battery, judges have insisted that there are some 'applications of force'[15] to which legally effective consent cannot be given, for the purpose of the offence of battery. The leading cases which supported the existence of such a category were concerned with issues as far removed from medical practice as prize-fights,[16] and flagellation for the purpose of sexual gratification.[17] Nevertheless, some of the approaches expounded in these cases had some bearing on medical procedures, and various writers examined the application of these cases to medical practice.[18]

been considered an essential element of the offence (see e.g. *R.* v. *Martin* (1840) 9 C. & P. 213, 215, 217; *R.* v. *Guthrie* (1870) L.R. 1 C.C.R. 241, 243; *R.* v. *Lock* (1872) L.R. 2 C.C.R. 10, 13; *R.* v. *Wollaston* (1872) 12 Cox C.C. 180, 182), the judgments in *R.* v. *Coney* (1882) 8 Q.B.D. 534 and *R.* v. *Donovan* [1934] 2 K.B. 498 have been seen by some to require a reformulation. But these cases can be subsumed within the traditional formulation by speaking of the absence of 'legally effective' consent. There is a hint of this approach in the judgment of Hawkins J. in *R.* v. *Coney* (1882) 8 Q.B.D. 534, 553. See also *A.-G.'s Reference (No. 6 of 1980)* [1981] Q.B. 718 D-E, cf. 719A.

[15] Even the lightest touch is regarded as an 'application of force', for the purpose of the crime and tort of battery.

[16] *R.* v. *Coney* (1882) 8 Q.B.D. 534. On prize-fights, see generally L. L. M. Minty, 'Unlawful Wounding; Will Consent Make it Legal?' (1956) 24 *Med.-Leg. J.* 54, 55–8; see also Note (1912) 28 *L.Q.R.* 125.

[17] *R.* v. *Donovan* [1934] 2 K.B. 498. *Archbold's Pleading, Evidence and Practice in Criminal Cases* (41st edn., 1982, ed. S. Mitchell), para. 20–124, cites *Donovan* in support of the proposition that 'Consent is no defence where severe blows are given for the purpose of gratifying perverted sexual passion', and goes on to state that it was 'followed in *R.* v. *Lawson and others*, May 25, 1936, C.C.A. where the law is reviewed'. Enquiries at the Bar Library, the Criminal Appeals Office, and the Public Record Office reveal that no report of the judgments in *R.* v. *Lawson* has been retained. A very brief note in *The Times*, 26 May 1936, indicates that the appellants had been convicted of indecent assault, and that the Court of Criminal Appeal (Lord Hewart C.J., du Parcq and Singleton JJ.) allowed the appeals, and quashed the convictions. There is no mention of the facts or law.

[18] The present writer discussed the matter in 'Medical Procedures and the Crime of Battery' [1974] *Crim. L.R.* 693–700. For a subsequent examination of these cases, see Adrian Lynch, 'Criminal Liability for Transmitting Disease' [1978] *Crim. L.R.* 612–25.

But the importance of these cases has been diminished by the *Attorney-General's Reference (No. 6 of 1980).*[19] The opinion of the Court of Appeal on this reference[20] is likely to be the starting-point for any future consideration of this matter in the courts.[21]

The Court of Appeal (which for convenience used the word 'assault' as including 'battery'[22]) started with the proposition that 'ordinarily an act consented to will not constitute an assault'. The court asked 'at what point does the public interest require the court to hold otherwise?' and gave the answer 'that it is not in the public interest that people should try to cause, or should cause, each other actual bodily harm for no good reason'.[23] In such cases, it was said, consent is not effective to prevent liability being incurred.

The phrase 'for no good reason' is important. The Court of Appeal did not say that it was not possible to give a legally effective consent to any application of force which was intended to cause, or which did cause, 'actual bodily harm'.[24] The court said:[25]

---

[19] [1981] Q.B. 715. The reference was made under s. 36 of the Criminal Justice Act 1972. Lord Lane C.J. read the opinion of the court. The other two judges were Phillips J. and Drake J.

[20] The court was asked to give its opinion on the following point of law: 'Where two persons fight (otherwise than in the course of sport) in a public place can it be a defence for one of those persons to a charge of assault arising out of the fight that the other consented to fight?' The answer of the court was 'No, but not, as the reference implies, because the fight occurred in a public place, but because, wherever it occurred, the participants would have been guilty of assault, subject to self-defence, if, as we understand was the case, they intended to and/or did cause actual bodily harm.' ([1981] Q.B. 719E-F.)

[21] The court stated that 'the diversity of view expressed in the previous decisions . . . make some selection and a partly new approach necessary' ([1981] Q.B. 719A).

[22] [1981] Q.B. 718D.

[23] Ibid. 719. The opinion continued: 'Minor struggles are another matter. So, in our judgment, it is immaterial whether the act occurs in private or in public; it is an assault if actual bodily harm is intended and/or caused. This means that most fights will be unlawful regardless of consent.'

[24] The court did not define 'actual bodily harm', but as *R.* v. *Donovan* was one of the few cases cited by counsel, and discussed in the opinion, it may be assumed that they used 'actual bodily harm' to refer to what was described as 'bodily harm' in *R.* v. *Donovan*. (It is difficult to conceive of bodily harm which is not 'actual': see generally Williams, *Textbook,* 154.) The words used to describe 'bodily harm' in *R.* v. *Donovan* were very similar indeed to those used of 'actual bodily harm' in the then-current edition of *Archbold's Pleading, Evidence and Practice in Criminal Cases;* see 28th edn., 1931, edd. R. E. Ross and T. R. F.

[*See opposite page for n. 24 cont. and n. 25*]

Nothing which we have said is intended to cast doubt upon the accepted legality of properly conducted games and sports, lawful chastisement or correction, reasonable surgical interference, dangerous exhibitions, etc. These apparent exceptions can be justified as involving the exercise of a legal right, in the case of chastisement or correction, or as needed in the public interest, in the other cases.

Although the approach adopted by the Court of Appeal prohibits a wide range of consensual contacts,[26] the court's opinion should not lead to difficulties in relation to medical practice.

Many touchings which occur in the course of medical practice do not involve 'any hurt or injury calculated to interfere with health or comfort'. In these cases, consent can prevent liability in battery, even if there is 'no good reason' for the touching. Surgery, and some other medical procedures, could be said to involve 'hurt or injury calculated to interfere with health or comfort' in a manner which is 'more than merely transient and trifling'. As has already been suggested, conduct which benefits bodily health should not be regarded as causing bodily harm. But even if it were regarded as causing bodily harm, there could be absolutely no doubt that it was possible to give a legally effective consent to such procedures.[27] There is clearly a good reason for them.

Sometimes medical procedures which were intended to benefit the patient will fail in their object, and will cause what is undoubtedly bodily harm. If an application of force was not intended to cause bodily harm, and the person responsible did not take an unjustifiable risk as to the causing of bodily harm, then the undesired consequence should not render ineffective consent which would otherwise have been effective.[28] In the

Butler, p. 953. In this discussion 'bodily harm' will be used as a synonym for 'actual bodily harm'.

[25] [1981] Q.B. 719E.

[26] The court appears to have been aware that its formulation applied to an unnecessarily wide range of contacts, for the opinion concluded with the statement 'We would not wish our opinion on the point to be the signal for unnecessary prosecutions.'

[27] See e.g. Stephen, *Digest*, 148; *Bravery* v. *Bravery* [1954] 1 W.L.R. 1169, 1180; *Corbett* v. *Corbett* [1971] P. 83, 99; *R.* v. *Hyam* [1975] A.C. 55, 74, 77.

[28] But see the 'answer' in *A.-G.'s Reference (No. 6 of 1980)*, quoted in n. 20 above. The reference to 'and/or' in that answer is unsatisfactory. The 'good reason' qualification may be particularly important in cases where bodily harm is caused unintentionally.

course of medical practice there is often good reason to attempt to benefit a patient's health, even though there is a risk of harm resulting.[29] Here, too, consent will undoubtedly prevent liability being incurred.

Some medical procedures are not intended to benefit the person on whom they are performed.[30] Indeed, sometimes a procedure is performed on a person in the knowledge that it will certainly be to that person's bodily detriment. This is the case when a kidney is removed from a healthy person, for transplantation into someone who is in need of it. The operation is a major one, and is not without risks.[31] But it is not unreasonably dangerous, and the probable benefit to the recipient far outweighs the probable detriment to the donor. Hence, if called upon to deal with a case in which a kidney had been removed from a consenting adult, for transplantation into someone in need of it, the courts may confidently be expected to take the view that the operation did not amount to the offence of battery.[32] Even though the operation causes serious bodily harm, there is clearly a good reason for it. There is also a good reason for some non-therapeutic medical experimentation, even if it may cause bodily harm.[33]

Where judges regard an activity as socially acceptable they are unlikely to question the reasons for it. In the *Attorney-General's Reference (No. 6 of 1980)* the court spoke of the 'accepted legality' of properly conducted games and sports, of dangerous exhibitions, and of 'reasonable surgical interference'. The need for these 'apparent exceptions' only arises

[29] See e.g. *R. v. Hyam* [1975] A.C. 55, 74, 77-8.

[30] In *Bravery v Bravery* [1954] 1 W.L.R. 1169, 1180, Denning L.J. accepted that there was a just cause for sterilization to prevent the transmission of a hereditary disease.

[31] See R. G. Simmons *et al.*, *Gift of Life* (1977), 165-75; A. B. Cosimi, 'The Donor and Donor Nephrectomy', in *Kidney Transplantation* (1979, ed. P. J. Morris), 69, 71, 73-8; Editorial, 'Living Related Kidney Donors' [1982] 2 *Lancet* 696.

[32] Edmund Davies, 'Transplants', 634. See also R. Ormrod, 'Medical Ethics' [1968] 2 *Br. Med. J.* 7, 9-10; *Urbanski v. Patel* (1978) 84 D.L.R. (3d) 650, esp. 651, 670-1.

[33] For a case arising out of non-therapeutic experimentation, see *Haluskha v. University of Saskatchewan* (1965) 53 D.L.R. (2d) 436. The 'good reason' could be found either in the possibility of an eventual benefit to the health of others (and, sometimes, the subject), or in the advancement of knowledge as an end in itself. See also Bernard Häring, *Medical Ethics* (1972), 214-15.

where an application of force is intended to cause, or does in fact cause, bodily harm. As the Court of Appeal was prepared to accept that dangerous exhibitions are needed in the public interest, it would be extraordinary if a later court took a restrictive view of the scope of permissible medical interventions. A court is not likely to inquire closely into whether there are good reasons for a particular intervention. There is no danger of a court attempting to decide whether there were good reasons for removing a kidney from a living donor, instead of keeping the patient on dialysis in the hope that a suitable cadaver kidney would become available. And there is now very little danger of a court seeking to manipulate the offence of battery so as to prevent individuals reaching their own decisions about whether to be sterilized,[34] or undergo cosmetic surgery.[35] Opinions vary as to the desirability of such operations in particular circumstances.[36] But it is doubtful whether judges would regard these operations as sufficiently against the public interest to warrant their

[34] In *Bravery* v. *Bravery* [1954] 1 W.L.R. 1169, 1180, an appeal from the dismissal of a petition for divorce on grounds of cruelty, Denning L.J. expressed the view that 'where a sterilisation operation is done so as to enable a man to have the pleasure of sexual intercourse, without shouldering the responsibilities attaching to it' the operation 'is illegal, even though the man consents to it'. However, Sir Raymond Evershed M.R. and Hodson L.J. dissociated themselves from these observations: see ibid. 1175. For a critique of Denning L.J.'s reasons, see G. W. Bartholomew, 'Legal Implications of Voluntary Sterilization Operations' (1959) 2 *Melbourne University Law Review* 77, 93–4; and see also, now, Editorial, 'Vasectomy Reversal' [1980] 2 *Lancet* 625-6. Sterilization is now a widely-accepted method of birth control, and s. 1 of the National Health Service (Family Planning) Amendment Act 1972 provides for voluntary vasectomy services to be provided by local health authorities in England and Wales on the same basis as contraception services under s. 1 of the National Health Service (Family Planning) Act 1967. *Halsbury* (vol. xi, para. 23, n. 8) is surely correct in stating that nowadays the legality of such operations 'cannot be doubted'. See also e.g. *R.* v. *Miskimmin*, *The Times*, 15 June 1974, p. 3 (news report); *Re D. (A Minor) (Wardship: Sterilisation)* [1976] Fam. 185, 196; *Wells* v. *Surrey Area Health Authority*, *The Times*, 29 July 1978, p. 3 (news report); *Cataford* v. *Moreau* (1978) 114 D.L.R. (3d) 585; *Re Eve* (1981) 115 D.L.R. (3d) 282.

[35] For a Canadian view, see *Petty* v. *MacKay* (1979) 10 C.C.L.T. 85. See also Stephen, *Digest*, 149 n. 3; *White* v. *Turner* (1981) 120 D.L.R. (3d) 269.

[36] *Quaere*, in what circumstances such operations could properly be regarded as causing bodily harm. These operations are sometimes performed for therapeutic purposes. Given some broad definitions of 'health', (see generally Daniel Callahan, 'The W.H.O. Definition of Health' (1973) 1 *Hastings Center Studies* 77-87), many of these operations could be regarded as for the benefit of the health of the patient.

being regarded as constituting the offence of battery, despite the presence of consent.[37]

Were a patient to consent to having his limbs amputated, for no good reason, his consent would not prevent the amputation from amounting to the offence of battery. But the judges' insistence that there are some applications of force to which consent cannot be given, for the purpose of the offence of battery, should not hinder modern medical practice.

II TORT OF BATTERY

Bodily touchings which occur in the course of medical practice come within the potential scope of the tort, as well as the crime, of battery.[38] Where it is possible to give a legally effective consent to a medical procedure, for the purpose of the crime of battery, there is no doubt that consent will also prevent liability under the tort.[39]

[37] See generally P. D. G. Skegg, 'Medical Procedures and the Crime of Battery' [1974] *Crim. L.R.* at 699-700. In *R.* v. *Coney* (1882) 8 Q.B.D. 534, 549 Stephen J. said: 'The principle as to consent seems to me to be this: When one person is indicted for inflicting personal injury upon another, the consent of the person who sustains the injury is no defence to the person who inflicts the injury, if the injury is of such a nature, or is inflicted under such circumstances, that its infliction is injurious to the public as well as to the person injured.' In his *Digest of the Criminal Law* Stephen had expressed a different view, and in the two subsequent editions of the *Digest* which he prepared he left unchanged the statement that 'Every one has a right to consent to the infliction upon himself of bodily harm not amounting to a maim.' (For a fuller account, see P. D. G. Skegg, op. cit., 699, n. 38.) Professor Glanville Williams has used passages from Stephen's *Digest* to support a restrictive interpretation of his judgment in *R.* v. *Coney* (see Williams, *Textbook*, 541). But the fact that Stephen did not amend these passages could be regarded as demonstrating that he recognized that the approach he propounded in *R.* v. *Coney* did not receive the support of the majority of the judges in that case. (Professor Glanville Williams states that when Stephen J. spoke in *R.* v. *Coney* of an injury injurious to the public 'he must have meant an injury that was either (1) a maim or dangerous to life or (2) inflicted in circumstances likely to produce a breach of the peace (the former prize-fight)'. But in *R.* v. *Coney* Stephen J. said that it was 'against the public interest that the lives *and the health* of the combatants should be endangered by blows' (8 Q.B.D. 549; emphasis added). An injury may affect health even though it is not a maim or dangerous to life.)

[38] It makes no difference whether the touching is by hand (e.g. *Latter* v. *Braddell* (1881) 50 L.J.Q.B. 166, 448) or with some instrument controlled by the doctor (e.g. *S.* v. *McC*; *W.* v. *W.* [1972] A.C. 24, 57).

[39] On the absence of consent as an element of the tort of battery, see e.g. *Hegarty* v. *Shine* (1878) 4 L.R. Ir. 288, 293, 296.

Even if it were not possible to give a legally effective consent to a particular medical procedure, for the purpose of the crime of battery, it might nevertheless be possible to give an effective consent to it, for the purpose of the tort of battery. The reason why it is not possible to consent to some applications of force, for the purpose of the crime, is the public interest involved.[40] This public interest is protected adequately by the criminal law, and on principle consent should prevent the recovery of damages in battery.[41] There is some authority to support this view,[42] and the only authority to the contrary stems from a *dictum* in a case decided in 1693,[43] which was followed once in 1747.[44] This *dictum* is best explained in terms of 'the double nature—criminal and civil—of the old writs of trespass',[45] and should no longer be considered applicable.[46] The more recent authority is to be preferred.

Were it accepted that it was not possible to give a legally effective consent to certain medical procedures, for the purpose of the tort of battery, there would still be an obstacle to the recovery of damages in some cases. The 'patient' would often have aided and abetted a criminal act. Despite the limited applicability of the maxim *ex turpi causa non oritur actio*[47]

---

[40] *R.* v. *Coney* (1882) 8 Q.B.D. 534, 549, 553; *A.-G.'s Reference (No. 6 of 1980)* [1981] Q.B. 715, 719. See also *Hegarty* v. *Shine* (1878) 4 L.R. Ir. 288, 294.

[41] See J. G. Fleming, *Law of Torts* (5th edn., 1977), 80; *Salmond and Heuston on the Law of Torts* (18th edn., 1981, edd. R. F. V. Heuston and R. S. Chambers), 476; H. Street, *Law of Torts* (7th edn., 1983), 69. *Contra Pollock's Law of Torts* (15th edn., 1951, ed. P. A. Landon), 113. See also P. H. Winfield, *Province of the Law of Tort* (1931), 88-9; *Winfield and Jolowicz on Tort* (11th edn., 1979, ed. W. V. H. Rogers), 663-4.

[42] *Wade* v. *Martin* [1955] 3 D.L.R. 635, 638. See also *R.* v. *Coney* (1882) 8 Q.B.D. 534, 553; *Hegarty* v. *Shine* (1878) 4 L.R. Ir. 288, 293; *Lane* v. *Holloway* [1968] 1 Q.B. 379, 386; *Murphy* v. *Culhane* [1977] Q.B. 94, 98; Devlin, *Samples*, 87.

[43] *Matthew* v. *Ollerton* (1693) Comb. 218. *Pollock's Law of Torts* (15th edn., 1951, ed. P. A. Landon), 113, n. 55, speaks of 'the slender authority of that reporter'.

[44] *Boulter* v. *Clarke* (1747) Bull. N.P. 16. But see *Milner* v. *Wilson* (1755) Barnes 364.

[45] W. S. Holdsworth, *History of English Law*, vol. iii (4th edn., 1935), 318. The Crown retained a theoretical interest in every action of trespass until 1694, when the penalty was abolished by 5 & 6 William & Mary, c. 12.

[46] This thesis is developed in F. H. Bohlen, 'Consent As Affecting Civil Liability for Breaches of the Peace' (1924) 24 *Columbia Law Review* 819, 825-9.

[47] 'No disgraceful matter can ground an action.'

in the law of torts,[48] it might well apply to a plaintiff who was trying to benefit from a criminal act to which he had consented.[49]

III CRIME OF CAUSING GRIEVOUS BODILY HARM

Consent which is effective for the purpose of the crime of battery will also be effective to prevent a doctor committing other crimes of which assault or battery is a necessary element.[50] But an assault or a battery is not an essential element of the most serious non-fatal offence against the person, that of intentionally causing grievous bodily harm.[51] It is clearly important to determine whether this offence has any application to medical procedures and, if so, whether consent will prevent liability being incurred.

Section 18 of the Offences against the Person Act 1861 makes it an offence 'unlawfully and maliciously by any means whatsoever' to 'cause any grievous bodily harm to any person . . . with intent to . . . do some . . . grievous bodily harm to any person'. 'Grievous bodily harm' is nowadays

[48] *National Coal Board* v. *England* [1954] A.C. 403, 418-20, 424-5, 428-9. See also *Smith* v. *Jenkins* (1970) 119 C.L.R. 397 (negligence).

[49] *Wade* v. *Martin* [1955] 3 D.L.R. 635, 638; *Godbolt* v. *Fittock* (1963) 80 W.N. (N.S.W.) 1110; *Tomlinson* v. *Harrison* [1972] 1 O.R. 670; *Murphy* v. *Culhane* [1977] Q.B. 94, 98. See also *Lane* v. *Holloway* [1968] 1 Q.B. 379, 386; *Boeyen* v. *Kydd* [1963] V.R. 235, 237; *Smith* v. *Jenkins* (1970) 119 C.L.R. 397, 403 (but see *Jackson* v. *Harrison* (1978) 138 C.L.R. 438); *Pallante* v. *Stadiums Pty. Ltd. (No. 1)* [1976] V.R. 331; *Ashton* v. *Turner* [1981] Q.B. 137; P. J. Rowe, 'Illegality as a Defence in Tort' (1981) *New L.J.* 570-1.

[50] See e.g. Offences against the Person Act 1861, s. 47 (assault occasioning actual bodily harm).

[51] *R.* v. *Austin* (1973) 58 Cr. App. R. 163; *R.* v. *Lambert* (1976) 65 Cr. App. R. 12; *R.* v. *Nicholls* [1978] *Crim. L.R.* 247. Following the decision of the Court of Appeal in *R.* v. *Wilson* [1983] 1 W.L.R. 356, an assault or battery is not an essential element of the offence of maliciously inflicting grievous bodily harm, contrary to s. 20 of the Offences against the Person Act 1861. Most of the discussion of the offence of causing grievous bodily harm with intent is applicable to the offence of maliciously inflicting grievous bodily harm. But the fault elements of the two offences are very different. In the context of s. 20, 'maliciously' has been interpreted so as to permit the conviction of someone who simply foresaw that 'some physical harm to some other person, albeit of a minor character, might result': *R.* v. *Mowatt* [1968] 1 Q.B. 421, 426. Cf. *R.* v. *Cunningham* [1957] 2 Q.B. 396, 399-400 (s. 23). But if the circumstances were such that it was reasonable to risk causing harm, a doctor would not be held to have acted 'maliciously' simply because he was aware that harm might result from his intervention: cf. *R.* v. *Stephenson* [1979] Q.B. 695, 703.

treated as a synonym for really serious bodily harm.[52] Hence a medical procedure which does not cause really serious bodily harm does not come within even the potential scope of the offence. Even where a medical procedure did cause grievous bodily harm, a doctor would not be guilty of the offence if he did not intend to cause such harm.[53]

If it is accepted that an operation which benefits bodily health should not be regarded as causing bodily harm,[54] then most operations will not come within the potential scope of the offence.[55] But some will. Once again, a good example is the removal of a kidney from a living donor, for the sole purpose of benefiting the health of a potential recipient. It is important to determine whether such operations are ever justified for the purpose of section 18, and, if they are, what role consent plays in this.

Section 18 does not make it an offence for anyone ever to cause grievous bodily harm, with intent to do so. As with many other offences in the Offences against the Person Act 1861, there is a specific requirement that the conduct described be committed 'unlawfully'.[56] Judges have not been entirely consistent in their approach to this requirement. In at least one case judges appear to have assumed that it is necessary for the conduct to be unlawful, quite apart from the offence under consideration.[57] But there is considerable support for a different and better approach to the requirement that the conduct specified be carried out 'unlawfully'. A good illustration is provided by the treatment of section 58

---

[52] *D.P.P.* v. *Smith* [1961] A.C. 290, 334; *R.* v. *Hyam* [1975] A.C. 55, 68-9, 85, 94; *R.* v. *Cunningham* [1982] A.C. 566, 574. On the application of the *Smith* definition to s. 18, see *D.P.P.* v. *Smith*, above, 334; *R.* v. *Metharam* [1961] 3 All E.R. 200, 202.

[53] On the meaning of 'intent' in this context, see *R.* v. *Belfon* [1976] 1 W.L.R. 741.

[54] See pp. 30-2, above.

[55] In most cases (but see n. 10, above), the final result would be the same, even if all operations intended to benefit bodily health were regarded as intended to cause bodily harm. Where an operation has been performed for the benefit of the patient's health, and consent has been given, it would not be regarded as unlawful.

[56] S. 18, like s. 20, commences 'Whosoever shall unlawfully and maliciously . . .'. On the meaning of 'maliciously' in these contexts, see Smith and Hogan, 373-5.

[57] *R.* v. *Clarence* (1888) 22 Q.B.D. 23, 36, 40-1, 47, 59.

of the Offences against the Person Act 1861 in *R.* v. *Bourne*.[58]
The reference to 'unlawfully' was not viewed as a requirement that the attempt to procure an abortion must be unlawful, quite apart from the offence under consideration. It was
treated as an indication that in certain circumstances it would
be lawful to attempt to procure an abortion.[59] Understood in
this way, the requirement of unlawfulness is simply an indication of the possibility of the conduct being justified in
certain circumstances.[60] This approach finds support in a
subsequent case on section 18, where 'unlawfully' was
treated as a synonym for 'without lawful excuse'.[61]

The fact that section 18 proscribes only the unlawful causing of grievous bodily harm can be used as a basis for the
argument that certain medical procedures, which intentionally
cause grievous bodily harm, are lawful.[62] Of course, consent
would not always be sufficient to prevent liability being
incurred. Coke reports a case in which 'a young, strong, and
lusty Rogue, to make himself impotent, thereby to have the
more colour to beg or to be relieved without putting himself
to any labour, caused his companion to strike off his left
hand'.[63] In these circumstances the consent of the amputee
would not prevent the amputation from amounting to the
offence of causing grievous bodily harm, contrary to section 18 of the Offences against the Person Act.[64] Consent

[58] [1939] 1 K.B. 687.

[59] Ibid. 691 per Macnaghten J. See also *Royal College of Nursing* v. *Department of Health and Social Security* [1981] A.C. 800, 825F.

[60] See also *R.* v. *Prince* (1875) L.R. 2 C.C.R. 154, 178 (s. 55); *R.* v. *Austin*
[1981] 1 All E.R. 374, 378 (s. 56).

[61] *R.* v. *Hogan* (1973) 59 Cr. App. R. 174, 176 per Lawton J. (This statement
is not affected by *R.* v. *Humphrys* [1977] A.C. 1.) See also *R.* v. *Odgers* (1843)
2 Mood. & R. 479, 482-3 (Offences against the Person Act 1837, s. 4, on which
s. 18 is based); *R.* v. *Newman* [1948] V.L.R. 61, 67. Cf. *Albert* v. *Lavin* [1982]
A.C. 546, 561G (D.C.).

[62] It is highly probable that this approach would be adopted, in this context.
If therapeutic operations were regarded as causing grievous bodily harm the courts
would certainly adopt this approach.

[63] *Wright* (1603) 1 Co. Inst. 127a-b.

[64] In *R.* v. *Draper and Faiers* (1982, Central Criminal Court) the defendants
had, with the consent of the 'victim', cut off his right hand with an axe. The
defendants pleaded guilty to a charge of causing grievous bodily harm with intent:
see *Archbold's Pleading, Evidence and Practice in Criminal Cases* (41st edn., 1982,
ed. S. Mitchell), para. 20-124. For a fuller account of the facts, see *The Times*, 19
August 1981, p. 3 (news report of hearing in magistrates' court). See also (1983)
441 Parl. Deb. H.L. 676-7 (excision of clitoris: statement by Lord Hailsham L.C.).

would never of itself be sufficient to prevent the intentional causing of grievous bodily harm from amounting to this offence.[65]

To revert to the example of the removal of a kidney from a living person for transplantation to another: as there is a shortage of kidneys for transplantation,[66] and as transplants from living donors are at least as successful as those from cadavers,[67] the courts may be expected to accept that there is a 'just cause or excuse',[68] or 'good reason',[69] for such operations. Where consent is also present,[70] such operations will not amount to the offence of causing grievous bodily harm.[71]

IV CRIME OF MAIM

In practice, the common law offence of maim has long been supplanted by statutory offences. But it has not been expressly abolished,[72] and a judge has made an extrajudicial statement which suggests that there is at least a theoretical possibility of the offence of maim applying to operations in which a kidney

[65] Cf. *R.* v. *Clarence* (1888) 22 Q.B.D. 23, 48. Very occasionally the presence of consent may be a factor in determining whether a procedure comes within the potential scope of the offence. For example, whether cosmetic surgery counts as 'bodily harm' may sometimes depend, not simply on the procedure performed, but on the patient's attitude to it.

[66] See Medical Services Study Group of the Royal College of Physicians, 'Donation of Kidneys', (1981) 283 *Br. Med. J.* 286-7.

[67] They are usually more successful: see generally A. B. Cosimi, 'The Donor and Donor Nephrectomy', in *Kidney Transplantation* (1979, ed. P. J. Morris), 69, 70.

[68] Cf. *Bravery* v. *Bravery* [1954] 1 W.L.R. 1169, 1181.

[69] Cf. *A.-G'.s Reference (No. 6 of 1980)* [1981] Q.B. 715, 719D.

[70] Whether it is ever lawful to perform, without consent, a medical procedure which intentionally causes grievous bodily harm depends very much on the meaning attributed to 'bodily harm'. If major surgical operations which benefit bodily health were regarded as causing really serious bodily harm, doctors would sometimes be justified, for the purpose of s. 18, in proceeding without consent. But if no procedure which benefits physical or psychological health were to be regarded as bodily harm, then a doctor would never be justified in performing, without consent, an operation which intentionally caused grievous bodily harm.

[71] See Edmund Davies, 'Transplants', 634. ('I should be surprised if a surgeon were . . . convicted of causing bodily harm to one of full age and intelligence who freely consented to act as donor—always provided that the operation did not present unreasonable risk to that donor's life or health.') See also R. Ormrod, 'Medical Ethics' [1968] 2 *Br. Med. J.* 7, 9, 10.

[72] Cf. *R.* v. *Owen* [1976] 1 W.L.R. 840 (revival of 'the obsolescent offence of embracery': ibid. 842).

is removed from a healthy living donor, for transplantation into a person who is in need of it.[73] It is therefore desirable to consider the extent to which the offence of maim would apply to medical procedures, and the related issue of whether consent would be effective to prevent liability.

The authorities[74] have long distinguished between acts which permanently disable and weaken a man,[75] rendering him less able in fighting; and acts which simply disfigure. The former are maims, the latter are not. There is no shortage of examples of injuries which fall within one category rather than the other. Over many centuries, it has been agreed that it is a maim to cut off, disable, or weaken an arm or foot. It has also been agreed that it is a maim to deprive a man of an eye, foretooth, or 'those parts, the loss of which in all animals abates their courage'.[76] However, it has also long been accepted that it is not a maim to cut off an ear or nose, as such injuries are said not to affect a man's capacity for fighting.

The fact that a particular injury has in the past been classified as a maim need not be decisive in any future case. Changes in military practice, or increased medical knowledge, could lead to certain injuries ceasing to be regarded as maims, and other injuries coming to be regarded as maims. When Bracton wrote that it was a maim to break the incisors, this

[73] R. Ormrod, op. cit., 9 (cf. *Jennings* v. *United States Government* [1982] 3 All E.R. 104, 107f–g per Ormrod L.J. (D.C.)). See also Edmund Davies, 'Transplants', 634.

[74] Among the more important accounts of the offence of maim are *Bracton on the Laws and Customs of England* (trans. etc. S. E. Thorne), vol. ii (1968), 409–10; *Britton* (trans. etc. F. M. Nichols, 1865), vol. i, 122–3; 1 Co. Inst. 127 a–b, 288a, 3 Co. Inst. 118 (and also 1 Co. Inst. 126a–b, 3 Co. Inst. 62–3); 1 Hawk. P.C. (8th edn.), 107–8 (ch. XV, ss. 1–4); 3 Bl. Com. 121, 4 Bl. Com. 205–6; 1 East P.C. 393, 400–3. See also Stephen, *Digest*, 148–9.

[75] It is often said that the offence of maim does not apply to maiming injuries to any woman, but the rationale of the offence given by some authorities (see e.g. 1 Co. Inst. 127a, 4 Bl. Com. 205) would be consistent with the offence of maim nowadays applying to maiming injuries to at least some women. The view that women were not the subject of maim may have resulted from the fact that women were not required to engage in military service, and the fact that castration has been a standard example of maim. Just as the courts now accept that affrays may be committed in private as well as public places (*R.* v. *Button and Swain* [1966] A.C. 591), so they could take the view that nowadays women as well as men may be the victim of maim.

[76] 4 Bl. Com. 205; *Russell on Crime* (12th edn., 1964, ed. J. W. C. Turner), vol. i, 625 (adding a comma after 'animals').

was because 'such teeth are of great assistance in winning a fight'[77]—by, it seems, biting. When, seven centuries later, Stephen wrote that it would sometimes have been an offence to pull out a soldier's front teeth, despite the soldier's consent, he explained that this was because it was an essential part of a common soldier's drill to bite cartridges.[78] The extraction of teeth would no longer bring anyone within even the potential scope of an offence of maim.

Most medical procedures do not permanently disable a person and render that person less able in fighting.[79] They therefore fall outside even the potential scope of any offence of maim.[80] This is as true of the removal of a healthy kidney for transplantation as it is of the removal of a diseased appendix. But even if a medical procedure did come within the potential scope of an offence of maim, it would not follow that a doctor would commit an offence of maim in going ahead with it. Just as the infliction of a maim was sometimes permitted in self-defence,[81] so a maiming operation would not amount to the offence of maim if there was a good reason for it. Hence, even if castration could still be regarded as coming within the potential scope of maim, it would be justified if performed for a therapeutic purpose.[82]

---

[77] Bracton, op. cit., vol. ii, 410.

[78] Stephen, *Digest*, 149, n. 3.

[79] On the requirement that an injury be permanent for it to constitute a maim, see e.g. 3 Bl. Com. 121. See also *R.* v. *Jeans* (1844) 1 Car. & Kir. 539. Even where a medical procedure permanently disabled the patient, and could be regarded as a maim, the doctor would not normally have intended, or been reckless as to, that consequence. On principle, intention or recklessness as to the injury should nowadays be required.

[80] Some medical procedures involve the amputation of limbs which have been specifically mentioned in discussions of maim. However, the amputation of an arm or leg would only come within the potential scope of the offence if it had the effect of permanently disabling the subject in fighting. See 1 Co. Inst. 288a (' "Maihem" . . . signifieth a corporal Hurt, whereby he loseth a Member, *by reason whereof* he is less able to fight'); 3 Bl. Com. 121 ('for ever disabled from making so good a defence against future external injuries, *as he otherwise might have done*') (emphasis added). As the injury which led to the amputation would normally have itself disabled the patient, the operation necessitated by that injury should not come within the potential scope of maim.

[81] See 1 East P.C. 402, which implies other interests may sometimes be balanced against the interest protected by the law of maim. On self-defence and maim, see also 3 Bl. Com. 121; *Cockcroft* v. *Smith* (1705) 1 Ld. Raym. 177, 2 Salk. 642, 11 Mod. 43.

[82] Cf. *Corbett* v. *Corbett* [1971] P. 83, 99A. See generally R. B. Welbourn,

The offence of maim would very rarely apply to any procedure performed in the course of medical practice, even if consent had not been given. But if something was done which did come within the potential scope of maim—as where a member of the armed forces persuaded a friend to cut off his trigger finger for him, in an attempt to obtain a discharge[83]—consent would normally[84] be irrelevant.[85] This is because the offence was said to protect the interests of the Sovereign in the services of those who owed her allegiance.[86] The subject was not in a position to waive his Sovereign's supposed interests in the matter.

'Castration' in *Dict. Med. Ethics*, 49-51. In *Cowburn* [1959] *Crim. L.R.* 590, Cowburn's counsel asked the Court of Criminal Appeal to assure the prison authorities that it would not be unlawful or contrary to public policy for Cowburn, a sexual psychopath, to be voluntarily castrated while in prison. The judges refused to give such an assurance. However, this should not be interpreted as implying anything as to the legality of such operations. The slightly fuller report in *The Times*, 12 May 1959, makes it very clear that the reason for this refusal was their view that it was not the function of the court to give directions on what takes place in prison.

[83] For an example of this being done, see B. Cox, *Civil Liberties in Britain* (1975), 286.

[84] The reason for this qualification is that very exceptionally consent may be relevant in deciding whether a particular medical procedure was, in the circumstances, therapeutic. If the procedure appeared to constitute a maim, the question whether it was therapeutic—and hence whether there was a just cause or excuse for it (cf. *Corbett* v. *Corbett* [1971] P. 83, 99A)—might in theory be relevant in determining whether it amounted to any offence of maim.

[85] *Wright* (1603) 1 Co. Inst. 127a-b; see also Bracton, op. cit., vol. ii, pp. 408. But see generally Williams, *Textbook*, 539-40. (Professor Glanville Williams points out that in *Wright* the parties 'had entered into a conspiracy to defraud the public' and states that 'the brief report does not state whether they were convicted of this conspiracy or of maim'. However, Coke gave his account of the case in the course of his discussion of maim, and stated that 'both of them were indited, fined and ransomed therefore, and that by the opinion of the rest of the Justices, for the cause aforesaid' (1 Co. Inst. 127b). The 'cause aforesaid' related to the principle underlying the offence of maim. See 1 Co. Inst. 127a (where the same phrase is used), and also 3 Co. Inst. 118.) Consent may, of course, affect the liability of the person who is maimed. It was only where consent had been given that he could be liable. See generally 1 East P.C. 400-1; 1 Hawk, P.C. (8th edn.) 108; Williams, *Textbook*, 538, 540.

[86] See 1 Co. Inst. 127a, 4 Bl. Com. 205.

INDIVIDUAL CAPACITY TO CONSENT
TO MEDICAL PROCEDURES

[T]here are many girls under sixteen who know full
well what it is all about and can properly consent.

Lord Parker C.J., 1965[1]

Once it is apparent that a medical procedure is one to which
some people can give a legally effective consent, for the
purpose of the crime or tort in question,[2] it becomes important to determine whether the patient can give a legally
effective consent, or whether anyone else can give such a
consent to the performance of the procedure on the patient.[3]
This chapter will deal first with consent of the patient, and
then with consent of others. In both parts it will be necessary
to pay particular attention to the capacity to consent to
medical procedures on minors,[4] for this is the matter which
has given rise to the greatest uncertainty and controversy.

I CONSENT OF PATIENT

The courts have rarely dealt with the question of individual
capacity to consent. Their concern has been directed towards
whether the person consented to the touching in question.

---

[1] *R.* v. *Howard* [1965] 3 All E.R. 684, 685.

[2] See ch. 2.

[3] There are substantive and procedural differences between the crime and the
tort of battery, reflecting to some extent the different purposes of the criminal
law and the law of torts. But it may be assumed that, where there are no good
reasons to the contrary, authorities on the crime will be applicable to the tort,
and vice versa. (See *Scott* v. *Shepherd* (1773) 2 Black. W. 892, 899; Offences
against the Person Act 1861, s. 45.) In this chapter, and in the two chapters which
follow, the crime and the tort will be considered together. However, on occasions,
possible differences between them will be discussed.

[4] For helpful discussions of this issue, with reference to the law in the United
States and Canada, see A. R. Holder, *Legal Issues in Pediatrics and Adolescent
Medicine* (1977), ch. 5; B. M. Dickens, *Medico-Legal Aspects of Family Law*
(1979), ch. 6.

Where he has not done so, it is of little consequence whether this was because he was incapable of consenting or because, although capable, he did not in fact consent.

The general principle

Capacity to give a legally effective consent depends upon capacity to understand and come to a decision on what is involved, and the capacity to communicate that decision.[5] The essentially factual issues which determine individual capacity to consent are well illustrated by two Commonwealth cases. The first, a New Zealand case,[6] resulted from the taking of a blood sample. The doctor had been requested by the police to examine a man who, they suspected, was too drunk to be lawfully driving a car. Although described by the doctor as 'pretty far gone', the suspect stoutly maintained that he was sober. To settle the point 'one way or other', as the doctor put it, the doctor proposed that he should take a blood sample. The man then rolled up his sleeve so that the blood could be taken from a vein in his forearm. The test revealed a blood alcohol level in excess of the statutory maximum,[7] and the man was subsequently convicted under the appropriate legislation. He then brought an action against the doctor, alleging that he had been too drunk to give a legally effective consent. The court held that, at the time the sample was taken, the man was incapable of consenting, and awarded him damages. This case may be contrasted with a Canadian one,[8] which also involved the taking of a blood sample. At the time the sample was taken the man was still showing signs of being affected by liquor, but the judge was satisfied that the man 'was in no way bereft of his powers of

---

[5] The latter requirement is important where the patient is conscious, but suffers from a medical condition which prevents him from communicating his assent or dissent. Such cases are comparatively rare, and no further reference will be made to this requirement.

[6] *Anon.* (1966), unreported, discussed in Medical Protection Society's *Annual Report and Accounts*, 1966, No. 75, pp. 36-7.

[7] The test showed 170 milligrammes of alcohol per 100 millilitres of blood. This is just over twice the permitted maximum under the Road Traffic Act 1972 (U.K.), ss. 6, 12(1) (substituted by the Transport Act 1981, s. 25(3), Sch. 8).

[8] *R.* v. *Ford* [1948] 1 D.L.R. 787 (Alta.).

decision and that he knew quite well what he was doing when he came to the decision to give the sample'.[9]

There is no reason to believe that, in the absence of special statutory provisions, the rules governing capacity to consent vary with different categories of person. Nevertheless, it is desirable to consider separately the capacity of minors, and the capacity of persons suffering from a mental disorder.

Minors

There has long been uncertainty in medical circles about the capacity of minors to consent to medical procedures. Some of the uncertainty was overcome by the Family Law Reform Act 1969. As well as reducing the age of majority from twenty-one to eighteen,[10] the Act includes a provision dealing with the consent to medical treatment[11] of minors of sixteen and seventeen years of age.

Section 8(1) provides that:

> The consent of a minor who has attained the age of sixteen years to any surgical, medical or dental treatment which, in the absence of consent, would constitute a trespass to his person, shall be as effective as it would be if he were of full age; and where a minor has by virtue of this section given an effective consent to any treatment it shall not be necessary to obtain any consent for it from his parent or guardian.

Treatment which in the absence of consent would constitute a 'trespass to his person'[12] will normally come within the purview of one or more crimes, so the section applies in the criminal law as well as in the law of torts.

Where the minor has attained the age of sixteen years there can be no doubt as to his capacity to consent to medical[13]

[9] Ibid. 793. See also *R.* v. *Lang* (1975) 62 Cr. App. R. 50, 52 ('We have no doubt that there is no special rule applicable to drink and rape. If the issue be, as here, did the woman consent? the critical question is . . . whether she understood her situation and was capable of making up her mind.'). Cf. Stephen, *Digest*, 147.

[10] Family Law Reform Act 1969, s. 1.

[11] See also Family Law Reform Act 1969, s. 21(2).

[12] Trespass to the person includes the tort of assault and the tort of battery, as well as the tort of false imprisonment.

[13] 'Medical' will be used in this discussion to comprehend surgical, medical, and dental procedures.

'treatment'. His consent is, by virtue of section 8(1), 'as effective as it would be if he were of full age'. Furthermore, section 8(1) specifically states that, where the minor has by virtue of the section given an effective consent to any treatment, 'it shall not be necessary to obtain any consent for it from his parent or guardian'.

Section 8(2) provides that:

> In this section 'surgical, medical or dental treatment' includes any procedure undertaken for the purposes of diagnosis, and this section applies to any procedure (including, in particular, the administration of an anaesthetic) which is ancillary to any treatment as it applies to that treatment.

The specific reference to diagnostic procedures, and to procedures ancillary to treatment, may be interpreted as implying that other procedures which are not an integral part of the treatment of an existing illness are not to be regarded as 'treatment' in this context. When the Ontario Commissioners for the Conference on Uniformity of Legislation in Canada produced a draft Medical Consent of Minors Act, with a definition of 'medical treatment' very similar to that in section 8(2) of the Family Law Reform Act 1969,[14] the Alberta Commissioners commented:[15]

> We are not satisfied that the definition of 'medical treatment' . . . is adequate. It refers only to 'treatment' and our concern is that the word 'treatment' may not extend to an examination of a patient prior to treatment nor to procedures that are in their nature preventative only, such as the prescribing or implantation of a contraceptive device in a minor female and an abortion performed on a minor female.

Although the concept of 'treatment' could be taken to cover innoculation and other preventive measures intended for the

[14] See *Proceedings of the Fifty-Sixth Annual Meeting of the Uniform Law Conference of Canada*, 1974, pp. 118, 120. For the text of the Act, as adopted and recommended for enactment, see *Proceedings of the Fifty-Seventh Annual Meeting of the Uniform Law Conference of Canada*, 1975, pp. 162-3.

[15] Letter, G. Acorn (on behalf of the Alberta Commissioners) to R. C. Smethurst (Secretary of the Conference of Commissioners), 27 November 1974, quoted in [G. M. van der Ven], *Consent of Minors to Medical Treatment* (Institute of Law Research and Reform, University of Alberta, Background Paper No. 9, 1975), p. 23.

benefit of the health of the patient, it is most unlikely that it would be held to comprehend medical procedures which were not intended to benefit the health of the minor. Most blood donations and most non-therapeutic experiments could not be regarded as 'treatment', for the purpose of section 8.

The fact that section 8 has no application to any medical procedures performed on minors under the age of sixteen, or to medical procedures not intended to benefit the health of minors of sixteen or seventeen years of age,[16] does not rule out the possibility of minors giving a legally effective consent in these cases. Section 8(3) provides that:

Nothing in this section shall be construed as making ineffective any consent which would have been effective if this section had not been enacted.

There is therefore still the possibility of consent being given on the basis of the minors' common law capacity.

Opinions concerning the common law capacity of minors to consent to medical procedures fall into three broad categories: that all minors are by reason of their age incapable of giving a legally effective consent; that all minors under some 'age of consent', invariably sixteen, are by reason of their age incapable of giving a legally effective consent; and that no minor is incapable by reason of his age alone, but that it all depends on his capacity to understand and come to a decision on the procedure in question.

The view that at common law all minors are incapable of consenting to medical procedures results from a fundamental misconception of the position of such procedures in relation to the criminal and the civil law. Medical procedures are not in a different category from other bodily touchings.[17] If minors were incapable by reason of their age alone of consenting to medical procedures, it would follow that they were incapable of consenting to other touchings. This would have interesting consequences. There would not have been any

---

[16] But see Family Law Reform Act 1969, s. 21(2), which provides that the consent of a minor who has attained the age of sixteen years to the taking from himself of a blood sample—where a court has directed that blood tests be used to assist in determining paternity—'shall be as effective as it would be if he were of full age'.

[17] See Devlin, *Samples*, 84–5.

need for the Tattooing of Minors Act 1969, for a tattooist who tattooed a minor with only that minor's consent would commit a battery.[18] So, too, would anyone who embraced a girl who had not attained her majority—unless, on one view, the consent of one of her parents had first been obtained. Furthermore, a minor would not be able to give a legally effective consent to a haircut. There is no reason to believe that this is so, and cases have been decided on the assumption that minors can consent to medical touchings,[19] and to other applications of force.[20]

The view that minors who have not attained the age of sixteen years are incapable of consenting to medical procedures is widely held. But it, too, rests on a misconception as to the position of medical procedures which, as already stated, the common law deals with on the same basis as other bodily touchings. The fact that persons of sixteen years and above are usually free to choose their own doctors under the National Health Service,[21] and to enter mental hospitals as voluntary boarders,[22] does not imply that persons under that age are incapable of consenting to medical procedures. Furthermore, even if these provisions were based on such an assumption, that would not of itself affect the common law position.[23] Some doctors who believe that minors under the age of sixteen are incapable of consenting to medical procedures appear to be influenced by the fact that the age of sixteen is widely regarded as the 'age of consent' in relation to sexual matters. But, if anything, this aspect of the law supports the view that persons under sixteen are sometimes capable of consenting. Although their consent is no defence to various statutory offences, because of specific provisions

[18] But see R. v. Dilks (1964) 4 Med. Sci. Law 209. Cf. Burrell v. Harmer (1966) 116 New L.J. 1658, [1967] Crim. L.R. 169.

[19] See e.g. R. v. Case (1850) 4 Cox C.C. 220; Agnew v. Jobson (1877) 13 Cox C.C. 625.

[20] See e.g. R. v. Donovan [1934] 2 K.B. 498; R. v. Dilks (1964) 4 Med. Sci. Law 209, and cases cited in n. 25, below.

[21] National Health Service (General Medical and Pharmaceutical Services) Regulations 1974 (S.I. 1974/160), regs. 14 and 32.

[22] Mental Health Act 1959, s. 5(2).

[23] See Inland Revenue Commissioners v. Dowdall, O'Mahoney & Co. [1952] A.C. 401, 426; Davies v. Davies, Jenkins & Co. Ltd. [1968] A.C. 1097, 1121; West Midland Baptist Association v. Birmingham Corporation [1970] A.C. 874, 898, 911.

to this effect,[24] it is well established that it may be effective for the purpose of crimes for which there is no such provision.[25] The statement of Lord Parker C.J. in a case concerning rape,[26] which was quoted at the beginning of this chapter, is equally true of medical procedures.

The common law does not fix any age below which minors are automatically incapable of consenting to medical procedures. It all depends on whether the minor can understand what is involved in the procedure in question. In the Canadian case of *Johnston* v. *Wellesley Hospital*,[27] Addy J. said the law was 'well expressed' in a passage in Lord Nathan's book on *Medical Negligence*[28] where it was said that:

the most satisfactory solution . . . is to rule that an infant who is capable of appreciating fully the nature and consequences of a particular operation or of particular treatment can give an effective consent thereto, and in such cases the consent of the guardian is unnecessary . . .

This is a helpful statement, but it would be a mistake to place great stress on the need to appreciate 'fully' the nature and consequences of a procedure. Many adults do not 'fully' understand the nature and consequences of a medical procedure (or, for that matter, a sexual touching), but that does not necessarily invalidate their consent. A sufficient understanding need not be a full understanding.[29] A minor who, in Addy J.'s words, is 'as fully capable of understanding the possible consequences of a medical or surgical procedure as an adult' is capable of giving an effective consent—even if, like many adult patients, he is not capable of appreciating 'fully' the nature and consequences of the procedure.[30]

[24] See e.g. Sexual Offences Act 1956, ss. 14, 15.

[25] See, for example, the following cases, in each of which the consent of the child, to a touching of a sexual nature, was effective to prevent a conviction: *R.* v. *Banks* (1838) 8 C. & P. 574 (nine-year-old); *R.* v. *Martin* (1840) 9 C. & P. 213, 215, 2 Moo. C.C. 123 (eleven-year-old); *R.* v. *Johnston* (1865) Le. & Ca. 632 (ten-year-old). See also *R.* v. *Guthrie* (1870) L.R. 1 C.C.R. 241, 243.

[26] *R.* v. *Howard* [1965] 3 All E.R. 684, 685.

[27] (1970) 17 D.L.R. (3d) 139, 144-5 (Ont.). See also *Booth* v. *Toronto General Hospital* (1910) 17 O.W.R. 118, 120.

[28] Lord Nathan, *Medical Negligence* (1957), 176.

[29] See ch. 4, pt. I, esp. pp. 77–80.

[30] Where a minor has the capacity to consent, and has in fact consented, to the procedure in question, a doctor will not incur liability in battery if he performs the procedure, even if both parents object.

The judgment of Heilbron J. in *Re D. (A Minor) (Ward-ship: Sterilisation)*[31] lends support to the view that at common law capacity to consent depends on capacity to understand what is involved in the procedure in question.[32] The case concerned a proposal to sterilize an eleven-year-old girl suffering from Sotos syndrome. The girl was said to have the understanding of a child of less than ten years of age. Heilbron J. did not suggest that there was any rule of law which automatically prevented a minor from consenting to a medical procedure. She said that the evidence showed that the girl was 'unable as yet to understand and appreciate the implications of this operation and could not give a valid or informed consent', but that 'the likelihood is that in later years she will be able to make her own choice'.[33]

Although in some cases it would not require any evidence beyond the tender age of the child to convince the court that the child was incapable of consenting,[34] many children under the age of ten would probably be capable of consenting to relatively minor and straightforward procedures,[35] such as the binding up of a wound. Doctors have reported that children of ten years of age are able to understand what is involved in the taking of a blood sample for research purposes, and are usually very willing to participate in such procedures.[36] But it would be unwise to assume that minors who have not reached their teenage years are capable of consenting to major procedures. An Australian judge once stated, extra-judicially, that 'in most cases of dangerous operations or amputations' a judge or jury would take the view that a minor under fourteen years of age was incapable of consenting.[37]

[31] [1976] Fam. 185 (hereinafter cited as *Re D.*). See generally Editorial, 'Sterilisation of Mentally Retarded Minors' (1980) 281 *Br. Med. J.* 1025-6, and subsequent correspondence, ibid. 1281-2.

[32] See also the extrajudicial comments of Ormrod L.J.: Ormrod, 'Ethics', 25-6.

[33] [1976] Fam. 196. See also ibid. 193.

[34] See e.g. *B (B.R.)* v. *B (J.)* [1968] P. 466, 473. See also *R.* v. *Harling* [1938] 1 All E.R. 307, 308; *R.* v. *Howard* [1965] 3 All E.R. 684, 685 (rape).

[35] See Speller, *Hospitals*, 194, n. 1 ('[A] comparatively young child can consent to the administration of a sticking plaster over a grazed knee . . .').

[36] J. A. Dodge and J. Evans, Letter, 'Research on Infants' [1977] 1 *Lancet* 852.

[37] N. O'Bryan, 'The Consent of the Patient to Surgical and Medical Procedures' (1961) 8 *Proceedings of the Medico-Legal Society of Victoria* 138, 155.

Although it might be convenient for doctors and hospital administrators if there were a fixed 'age of consent' to medical touchings, English law does not fix any one age. A child may have a sufficient intellectual capacity to consent to one procedure, but not another. Some children of the same age may lack the capacity to consent to either procedure. There is obviously room for considerable difference of opinion whether the minor was capable of understanding, and did in fact understand, what was involved in a particular procedure. This makes it especially important for the doctor to ensure that the minor understands the relevant considerations. The courts are unlikely to question the capacity of a normal seventeen-year-old to consent to the removal of blood for transfusion, but they are likely to be much more wary with a fourteen-year-old who purports to consent to the removal of one of his kidneys, for transplantation to his twin brother. Nevertheless, there is reason to believe that many minors of fourteen years of age are capable of consenting to such an operation. American courts have found that minors of that age fully understood the nature of a nephrectomy and its possible consequences, and freely consented to it.[38] From the doctor's point of view, the danger is that, in the unlikely event of proceedings being brought, a judge or jury who disapproved of the removal on moral grounds would hold, without making any proper examination of the minor's intellectual capacity, that he was in fact incapable of consenting.[39]

It has been suggested that there is a rule of law whereby minors cannot give an effective consent to touchings which are to their detriment.[40] So far as the criminal law is concerned, there is no reason to believe that at common law minors are in a different position from adults in this matter.[41] It was for this reason that statutes were required to restrict

[38] *Huskey* v. *Harrison* (1957); *Foster* v. *Harrison* (1957); unreported Massachusetts cases, discussed in W. J. Curran, 'A Problem of Consent: Kidney Transplantation in Minors' (1959) 34 *New York University Law Review* 891-8. For a selection of documents relating to these cases, see J. Katz, *Experimentation with Human Beings* (1972), 964-72.

[39] Cf. *Burrell* v. *Harmer* (1966) 116 *New L.J.* 1658, [1967] *Crim. L.R.* 169.

[40] Whether there should be such a rule is, of course, another question.

[41] *R.* v. *Donovan* [1934] 2 K.B. 498 proceeds on this assumption. See also *R.* v. *Dilks* (1964) 4 *Med. Sci. Law* 209, and the cases cited n. 25, above.

sexual contacts and the tattooing of minors. But it was once said that 'the whole idea of civil law . . . that a minor is completely incapable of consenting to any act which is to her prejudice' would prevent the law from permitting a minor to donate an organ.[42] This principle is broadly true as far as the law of contract is concerned, but there is no reason to believe that it applies to the law of torts. In the course of sporting and other activities children consent to bodily contacts which are not always for their benefit. The adoption of a rule whereby minors are incapable of consenting to any acts which are to their prejudice would have far-reaching effects, not merely on the tort of battery, but also in other areas of the civil law.[43] As yet, there is little reason to believe that the courts will uphold the existence of such a rule.

Mentally disordered persons

The fact that a person is suffering from a mental disorder, as defined in the Mental Health Act 1959,[44] does not of itself preclude that person from giving a legally effective consent.[45] Whether the person is capable of doing so depends upon whether that person can understand and come to a decision upon what is involved.[46] Most patients in mental hospitals are

[42] Lord Kilbrandon, in *Ethics and Medical Progress* (1966, edd. G. E. W. Wolstenholme and M. O'Connor), 214. Lord Kilbrandon was not dealing specifically with the tort of battery, but was discussing the possibility of a statutory provision, authorizing the donation of organs by minors.

[43] It might be argued that it would, for example, prevent minors making gifts to charitable organizations.

[44] S. 4(1) of the Mental Health Act 1959 provides that 'In this Act "mental disorder" means mental illness, arrested or incomplete development of mind, psychopathic disorder, and any other disorder or disability of mind, and "mentally disordered" shall be construed accordingly.' The terms are used in this sense in this chapter. On the definition of mental disorder, see also Mental Health (Amendment) Act 1982, ss. 1-2.

[45] Cf. *Bolam* v. *Friern Hospital Management Committee* [1957] 1 W.L.R. 582 (action in negligence—voluntary patient in mental hospital, suffering from depression—capacity to consent assumed).

[46] Cf. *Mason* v. *Mason*, *The Times*, 22 May 1972 (Question of whether voluntary mental patient could validly consent to the grant of a decree of divorce under Divorce Reform Act 1969, s. 2(1) (d); Sir George Baker P. adopted test of whether the person knew and understood at the time what he was doing.) See also Family Law Reform Act 1969, s. 21(4); *R.* v. *Morgan* [1970] V.R. 337, 341-2 (capacity of mentally retarded girl to consent to sexual intercourse); *Re Beaney* [1978] 1 W.L.R. 770 (degree of understanding required for making a contract, or a gift

capable of giving a legally effective consent, including many who are compulsorily detained. Doctors are sometimes free to proceed without consent,[47] but even then a patient will sometimes have the capacity to give a legally effective consent, which would of itself prevent the doctor's conduct from amounting to the tort or crime of battery.[48]

II CONSENT OF OTHERS

A person who is capable of consenting to the performance of a particular medical procedure on himself is capable of giving a legally effective consent to its performance on another, where he has been authorized by that person, or by law, to do so. Authorization by the patient does not raise any special difficulties: the ordinary principles of agency apply.[49] More difficult is the question of the extent to which a person may have independent legal authority to consent to medical procedures on others. It is proposed to deal first with the power to give a legally effective consent to medical procedures on minors. This will be followed by an examination of whether there is a special power to consent to medical procedures on

inter vivos); *Review of the Mental Health Act 1959* (Cmnd. 7320; 1978), para. 6. 23; L. O. Gostin, 'Observations on Consent to Treatment and Review of Clinical Judgment in Psychiatry: A Discussion Paper' (1981) 74 *J. Roy. Soc. Med.* 742, 743-4.

[47] See ch. 5, n. 3.

[48] But see s. 43 of the Mental Health (Amendment) Act 1982, which applies to treatment for mental disorder which involves 'any surgical operation for destroying brain tissue or for destroying the function of brain tissue', and also to 'such other forms of treatment as may be specified for the purposes of this section by regulations made by the Secretary of State'. Except in circumstances specified in s. 48 of the Act, such treatment is not to be given to a detained or to a voluntary patient (ss. 42, 50) unless the patient has consented to it; three other persons, including a medical practitioner, have certified that the patient 'is capable of understanding the nature, purpose, and likely effects of the treatment in question and has consented to it'; and the medical practitioner involved in the certification process has certified, after required consultation, that 'having regard to the likelihood of the treatment alleviating or preventing a deterioration of the patient's condition, the treatment should be given'. See also s. 44 (forms of treatment of detained patients requiring consent or a second opinion), s. 45 (consent etc. to a plan of treatment), and s. 46 (withdrawal of consent).

[49] See e.g. *Jackson & Co.* v. *Napper* (1886) 35 Ch. D. 162, 172; *Grand Trunk Railway Co. of Canada* v. *Robinson* [1915] A.C. 740, 747. See also N. O'Bryan, op. cit., n. 37 above, 151.

persons suffering from a mental disorder, and finally a consideration of whether there is some general principle whereby persons are sometimes able to give a legally effective consent to medical procedures on others.

Consent to procedures on minors: introduction

Although it has long been assumed that parents can sometimes give a legally effective consent to medical procedures to be performed on their children, it was not until the late 1960s that such a power was clearly recognized in reported English decisions.[50] These decisions were primarily concerned with blood tests for forensic purposes, but they provided clear judicial recognition of a parental power to consent in some circumstances. There can now be no doubt that legally effective consent can be given by a parent, who has not been deprived of the custody and control of an infant, where the procedure is in the best interests of the child and the child is incapable of consenting on its own behalf. Of course, some cases are less straightforward.

In most cases either parent can give a legally effective consent to certain medical procedures on at least young children,[51] as can anyone upon whom parental powers have been conferred by statute.[52] Authorization can also be given by a

[50] In 1960 Lord Devlin (as he now is) said, in the course of a lecture to a medical society, that it was uncertain whether anyone could consent to medical treatment on a child: Devlin, *Samples*, 86. But see now e.g. *Re L.* [1968] P. 119; *B. (B.R.)* v. *B. (J.)* [1968] P. 466. These cases remain authority for the proposition that parents (and hence the High Court exercising the Crown's prerogative powers as *parens patriae*) can authorize medical procedures, even if it be accepted (see *S.* v. *McC.*; *W.* v. *W.* (1970) [1972] A.C. 24, esp. 43-4, 46-51, 59) that at common law the High Court sometimes has the power, independent of its custodial jurisdiction, to require that a sample of a minor's blood be taken for testing for forensic purposes. See also Family Law Reform Act 1969, ss. 8(1), 21(3).

[51] *Re L.* [1968] P. 119, 132; Guardianship Act 1973, s. 1(1). The father of an illegitimate child, or a step-parent, cannot, as such, consent to medical procedures on the child: see generally Children Act 1975, s. 85(7); *Re N. (Minors) (Parental Rights)* [1974] Fam. 40. Where one parent has the capacity to consent to the procedure in question, and does in fact do so, a doctor would not incur liability in battery if he performed the procedure against the wishes of the other parent. But where a minor's parents disagree on any question affecting the welfare of the child, either parent may apply to the court for its direction: see Guardianship Act 1973, s. 1(3).

[52] See e.g. Adoption Act 1976, s. 12; Child Care Act 1980, ss. 10(2), 18(1). Consent can also be given by a guardian of the child and, in many circumstances, by a person *in loco parentis*: see generally P. D. G. Skegg, 'Consent to Medical

Judge of the High Court, in the exercise of that Court's wardship jurisdiction.[53]

It is convenient to consider separately those instances where the minor is incapable of consenting, and those instances where the minor has the capacity to consent on his own behalf. Within each category a distinction will be drawn between those procedures which are intended to benefit the minor and those which are not intended to have this effect.

Minor incapable of consenting to the procedure in question

It is certain that a parent or other appropriate person can give a legally effective consent to a procedure which that person, and the doctor, reasonably believe to be in the best interests of the minor's health.[54] This category may be taken to include many procedures for the purpose of assessment and prevention, as well as those for the treatment of an existing condition.[55]

In most cases there will be no doubt that the procedure is intended to benefit the health of the minor. Problems—of a factual, rather than purely legal, character—arise in some cases where the benefit is, at best, indirect. For example, there is an obvious distinction between the situation in which a minor is extremely likely to benefit from the knowledge gained from a non-therapeutic experimental procedure, and that in which there is no likelihood of his benefiting. But there are many cases that lie between these extremes.[56]

Procedures on Minors' (1973) 36 *M.L.R.* 370, 375-6.

[53] See e.g. *Re P. (A Minor)* (1981) 80 L.G.R. 301. For a discussion of the circumstances in which the court's authorization must be sought in respect of medical procedures on a ward of court, see N. V. Lowe and R. A. H. White, *Wards of Court* (1979), 74-7, 108-9; T. Radevsky, 'Wardship and Abortion' (1980) 130 *New L.J.* 813-14; N. V. Lowe, 'Wardship and Abortion—A Reply' (1981) 131 *New L.J.* 561-2. See also *Re D.* [1976] Fam. 185, 196D.

[54] A distinction could be drawn between the concept of 'best interests of the minor's health' and the concept of 'benefit of the minor's health', for it may be argued that not all procedures which are for the benefit of a minor are in the minor's best interests, as other procedures may be still more to the minor's benefit. But the two concepts were used interchangeably in the blood test cases (e.g. *Re L.* [1968] P. 119; *B. (B.R.)* v. *B. (J.)* [1968] P. 466) and the distinction will not be drawn here.

[55] See 'Responsibility in Investigations on Human Subjects', *Report of the Medical Research Council for the Year 1962-1963* (Cmnd. 2382; 1964), pp. 21-2.

[56] For a useful analysis, see G. E. Schreiner, 'Liability in Use of Investigational Drugs' (1963) 185 *J.A.M.A.* 259, 260.

More difficult are some of those instances in which the procedure may be said to be to the detriment of one aspect of a minor's health, although for the benefit of another aspect.[57] American courts have considered such matters in the context of medical transplantation. The first three cases[58] came before the Supreme Court of Massachusetts, and all involved the proposed removal of kidneys from healthy minors, for the purpose of transplantation into their identical twins. In each case, the court found that the removal of a kidney was for the benefit of the healthy twin. The reason given was that the death of its identical twin would have had a grave emotional impact, an impact which (it was said in the first case) 'could well affect the health and physical well-being of [the healthy twin] for the remainder of his life'.[59] Under English law, all the twins would probably have been capable of consenting on their own behalf, for in each case the court found that the potential donor fully understood the nature of the operation and its possible consequences, and freely consented to it.

However, two subsequent cases concerned persons who would not have been capable of consenting on their own behalf. In one of these,[60] a Washington court held that the proposed removal of skin from a three-year-old boy, for the purpose of transplanting it to his twin brother (who had been badly burnt), was for the benefit of the healthy twin. The reason given was the value of the preservation of the family unit, and the demonstrated affinity of the twins for each

[57] Although surgical removal of reproductive organs is clearly to the detriment of a patient's reproductive capacity, it is sometimes for the benefit of the patient's health. For a difficult example concerning sterilization, consider the facts in *Re D.* [1976] Fam. 185. Cf. *Re Eve* (1981) 115 D.L.R. (3d) 283. (1981) 115 D.L.R. (3d) 283.

[58] *Masden* v. *Harrison* (1957); *Huskey* v. *Harrison* (1957); *Foster* v. *Harrison* (1957). These cases have not been reported, but are discussed at length in W. J. Curran, op. cit. n. 38, 892-8. For a discussion of subsequent cases in Massachusetts, see C. H. Baron, M. Botsford, and G. F. Cole, 'Live Organ and Tissue Transplants from Minor Donors in Massachusetts' (1975) 55 *Boston University Law Review* 159-93.

[59] *Masden* v. *Harrison* (1957), per Counihan J. The full text of Counihan J.'s judgment is to be found in C. E. Wasmuth and C. E. Wasmuth, *Law and the Surgical Team* (1969), 342-5.

[60] *McMahon* v. *McMahon* (1963), unreported, but discussed at length in P. W. Herron and L. F. Marion, 'Homografting in the Treatment of Severe Burns, Using An Identical Twin as a Skin Donor' (1967) 75 *Pacific Medicine and Surgery* 4-10.

other, even at this early stage.[61] The other case[62] involved the proposed removal of a kidney from a mentally retarded adult, for the purpose of transplanting it into his brother. The potential donor had a mental age of about six years, but the trial court accepted evidence that he was emotionally and psychologically dependent on his brother, 'and that his well being would be more severely jeopardized by the loss of his brother than by the removal of a kidney'. The majority in the Kentucky Court of Appeals was prepared to accept the finding that in these circumstances the removal of the kidney was in the potential donor's best interests.

In dealing with cases such as these, it is necessary to weigh the likelihood of being able to save the potential recipient's life by making use of the proposed donor's organ or tissue; the likelihood of being able to achieve the same end by making use of some alternative source or treatment; the likely and the possible consequences to the proposed donor's health if the potential recipient dies; and the likely and the possible consequences to the donor's health if the organ or tissue is removed for transplantation. English courts would be free to balance the considerations in the same way as some American courts have done, but it would be unwise to assume that they would necessarily hold such operations to be for the donor's benefit.[63] In such cases, the approach of an English

[61] See also *Hart v. Brown* (1972) 289 A. 2d 386 (Conn.); *Howard v. Fulton and Dekalb Hospital Authority* (1973) 42 U.S. L.W. 2322; A. M. Capron, 'Informed Consent in Catastrophic Disease Research and Treatment' (1974) 123 *University of Pennsylvania Law Review* 340, 425 n. 209.

[62] *In the matter of Strunk an Incompetent* (1969), aff'd. *sub. nom. Strunk v. Strunk* (1969) 445 S.W. 2d 145 (Ky.). The fullest account of this case, particularly in the lower courts, is to be found in J. C. Savage, 'Organ Transplantation With an Incompetent Donor: Kentucky Resolves the Dilemma of *Strunk v. Strunk*' (1970) 58 *Kentucky Law Journal* 129, 142–54. See also *Re Dickinson* (Connecticut, 1960), unreported, discussed in J. C. Savage, above, 137 n. 26. In *Re Richardson* (1973) 284 So. 2d 185 (La.), the court refused to authorize the removal of a kidney from a seventeen-year-old with a mental age of three or four years, for transplantation to his thirty-two-year-old sister. For a full account of *Re Richardson*, including material which does not appear in the published law report, see R. Stetter, 'Kidney Donation from Minors and Incompetents' (1975) 35 *Louisiana Law Review* 551–61. See also *Re Pescinski* (1975) 226 N.W. 2d 180 (Wis.).

[63] See Edmund Davies, 'Transplants', 635. However, Lord Kilbrandon, in a speech to a university law society, has described the Massachusetts decisions as 'a courageous piece of sophisticated reasoning': D. W. Meyers, *The Human Body and the Law* (1970), 123.

court might be the same as that of one of the judges who dissented in the Kentucky case.[64] He did not rule out altogether the possibility of the removal of an organ or tissue being for the benefit of a donor, but he said that in the case in question the opinions concerning psychological trauma were 'at best most nebulous'. He was influenced by the fact that there was no guarantee that the transplant would be a success, and that, whereas the life of the proposed donor was not at present in danger, the removal of a kidney would create some peril.

The concept of benefit to the minor is not restricted to benefit to the minor's health.[65] For example, the taking of a blood sample for forensic purposes may be in a minor's best interests, even though it is not shown to benefit his health.[66] Financial benefit may outweigh any possible detriment to health.[67] This raises interesting possibilities with non-therapeutic experimentation as well as with transplantation. Suppose blood from a minor with a rare blood group was urgently required for transfusion. It could be argued that the removal of a quantity of his blood would be for his benefit if, in consideration for the removal, a substantial sum of money was paid into a bank account opened in the minor's name. Judges might find it difficult not to accept this approach if no substantial pain, discomfort, risk, or detriment to health was involved. However, where any of these factors is present, English judges may be expected to be most reluctant to accept the notion that any sum of money fully compensates for, say, the loss of an organ or of non-regenerative tissue. Otherwise, it would be possible to argue that the removal of

[64] *Strunk* v. *Strunk* (1969) 445 S.W. 2d 145, 150–1, per Steinfeld J.

[65] *Re L.* [1968] P. 119, 168.

[66] See e.g. *B. (B.R.)* v. *B. (J.)* [1968] P. 466. Given as broad a concept of 'health' as that found in the Preamble to the Constitution of the World Health Organization ('Health is a state of complete physical, mental and social well-being and not merely the absence of disease or infirmity'), a strong case could be made for the view that, in many of the blood test cases, the determination of the minor's paternity was for the benefit of the minor's health.

[67] In a number of the blood test cases, judges alluded to financial considerations. See e.g. *B. (B.R.)* v. *B. (J.)* [1968] P. 466, 479; *S.* v. *McC.*; *W.* v. *W.* [1972] A.C. 24, 42. Cf. *Doyle* v. *White City Stadium* [1935] 1 K.B. 111, where it was held that the infant boxer's contract with the British Boxing Board of Control was for his benefit. Had the question of possible detriment to his health been raised, the court would presumably have held that this factor was outweighed by the possibility of financial and other benefits.

a kidney was for the minor's benefit, merely because there had been paid into his bank account a sum in excess of that which he would receive in a personal injury claim for the loss of the organ, and for the associated discomfort and inconvenience.

Medical procedures which doctors wish to perform on a minor are usually intended for the benefit of that minor's health. But some are not.[68] The most important category of such procedures are those which are performed for non-therapeutic experimental purposes.[69] The ensuing discussion of capacity to consent to procedures not intended to benefit the minor will therefore focus on those procedures which are carried out for the purpose of medical research, without any expectation of benefiting the person in question.

There are undoubtedly some limits to the range of procedures to which a parent can give a legally effective consent,[70] and doctors and others have sometimes assumed that a parent is precluded from consenting to any procedure which is not intended for the minor's benefit. If this is so, doctors risk criminal and civil liability whenever they take blood samples from small children, solely for research purposes.[71] Parental consent will make no difference.

One much-quoted opinion is to be found in the Medical Research Council's statement on 'Responsibility in Investigations on Human Subjects'. This asserted that 'In the strict view of the law parents and guardians of minors cannot give consent on their behalf to any procedures which are of no particular benefit to them and which may carry some risk of harm.'[72] This view was based on the advice of the Treasury

[68] For the special statutory provisions dealing with blood tests to determine paternity, see Family Law Reform Act 1969, ss. 20-25, esp. s. 21(3).

[69] See generally 'Guidelines to Aid Ethical Committees Considering Research Involving Children' (1980) 55 *Archives of Disease in Childhood* 75-7, (1980) 280 *Br. Med. J.* 229-31. These Guidelines, prepared by a Working Party set up by the British Paediatric Association, were discussed in an Editorial, 'Clinical Research on Children' (1982) 8 *Journal of Medical Ethics* 3, 3-4.

[70] Edmund Davies, 'Transplants', 635; Lord Hailsham L.C., (1983) 441 Parl. Deb. H.L. 677. See also *R.* v. *March* (1844) 1 Car. & K. 496, 499 *in arguendo*.

[71] Despite the limited application of the maxim *de minimis non curat lex*, it is likely to apply where small additional quantities of blood are obtained for legitimate research purposes during diagnostic or treatment procedures. This does not expose the patient to any additional risk or discomfort.

[72] 'Responsibility in Investigations on Human Subjects', *Report of the Medical*

Solicitor, who subsequently explained that although he was confident about the correctness of the statement he could not cite any statute or decided case that was exactly in point.[73] The statement of the Medical Research Council is a little less restrictive than is sometimes assumed. It implies that parents can give a legally effective consent to procedures which are not for the benefit of the minor but which do not carry some risk of harm. Of course, much depends upon what is meant by 'risk of harm'. To weigh a new-born baby twice as frequently as usual, because of the requirements of a research project, may involve an added risk that the baby will be dropped. And while the taking of a blood sample normally involves little more than the transitory pain of a pin prick, there have been instances of complications resulting.[74]

In 1973 the Royal College of Physicians advised that clinical research investigation of a child which is not for the direct benefit of the child should be conducted 'only where the procedure entails negligible risk or discomfort' and 'subject to the provisions of any common or statute law prevailing at the time'.[75] This begged the question whether parents can give a legally effective consent to a procedure which involves negligible—but not non-existent—risk or discomfort. A circular issued by the Department of Health and Social Security advised Health Authorities that they ought not to infer from this recommendation that the fact that consent had been given by the parent or guardian, and that the risk involved is considered negligible, will be sufficient 'to bring such clinical research investigation within the law as it now stands'.[76]

Research Council for the Year 1962-1963 (Cmnd. 2382; 1964), 21, 23. (This statement was reproduced in full at [1964] 2 *Br. Med. J.* 178-80. The passage quoted in the text above is on p. 179.)

[73] Letter, H. Druitt to H. K. Beecher, 16 December 1968, reported in W. J. Curran and H. K. Beecher, 'Experimentation on Children' (1969) 210 *J.A.M.A.* 77, 81.

[74] See J. A. Dodge and J. Evans, Letter, 'Research on Infants' [1977] 1 *Lancet* 852.

[75] *Committee on the Supervision of the Ethics of Clinical Research Investigations in Institutions* (Royal College of Physicians of London, 1973).

[76] *Supervision of the Ethics of Clinical Research Investigation and Fetal Research* (Department of Health and Social Security, H.S.C. (I.S.) 153, 1975). See also Second Report from the Social Services Committee, House of Commons,

There is no English or other Commonwealth case in which a judge has stated that a parent can never give a legally effective consent to any procedure which is not intended to benefit a minor.[77] Nor is there any case in which a judge has adopted the views expressed in the statement of the Medical Research Council, or implied in the circular from the Department of Health and Social Security. Indeed, there is some judicial support for the view that parents may sometimes give a legally effective consent to the taking of a blood sample for non-therapeutic purposes.[78] But before examining the case in question it is as well to consider two other considerations which lend weight to the view that parents may consent to some non-therapeutic research procedures.

One consideration is the serious consequence of outlawing medical research which involves extremely slight risks but which may confer substantial benefit on others. Without past research involving the taking of blood samples from normal children, children would still be killed or crippled in consequence of infection with poliomyelitis.[79] In some fields medical progress will be hindered or prevented if parents are never able to give a legally effective consent to the taking of blood samples from their children for research purposes. For example, it is possible that research studies involving the taking of only a few millilitres of blood from a group of mentally handicapped children will assist in the genetic counselling of many parents.[80]

The other consideration is that society generally concedes

Session 1979–80, *Perinatal and Neonatal Mortality*, vol. i, para. 454; Department of Health and Social Security, *Reply to the Second Report from the Social Services Committee on Perinatal and Neonatal Mortality* (Cmnd. 8084; 1980), para. 167.

[77] The judgment in *Re D.* [1976] Fam. 185 did not contain any statements to this effect. Heilbron J. said that the proposed sterilization was for 'non-therapeutic reasons', and noted that the doctor referred to the issue of parental consent. But she did not give any guidance as to the efficacy of parental consent where the child is not a ward of the court, although she did make it clear that where the child is a ward of court a step as important as that proposed in this case requires the consent of the court. (See ibid. 193, 194, 196.)

[78] *S.* v. *McC.*; *W.* v. *W.* [1972] A.C. 24. On the question of the taking of blood samples to determine paternity, see now Family Law Reform Act 1969, ss. 20–25.

[79] Editorial, 'The Ethics of Research Involving Children as Controls' (1973) 48 *Archives of Disease in Childhood* 751.

[80] C. George, 'Ethical Committees', *World Medicine*, 22 March 1978, p. 9.

to parents some discretion about the risks to which they may expose their children. The circumcision of baby boys is not without risks,[81] and the preponderance of medical opinion in the United Kingdom is that this practice is not normally for the benefit of the health of the child.[82] But it has long been assumed that parents can give a legally effective consent to such procedures.[83] Similarly it is generally accepted that a parent may give a legally effective consent to the piercing of a young daughter's ears, for cosmetic reasons.[84] On a wider front, it is assumed that a parent has the authority to permit a visitor to pick up and kiss a baby, even though this exposes the baby to an additional risk of being dropped and of contracting an infection. Were the parent's consent ineffective, the visitor's action might amount to battery. To take another example, it is assumed that parents who want a quiet hour to themselves may permit a neighbour to take their unwilling child on an outing in a car, even though the child may suffer nausea in consequence and will be exposed to the risk of injury in an accident. If parental consent were ineffective the neighbour's conduct could be regarded as amounting to the tort of false imprisonment. These examples suggest that parents may expose their children to some degree of risk, even if the activity in question is not for the child's benefit.

In view of comments made in the House of Lords in a case concerning the taking of blood samples for forensic purposes,[85] there is reason to believe that the courts will accept that, when a minor is incapable of consenting, a parent can give a legally effective consent to any procedure to which a 'reasonable parent' would consent. The judgment

---

[81] For a claim for damages resulting from the negligent circumcision of a six-day-old boy, see *Gray* v. *LaFleche* [1950] 1 D.L.R. 337.

[82] See generally Editorial, 'The Case Against Neonatal Circumcision' [1979] 1 *Br. Med. J.* 1163–4, and subsequent correspondence [1979] 2 *Br. Med. J.* 554, 933, 1220–1.

[83] Cf. Williams, *Textbook*, 527 ('It is inconceivable that any judge would hold this immemorial usage to be illegal.').

[84] But see *R.* v. *Adesanya*, *The Times*, 16 July 1974, p. 3, 17 July 1974, p. 4 (news reports) discussed in Williams, *Textbook*, 527.

[85] *S.* v. *McC.*; *W.* v. *W.* [1972] A.C. 24. It is not suggested that this case provides binding authority on the issue under consideration; simply that it provides an indication of the attitude of some leading members of the judiciary, and that statements in the case can be used as the basis of a helpful test in relation to the capacity of parents to consent to medical procedures on minors.

of Lord Reid in that case gave some indication of how the courts would apply the 'reasonable parent' test in this context. Lord Reid implied that, when a blood test was in the public interest, a reasonable parent would not require it to be shown to be for the child's benefit before consenting to the taking of a blood sample from the child. On the contrary, he said that a reasonable parent would consent unless he thought that the test would clearly be against the child's interests.[86] Where the risk or discomfort involved in a non-therapeutic experimental procedure is only of the same order as that involved in the taking of a blood sample for forensic purposes, and the potential benefit to others could be regarded as commensurate with the pain and inconvenience caused, Lord Reid's statements may be cited in support of the view that a reasonable parent would consent.[87]

Although the 'reasonable parent' test enables a parent to give effective consent to some research procedures which are not for the child's benefit,[88] it would be a mistake to exaggerate the scope of lawful non-therapeutic experimentation which this development opens up. It is, for example, extremely unlikely that a court would accept that a reasonable parent would agree to a liver biopsy or cardiac catheterization where there was no prospect of benefit to the child.[89]

A reasonable parent would not normally put a child's interests in jeopardy, whether for the benefit of any other individual or of the public generally.[90] But a reasonable parent

[86] *S.* v. *McC.*; *W.* v. *W.* [1972] A.C. 44, 45. See also ibid. 48, 51, 57, 58.

[87] See B. M. Dickens, 'The Use of Children in Medical Experimentation' (1975) 43 *Med.-Leg. J.* 166, 169–70; B. M. Dickens, 'Contractual Aspects of Human Medical Experimentation' (1975) 25 *University of Toronto Law Journal* 406, 418; G. Dworkin, 'Legality of Consent to Nontherapeutic Medical Research on Infants and Young Children' (1978) 53 *Archives of Disease in Childhood* 443, 445. See also Williams, *Textbook*, 528.

[88] The reasonable parent might well distinguish between pain and risk. In some circumstances the reasonable parent might agree to the performance of a procedure which caused pain, even though the parent would not agree to a procedure which involved a significant risk of injury to health. The reasonable parent would rarely consent if the tests could equally well be carried out on older subjects, who would be capable of consenting on their own behalf.

[89] For helpful discussions of the circumstances in which consent may reasonably be given, see Editorial, 'Valid Parental Consent' [1977] 1 *Lancet* 1346–7; Editorial, 'Research Involving Children—Ethics, the Law, and the Climate of Opinion' (1978) 53 *Archives of Disease in Childhood* 441–2.

[90] *S.* v. *McC.*; *W.* v. *W.* [1972] A.C. 24, 44, 48, 57.

might do so where an organ or tissue could be removed from the child to save the life of its histo-compatible sibling (usually an identical twin). Results with transplantation of kidneys between histo-compatible siblings are so exceptionally good that the courts should accept that a reasonable parent would sometimes consent to the removal of a kidney from a healthy sibling, where no other action would give a comparable chance of success and the child was not opposed to the operation.[91] Reasonable parents frequently have to balance the interests of one child against those of another, and in the case of a kidney transplant the likely benefit to the recipient far outweighs the likely detriment to the donor. Although this might appear to put the small proportion of children who have histo-compatible siblings at a disadvantage compared with other children, it may be argued that, as such children are also the potential beneficiaries of such a practice, it would be unreasonable to prevent them from benefiting from their good fortune in having such exceptionally suitable potential donors. But such cases are exceptional and it remains highly unlikely that in other circumstances the courts would accept that a reasonable parent would consent to the performance on a child of a medical procedure which was not intended for the child's benefit, and which was significantly detrimental to the child's well-being.

Minor capable of consenting to the procedure in question
Writers have sometimes taken the view that parents may only give an effective consent when the minor is incapable of consenting on his own behalf.[92] This would be convenient if there was one 'age of consent' at, say, sixteen or eighteen. But there is not, and quite small children are capable of giving a legally effective consent to some medical touchings. Parents' authority would be severely restricted if their wishes could never prevail against the wishes of a nine-year-old who objected to going to the dentist, or to having a splinter removed from a finger.[93]

[91] See also H. E. M. Kay, 'Bone Marrow Transplantation: 1982' (1982) 285 *Br. Med. J.* 1296-8.

[92] See e.g. B. Tomkins, 'Health Care for Minors: The Right to Consent' (1974–75) 40 *Saskatchewan Law Review* 41, 54.

[93] A parent is under a statutory obligation to provide, arrange for, or permit

There is judicial support for the view that parents may sometimes give a legally effective consent even though the minor is capable of consenting on his own behalf.[94] Such a power is not unlimited, even with minors below the age of sixteen.[95] The difficulty is to determine the limits. An extrajudicial statement of Ormrod L.J. gives some indication of the approach which judges are likely to adopt. Speaking of wardship proceedings and medical treatment, he said:[96]

Teenagers will have definite views of their own, which are entitled to reasonable respect, although there may be situations where it is justifiable to impose adult views upon them. They may refuse transfusion or operation on religious or cultural grounds and it may be wrong to override such a refusal if to do so would gravely distress the patient or complicate his future in some way.

He did, however, go on to say that in a life-saving situation a judge would 'probably authorize the necessary medical procedure, if the evidence was sufficiently clear'.

For a general formulation it is not possible to improve on the reasonable parent test.[97] There is no difficulty about giving relatively uncontroversial examples of circumstances in which the reasonable parent would, or would not, consent. At one extreme there would be general agreement that a reasonable parent would normally override a twelve-year-old's objection to an operation which was necessary to preserve life, or to prevent grave injury to health. At the other extreme, the reasonable parent would not consent to a procedure on a fifteen-year-old, where the minor objected and the procedure

the medical treatment of his child in some circumstances. See Children and Young Persons Act 1933, s. 1.

[94] See B. (B.R.) v. B. (J.) [1958] P. 466, 473–4; S. v. McC.; W. v. W. [1972] A.C. 24, 45. Cf. Stephen, Digest, 148.

[95] S. 8(3) of the Family Law Reform Act 1969 could be interpreted as preserving a power to consent—in so far as it exists—in respect of minors who are sixteen or seventeen years of age. Any such power would be extinguished by marriage: see generally P. M. Bromley, Family Law (6th edn., 1981), 287.

[96] Ormrod, 'Ethics', 26. Cf. Hewer v. Bryant [1970] 1 Q.B. 357, 369 where Lord Denning M.R. said that even before the legal right of a parent to the custody of a child ends 'it is a dwindling right which the courts will hesitate to enforce against the wishes of the child, and the more so the older he is. It starts with a right of control and ends with little more than advice.'

[97] S. v. McC.; W. v. W. [1972] A.C. 24, 44, discussed above.

would confer only limited benefit to health, or could reasonably be postponed.[98]

There are, of course, many intermediate cases. Here it will be necessary to balance many factors, including the minor's age, the strength of his objections and the reasons for them. If an objection resulted from a fear of injections, or of hospitals, the reasonable parent might give it less weight than an objection on conscientious or well thought out grounds. One difficult intermediate case is that of a thirteen-year-old girl who objects to being vaccinated for rubella because she has a horror of injections, but whose mother is willing to consent to her daughter being vaccinated. The vaccination may prevent harm to any children that the girl may conceive, and hence may be said to be indirectly for the girl's benefit, since it will avoid worry during pregnancy, or an abortion, or the additional stress of bringing up a handicapped child. Although a parent who does not make such vaccination available to a daughter would be unlikely to risk conviction for wilfully neglecting a child in a manner likely to cause 'unnecessary suffering or injury to health',[99] a reasonable parent might well consent to the vaccination, even in the face of the daughter's objection.[1]

If a medical procedure is not intended for the benefit of a minor who is capable of consenting to it on his own behalf,

[98] *Quaere*, whether a reasonable parent would ever consent to an abortion being performed on a fifteen-year-old daughter who wished to continue with the pregnancy. Probably not, at least if the abortion was not necessary to prevent a substantial risk of death or grave permanent injury to the health of the girl in question. Ormrod L.J. once stated, extrajudicially, that 'refusal to submit to abortion should be conclusive, unless it is necessary to save the girl's life' (Ormrod, 'Ethics', 26). See also Medical Defence Union's *Annual Report 1972*. p. 27; Speller, *Hospitals*, 194; *Re Smith* (1972) 295 A. 2d 238 (Md.); *Planned Parenthood of Central Missouri* v. *Danforth* (1976) 428 U.S. 52, 73-4.

[99] Children and Young Persons Act 1933, s. 1. Although a parent (and any other person over the age of sixteen who has the custody, charge, or care of a child under that age) has a duty to provide, or to take steps to provide, medical care necessary to prevent 'unnecessary suffering or injury to health', it does not follow that there is a power to consent to such procedures if the minor is capable of consenting but refuses to do so. Persons who undertake to care for infirm persons are sometimes under a duty to provide necessary medical treatment and food, but it does not follow that the infirm person may be treated against his wishes, or forcibly fed (although see pp. 113-14, below).

[1] It is unlikely that a doctor would proceed if the girl offered physical resistance. But if she was prepared to submit, the efficacy of parental consent could be of crucial importance.

a reasonable parent would not consent if the minor objected or had not been consulted. In theory, the minor's consent suffices in such cases, but in practice it is usually wise to seek the consent of a parent as well.

Consent to procedures on mentally disordered persons

There is no general principle of law whereby the nearest relative of a mentally disordered person is authorized to consent to medical procedures on that person.[2]

It might sometimes be convenient for doctors if the Mental Health Acts authorized certain persons to consent to the treatment of mentally disordered persons who were incapable of consenting on their own behalf.[3] Where a mentally disordered person had been received into guardianship under the Mental Health Act 1959[4] the guardian used to have 'all such powers' in relation to that person as a father has in relation to a child under the age of fourteen years.[5] Such powers would have included that of consenting to medical treatment. However the Mental Health (Amendment) Act 1982 has amended this provision by specifying the powers which the guardian may exercise.[6] The powers include that of requiring the patient to attend at specified places and times for the purpose of medical treatment,[7] and the power to require access to be given, at any place where the patient is residing, to any registered medical practitioner.[8] But the

[2] But see Family Law Reform Act 1969, s. 21(4), for the circumstances in which a person having care and control of a mentally disordered person can consent to the taking of a blood sample to determine paternity. (S. 21 should be read in the context of Part III of the Act, and not as conferring a general power in relation to the taking of blood samples.)

[2] *Quaere*, whether consent could in theory be given under the procedure provided by Part VIII of the Mental Health Act 1959. See ibid. ss. 100–104, esp. s. 102(1) (a), (b), (d) and s. 103(1) (j). See generally J. Jacob, 'The Right of the Mental Patient to his Psychosis' (1976) 39 *M.L.R.* 17, 38–9.

[4] See Mental Health Act 1959, s. 34(1) (and also ss. 33(2), 42(2)). S. 34(1) confers the power 'subject to regulations made by the Minister'. The Mental Health (Hospital and Guardianship) Regulations 1960 (S.I. 1960/1241), r. 6(1), provide that the guardian shall ensure that everything practicable is done for the promotion of the mentally disordered person's physical and mental health.

[5] See Mental Health Act 1959, s. 34(1).

[6] Mental Health (Amendment) Act 1982, s. 8.

[7] Ibid. s 8(b). For the extended meaning of 'medical treatment' in this context, see Mental Health Act 1959, s. 147(1); Mental Health (Amendment) Act 1982, s. 63(2).   [8] Mental Health (Amendment) Act 1982, s. 8(c).

guardian is not authorized to consent to the medical treatment of the person who has been received into guardianship.

There will be many cases where the doctor is justified in proceeding without the consent of a mentally disordered person, but this will not be by virtue of the consent of others. It will be by virtue of statutory or non-statutory powers to treat the patient in the absence of consent.[9]

Consent to procedures on others generally

It is sometimes stated or assumed that, where a patient is incapable of consenting, an effective consent may be given by his spouse, or by some near relative.[10] Unfortunately, those who hold this view do not indicate the grounds on which it is based. There are several possibilities.

One is the doctrine of agency of necessity. Some writers have used this doctrine as the basis of a justification for a doctor proceeding without consent. They have suggested that a person who administers treatment in emergency conditions is acting as an agent of necessity.[11] In much the same way, it could be argued that if agency of necessity justifies someone in proceeding without consent, it would also empower that person to give a legally effective consent to treatment administered by some other person. This approach would be of little value, however, for in the circumstances in which it would operate the other person would already be justified in proceeding without consent.

Another possibility is also closely linked to a justification for performing medical procedures without consent. The law places a duty on some people in relation to the health of others, and it could sometimes be argued that this duty implies a power to administer medical treatment without consent.[12] On this basis, it could be said that any person who has the implied power to administer treatment without consent has a concomitant power to authorize someone else to

[9] See ch. 5, esp. n. 3.
[10] See e.g. D. J. Gee, *Lecture Notes on Forensic Medicine* (3rd edn., 1979), 50 (spouse).
[11] See e.g. *Report of the Committee on the Age of Majority* (Cmnd. 3342; 1967), para. 475.
[12] This was the approach adopted in *Leigh* v. *Gladstone* (1909) 26 T.L.R. 139. Cf. Children and Young Persons Act 1933, s. 1. See generally, pp. 113–15.

administer it in his place. But here, too, the person administering the treatment would invariably be justified in proceeding without consent.

The better view is that there is no general doctrine whereby a spouse or near relative is empowered to give a legally effective consent to medical procedures to be carried out on an adult.[13] Of course, doctors are sometimes justified in proceeding without the consent of the patient. But this is not because the consent of others justifies a doctor in proceeding without the patient's consent, but because in the circumstances the doctor is justified in proceeding despite the absence of legally effective consent.[14]

[13] For extrajudicial statements in support of this view, see Devlin, *Samples*, 86; N. O'Bryan, op. cit. n. 37, above, 151.

[14] Nevertheless, it is sometimes desirable for a doctor to obtain the agreement of a spouse, or a near relative, to his treating a patient without the patient's consent. Although such agreement does not affect the doctor's legal power to proceed without consent, it reduces any danger there might be of his being prosecuted or sued for doing so.

CONSENT TO MEDICAL PROCEDURES

> If at all possible, consistent with patient psychology,
> the doctor should obtain the patient's freely given con-
> sent after the patient has been given a full explanation.
>
> World Medical Association's
> Declaration of Helsinki, 1964[1]

Once it is accepted that it is possible to give a legally effective consent to a particular medical procedure,[2] and also that the person in question has the capacity to do so,[3] it becomes important to determine what sort of consent is required to prevent liability being incurred.[4]

Writers on medical law sometimes state that consent must be 'informed' and 'free'. These terms can be misleading. Consent may be in many respects uninformed, and given under considerable pressure, yet still be effective in law. Furthermore, a patient may be sufficiently informed to give a consent which precludes an action in battery, yet still have an action in negligence in consequence of the doctor's failure to disclose further information about the procedure.[5] Nevertheless, the terms 'informed' and 'free' do point to two basic issues, and provide convenient pegs upon which to hang a discussion.

It is proposed to deal first with the matter of 'informed' consent, and then with 'free' consent. In both cases it is convenient to commence with an examination of the obligations placed on a doctor by the tort and the crime of

---

[1] The passage quoted is from the section headed 'Clinical Research Combined with Professional Care'.

[2] See ch. 2.

[3] See ch. 3.

[4] For an excellent discussion, see G. Robertson, 'Informed Consent to Medical Treatment' (1981) 97 *L.Q.R.* 102–26.

[5] See *Chatterton* v. *Gerson* [1981] Q.B. 432. In *Reibl* v. *Hughes* (1980) 114 D.L.R. (3d) 1, 8–9, Laskin C.J.C. said that it would be better to abandon the term 'informed consent' when it tends to confuse battery and negligence. See, similarly, *White* v. *Turner* (1981) 120 D.L.R. (3d) 269, 282 per Linden J.

battery,[6] and then to consider the extent to which these obligations are sometimes supplemented by the tort of negligence and also, in the case of 'informed' consent, by the tort of deceit.

I 'INFORMED' CONSENT

A TORT AND CRIME OF BATTERY

In the absence of consent or some other legal justification, a doctor is not free to proceed with any medical procedure which involves a bodily touching. If he does so, with knowledge of the relevant facts,[7] he will commit the tort and the crime of battery. It will usually be obvious whether a legally effective consent has been given. The consent must be to the touching which does in fact take place. Consent to one operation being performed is clearly ineffective if the surgeon performs another,[8] just as consent to a particular surgeon performing an operation is ineffective if it is performed by some other surgeon.[9]

It would only be in the most exceptional circumstances that an English court would hold that an apparent consent

---

[6] It may be assumed that consent which is effective to prevent the performance of a medical procedure from amounting to the offence of battery will also prevent it from constituting any other offence against the person in which consent is, in the circumstances, inconsistent with liability.

[7] This chapter does not include a discussion of the extent to which a doctor would incur liability if he performed a medical procedure in the mistaken belief in facts which, if true, would undoubtedly prevent liability being incurred.

[8] See e.g. *Cull* v. *Royal Surrey County Hospital and Butler* [1932] 1 *Br. Med. J.* 1195, [1932] 1 *Lancet* 1377 (consented to abortion by curettage, doctor performed a hysterectomy); *Hamilton* v. *Birmingham Regional Hospital Board and Keates* [1969] 2 *Br. Med. J.* 456 (sterilized without consent during a Caesarean delivery; liability conceded). See also *Boase* v. *Paul* [1931] 1 D.L.R. 562, [1931] 4 D.L.R. 435; *Yule* v. *Parmley and Parmley* [1944] 4 D.L.R. 46, [1945] 2 D.L.R. 316, *sub. nom. Parmley* v. *Parmley and Yule* [1945] 4 D.L.R. 81; *Schweizer* v. *Central Hospital* (1974) 53 D.L.R. (3d) 494; *Allan* v. *New Mount Sinai Hospital* (1980) 109 D.L.R. (3d) 634, 641-3, (1981) 125 D.L.R. (3d) 276; *White* v. *Turner* (1981) 120 D.L.R. (3d) 269, 283; *Chatterton* v. *Gerson* [1981] Q.B. 432, 443B; *Grewal* v. *National Hospital for Nervous Diseases*, *The Times*, 15 October 1982.

[9] *Michael* v. *Molesworth* [1950] 2 *Br. Med. J.* 171, [1950] 1 *Lancet* 1168 (consented to a particular specialist performing an operation, performed by house surgeon). Although see *Burk* v. *S., B., and K.* (1951) 4 W.W.R. (N.S.) 520, 523. For two criminal cases on (fraudulently induced) mistake as to identity generally, see *R.* v. *Saunders* (1838) 8 C. & P. 265; *R.* v. *Williams* (1838) 8 C. & P. 286.

was ineffective to prevent liability for battery, because the person who purported to consent was insufficiently informed about the procedure in question. The leading English case is *Chatterton* v. *Gerson*.[10] A patient claimed damages for battery[11] and for negligence, because of the alleged failure of the doctor to give her adequate information before obtaining her consent. The doctor had sought to relieve the patient's pain by intrathecal injections of phenol solution. It was the doctor's practice to tell such patients that he hoped to relieve their pain by injecting a solution that would interrupt the nerve along which pain was signalled to the brain; that this would involve numbness in the area from which the pain signals had been transmitted, and numbness over an area larger than the pain source itself, and might involve temporary loss of muscle power. The judge found that the patient had been given the usual explanation, and held that in the circumstances the doctor was not liable for battery or for negligence.

Bristow J. said that in any context in which consent is a defence to what would otherwise be a crime or a civil wrong, 'the consent must be real'.[12] He went on to say that 'once the patient is informed in broad terms of the nature of the procedure which is intended, and gives her consent, that consent is real'.[13] The implication was that if the patient was not aware 'in broad terms of the nature of the procedure', the apparent consent could be regarded as unreal, and hence ineffective to prevent liability in battery.[14] Bristow J. did not give any examples taken from a medical context where an apparent consent would be ineffective. But he did make it clear that a mere failure to explain the 'risks and implications' of a procedure would not result in the consent being regarded

[10] [1981] Q.B. 432. See also *Wells* v. *Surrey Area Health Authority*, *The Times*, 29 July 1978, p. 3 (news report), an account of which is to be found in n. 12 on p. 98, below.

[11] In *Chatterton* v. *Gerson* the term 'trespass to the person' was used as a synonym for battery. See [1981] Q.B. 441G.

[12] [1981] Q.B. 442B-C.

[13] Ibid. 443A. See also *Kelly* v. *Hazlett* (1976) 75 D.L.R. (3d) 536, 558.

[14] On the advantages of being able to have recourse to the tort of battery, rather than simply to the tort of negligence, see *Chatterton* v. *Gerson* [1981] Q.B. 432, 442G-443A; *Reibl* v. *Hughes* (1980) 114 D.L.R. (3d) 1, 9 (although, on the question of proof of the absence of consent, see also *Latter* v. *Braddell* (1880-81) 50 L.J.Q.B. 166, 448 (C.A.) and H. Street, *The Law of Torts* (7th edn., 1983), 18-19, 67).

as 'unreal', and hence ineffective to prevent liability in battery.
To vitiate the reality of consent there must, he said, 'be a
greater failure of communication between doctor and patient
than that involved in a breach of duty if the claim is based
on negligence'.[15]

In *Chatterton* v. *Gerson* the judge found that the patient
had been 'under no illusion as to the general nature of what
an intrathecal injection of phenol solution nerve block would
be'.[16] But if a patient consented to an injection in the belief
that it was for the purpose of pain relief, when it was in fact
being given to immunize the patient against some infectious
disease, an English court might be expected to take the view
that the patient could recover damages for battery. There are
other circumstances in which an apparent consent could be
held to be ineffective because the person who purported to
give consent was not aware 'in broad terms of the nature of
the procedure'. If a patient consented to the removal of a
kidney in the belief that it was in the interests of his health,
when there was in fact no prospect of the removal benefiting
his health, and it was being removed solely for the purpose of
providing a kidney for transplantation, the patient's consent
to the removal of a kidney would not prevent liability in
battery. Similarly, if a woman consented to an abortion by
hysterectomy, without realizing that in consequence she
would not be able to bear children in future, it could reasonably be said that she was unaware of 'the general nature' of a
hysterectomy.[17] In consequence, her consent would be ineffective. However, a mere omission to warn the patient
of risks, or possible complications, of a nephrectomy or
hysterectomy would not render the patient's consent 'unreal', even where the patient had a remedy in negligence in
consequence of the failure to explain those risks and complications.

Canadian courts have sometimes accepted that patients

[15] [1981] Q.B. 442G (and see also, to the same effect, 443A–C). Having said
that the cause of action on which to base a claim for failure to go into risks and
implications is negligence, not trespass, Bristow J. said 'Of course if information
is withheld in bad faith, the consent will be vitiated by fraud.' (Ibid. 443A–B.)
See n. 24, below.   [16] [1981] Q.B. 443C.
[17] Cf. *Wells* v. *Surrey Area Health Authority*, *The Times*, 29 July 1978, p. 3
(news report). See also *Nash* v. *Sheen*, *The Times*, 13 March 1953.

could recover damages in battery in circumstances which, according to *Chatterton* v. *Gerson*, should be left to the tort of negligence.[18] But in consequence of the judgment of the Supreme Court of Canada in *Reibl* v. *Hughes*,[19] a failure to disclose even very serious risks will no longer give rise to an action in battery in Canada. This judgment makes it still more likely that English courts will continue to take the view that consent can be effective to prevent liability in battery, even if given in ignorance of risks which the doctor ought to have disclosed.

In criminal cases, the English courts have sometimes shown a willingness to manipulate the concept of consent to permit the conviction of someone whose behaviour was regarded as deserving of punishment.[20] It is not enough that consent was given to a touching of the same physical scope as that which took place.[21] It must also have been to a touching 'of the same nature' as that which took place.[22] Such an approach

[18] *Koehler* v. *Cook* (1975) 65 D.L.R. (3d) 766; *Zimmer* v. *Ringrose* (1978) 89 D.L.R. (3d) 646 (but see, on appeal, (1981) 124 D.L.R. (3d) 215); *Reibl* v. *Hughes* (1977) 78 D.L.R. (3d) 35, 42, 44 (revsd. (1978) 89 D.L.R. (3d) 112, 125-8, upheld on other grounds, (1980) 114 D.L.R. (3d) 1; on the specific issue of battery, see ibid. 8-11); *Lepp* v. *Hopp* (1979) 98 D.L.R. (3d) 464, esp. 486 (revsd. *sub. nom. Hopp* v. *Lepp* (1980) 112 D.L.R. (3d) 67). See also *Halushka* v. *University of Saskatchewan* (1965) 53 D.L.R. (2d) 436; *Schweizer* v. *Central Hospital* (1974) 53 D.L.R. (3d) 494, 495, 508.

[19] (1980) 114 D.L.R. (3d) 1, esp. 10-11. The judgment of the court was delivered by Laskin C.J.C. *Chatterton* v. *Gerson* (which had then been reported only in *The Times*, 7 February 1980) was not mentioned in the judgment. Less than six months earlier a passage in a judgment of the Supreme Court, also delivered by Laskin C.J.C., had implied that a failure to disclose risks prior to treatment could result in liability in battery. See *Hopp* v. *Lepp* (1980) 112 D.L.R. (3d) 67, 70. The judgment of the Supreme Court in *Reibl* v. *Hughes* can be regarded as taking a more restrictive view of the role of battery in 'informed consent' cases than does the judgment in *Chatterton* v. *Gerson*. The Supreme Court did not state that consent would be ineffective if the patient was not aware, in broad terms, of the nature of the procedure in question. Cf. *R.* v. *Maurantonio* (1967) 65 D.L.R. (2d) 674 (Laskin J.A., dissenting).

[20] See e.g. *Burrell* v. *Harmer* (1966) 116 *New L.J.* 1658. (The conduct in question is now proscribed by the Tattooing of Minors Act 1969, s. 1.) Cf. *R.* v. *Clarence* (1888) 22 Q.B.D. 23.

[21] The cases are usually argued, and decided, on the basis that fraud going to the nature of the act vitiates consent. But the better analysis is that in such cases there is no consent to the touching in question, because it is different from that to which consent was given (see *R.* v. *Clarence* (1888) 22 Q.B.D. 23, 27-8, 34, 44; *Papadimitropoulos* v. *R.* (1957) 98 C.L.R. 249, 260 (rape)).

[22] Two cases in which a patient's consent was held to be ineffective were *R.* v. *Rosinki* (1824) 1 Lewin 11, 1 Mood. 19, and *R.* v. *Case* (1850) 4 Cox C.C. 220.

gives a court considerable room for manœuvre. However, the English courts are likely to be very reluctant to regard a doctor as guilty of a criminal offence simply because, before treating the patient, he gave an inadequate explanation of the treatment, or concealed the risks involved. In the restricted range of cases in which a patient's consent will be regarded as 'unreal', for the purpose of the tort of battery,[23] it will probably also be regarded as 'unreal', for the purpose of the crime of battery and the related statutory offences.[24] But the criminal courts are not likely to go further in making fine distinctions between medical touchings of one 'nature' and another.

Consent will often be specific, but may sometimes be given in general terms.[25] Writers have sometimes questioned the effectiveness of general consent, but there seems no reason why a patient, any more than a games player,[26] should be obliged to give a separate consent to each particular touching. Courts will not be hasty to find that a patient has given a general consent, but they should not prevent a patient who so desires from giving an effective consent to whatever is necessary for the treatment of his illness.

Consent may be implied by conduct,[27] rather than expressed

[23] There is a strong case for the criminal law having some role in these cases. See generally Law Reform Commission of Canada, *Medical Treatment and Criminal Law* Working Paper 26, 1980.

[24] But it is clear that consent induced by a fraudulent misrepresentation which does not go to the nature of the act, or to the identity of the actor, will prevent a touching from constituting the crime of battery. See e.g. *R.* v. *Clarence* (1888) 22 Q.B.D. 23, and also *Papadimitropoulos* v. *R.* (1957) 98 C.L.R. 249 (rape). A wider range of misrepresentations and failures to disclose may vitiate consent for the purpose of the tort of battery. See *Hegarty* v. *Shine* (1878) 4 L.R. Ir. 288; *Reibl* v. *Hughes* (1980) 114 D.L.R. (3d) 1, 11 (*dicta*); and, especially, *Chatterton* v. *Gerson* [1981] Q.B. 432, 443A–B (*dicta*). It might be thought that the power to distinguish between touchings of one 'nature' and another, together with the tort of negligence and the tort of deceit, would be adequate to deal with such cases. But see J. G. Fleming, *The Law of Torts* (5th edn., 1977), 78–9; *Salmond and Heuston on the Law of Torts* (18th edn., 1981, edd. R. F. V. Heuston and R. S. Chambers), 473; *Winfield and Jolowicz on Tort* (11th edn., 1979, ed. W. V. H. Rogers), 662.

[25] See e.g. *Beatty* v. *Cullingworth*, *The Times*, 11 August and 17 November 1896, [1896] 2 *Br. Med. J.* 423, 1546. Cf. *Male* v. *Hopmans* (1965) 54 D.L.R. (2d) 592, 595 (negligence).

[26] On general consent to touchings in an ice-hockey match, see *R.* v. *Green* (1970) 16 D.L.R. (3d) 137. Cf. *R.* v. *Maki* (1970) 14 D.L.R. (3d) 164.

[27] For an extreme example of a jury being permitted to hold that consent was

in words. However, a doctor would often be unwise to assume that, merely because a patient has consulted him about a medical complaint, the patient has impliedly consented to treatment of it. The courts will uphold 'the right of a patient . . . to have an examination, a diagnosis, advice and consultations, and . . . thereafter . . . to determine what, if any, operation or treatment shall be proceeded with'.[28]

It is sometimes desirable that consent be expressed in writing. One of the standard consent forms has a space for the name of the operation to be inserted, and the patient acknowledges that the nature and purpose of the operation have been fully explained to him.[29] But if the operation performed was not of the same 'nature and purpose' as that explained, it would be open to the court to find that there was no consent to the operation in question.[30]

B TORT OF NEGLIGENCE

The tort of negligence may sometimes duplicate the obligation, placed on a doctor by the crime and the tort of battery, to obtain consent before carrying out a medical procedure.[31] However, in this context the tort of negligence has a more important role in supplementing the obligations which the crime and the tort of battery impose upon the doctor.

implied, see *Beatty* v. *Cullingworth*, op. cit., [1896] 2 *Br. Med. J.* 423, 1546, 1548 (appeal to Court of Appeal failed; House of Lords refused leave to appeal: *Marshall* v. *Curry* [1933] 3 D.L.R. 260, 265). However, the decision in *Mulloy* v. *Hop Sang* [1935] 1 W.W.R. 714 demonstrates that it would be unwise to assume that a court would always be prepared to stretch the facts in the way permitted in *Beatty* v. *Cullingworth*.

[28] *Parmley* v. *Parmley and Yule* [1945] 4 D.L.R. 81, 89 (S.C. Can.). See also *Stoffberg* v. *Elliott* [1923] C.P.D. 148, 149. On a doctor's implied authority to engage an anaesthetist, see *Villeneuve* v. *Sisters of St. Joseph* (1971) 18 D.L.R. (3d) 537, 552.

[29] See generally W. A. J. Farndale, *Law on Hospital Consent Forms* (1979), 19–29, and also Speller, *Hospitals*, 187–9, 201, 765–75.

[30] See generally *Halushka* v. *University of Saskatchewan* (1965) 53 D.L.R. (2d) 436; *Chatterton* v. *Gerson* [1981] Q.B. 432, 443C–D.

[31] For cases illustrating the way in which a doctor may be regarded as being in breach of his duty of care if he proceeds without first obtaining consent, see e.g. *Boase* v. *Paul* [1931] 1 D.L.R. 562, 566–7, [1931] 4 D.L.R. 435; *Parmley* v. *Parmley and Yule* [1945] 4 D.L.R. 81, 88–9 (S.C. Can.); and see also *Slater* v. *Baker and Stapleton* (1767) 2 Wils. K.B. 359, 362. *Contra Winn* v. *Alexander* [1940] 3 D.L.R. 778, 780; *Halushka* v. *University of Saskatchewan* (1965) 53 D.L.R. (2d) 436, 446. See also *Lepp* v. *Hopp* (1979) 98 D.L.R. (3d) 464, 486, *sub. nom. Hopp* v. *Lepp* (1980) 112 D.L.R. (3d) 67, 73.

A doctor will not incur liability in negligence unless it can be established that he owed a legal duty of care to the patient,[32] that he was in breach of that duty, and that the patient suffered damage in consequence. This discussion will concentrate on the amount of information a doctor must disclose about a proposed procedure, if he is to comply with the required standard of care.[33] But it must be stressed that a doctor is not liable in negligence simply because he fails to comply with the required standard of care. In the context of the duty to inform, this means that a patient has to establish that, had the doctor disclosed the information in question, he would not have undergone the treatment.[34]

It is often said that compliance with a common and approved practice is conclusive evidence of compliance with the required standard of care.[35] However, there is also high authority in support of the view that, although compliance with a common and approved practice is strong evidence of compliance with the required standard of care, it is not conclusive.[36]

[32] See generally Lord Nathan, *Medical Negligence* (1957), 6-11.

[33] Where an activity involves the exercise of a special skill, the usual test of the required standard of care—what any reasonable person would do in the circumstances—is replaced by the test of what any reasonable practitioner of the skill in question would do in the circumstances. See generally Nathan, op. cit., 19-36. See also *Whitehouse* v. *Jordan* [1981] 1 W.L.R. 246, 257H-258D, 263A-F, 268C-D.

[34] See e.g. *Chatterton* v. *Gerson* [1981] Q.B. 432, 442G-H (and 445B-D) (contrast battery, 442H-443A); *Sidaway* v. *Bethlem Royal Hospital* [1982] 1 *Lancet* 808, 809. As to the different test now accepted in such cases in Canada, see *Reibl* v. *Hughes* (1980) 114 D.L.R. (3d) 1, 15-17, 35; *White* v. *Turner* (1981) 120 D.L.R. (3d) 269, 286. For an interesting study which suggests that knowledge of the risks of a medical procedure will not induce patients to refuse consent, see R. J. Alfidi, 'Informed Consent: A Study of Patient Reaction' (1971) 216 *J.A.M.A.* 1325-9.

[35] A well-known statement along these lines is that of Maughan L.J. (dissenting) in *Marshall* v. *Lindsey C.C.* [1935] 1 K.B. 516, 540. See also 'the classic statement' (*Clark* v. *MacLennan* [1983] 1 All E.R. 416, 422j, per Peter Pain J.) of McNair J. in *Bolam* v. *Friern Hospital Management Committee* [1957] 1 W.L.R. 582, 586-7 (but see n. 39, below).

[36] There is an account of the leading English cases in *Clerk and Lindsell on Torts* (15th edn., 1982, gen. ed. R. W. M. Dias), para. 10-42; *Charlesworth on Negligence* (6th edn., 1977, ed. R. A. Percy), paras. 202-3. For an excellent discussion, see A. M. Linden, *Canadian Tort Law* (3rd edn., 1982), 161-72, esp. 164-6. See also J. L. Montrose, 'Is Negligence an Ethical or a Sociological Concept?' (1958) 21 *M.L.R.* 259-64; E. I. Picard, *Legal Liability of Doctors and Hospitals in Canada* (1978), 170-81; R. M. Jackson and J. L. Powell, *Professional Negligence* (1982), 10-11, 214-18; A. M. Dugdale and K. M. Stanton, *Professional Negligence* (1982), 192-6.

In many cases, including a number of medical ones,[37] a defendant has been held to be in breach of his duty of care, despite his compliance with a common and approved practice.

With matters involving technical medical expertise,[38] a court should be extremely cautious before condemning as negligent a procedure which was performed in accordance with a common and professionally approved practice. But by no means all decisions taken by doctors concern matters within the exclusive competence of the medical profession, and with these matters the courts should not act as if evidence of any common and approved practice was determinative.

There have been very few English cases dealing with the duty to disclose information about a procedure, before obtaining consent to it. Prior to the disappearance of the jury in actions in negligence there were two cases in which trial judges appeared unwilling to give a lead, or to encourage a jury to give a lead, in determining the extent of a doctor's duty of disclosure.[39] But in the later case of *Chatterton* v. *Gerson*[40] Bristow J. did not suggest that the matter could be settled by reference to professional opinion.[41] Having reviewed the evidence of the medical witnesses, he went on to explain the

[37] See e.g. *Marshall* v. *Lindsey C.C.* [1935] 1 K.B. 516, esp. 553, aff'd., *sub. nom. Lindsey C.C.* v. *Marshall* [1937] A.C. 97; *Clarke* v. *Adams* (1950) 94 *Sol. J.* 599; *Hucks* v. *Cole* [1967] 3 *Br. Med. J.* 624 (Q.B.), *The Times*, 9 May 1968, [1968] 2 *Br. Med. J.* 381 (C.A.). See also *Urry* v. *Bierer*, 15 July 1955 (C.A.).

[38] Compare *Whitehouse* v. *Jordan* [1981] 1 W.L.R. 246, esp. 250F per Lord Wilberforce ('the error, if error there was, lay centrally in the area of the exercise of expert judgment and experienced operation') with *Chapman* v. *Rix, The Times*, 22 December 1960 (where Lord Keith, dissenting, is reported to have said that he hardly regarded it as a medical question at all, though it had a medical background).

[39] See especially *Hatcher* v. *Black, The Times*, 2 July 1954. (The crucial passage in Denning L.J.'s direction to the jury is quoted in his book *The Discipline of the Law* (1979), 243–4.) The other case was *Bolam* v. *Friern Hospital Management Committee* [1957] 1 W.L.R. 582. There were passages in McNair J.'s summing-up which implied that professional opinion was determinative, but others which suggested that the jury were not bound by the expert evidence and that, having taken account of it, were free to make their own assessment of what was proper in the circumstances.

[40] [1981] Q.B. 432.

[41] Bristow J.'s statement that the duty of the doctor is to explain what he intends to do, and its implications, 'in the way a careful and responsible doctor in similar circumstances would have done' ([1981] Q.B. 443E) should be read in the light of the passage which followed. But see *Sidaway* v. *Bethlem Royal Hospital* [1982] 1 *Lancet* 808.

circumstances in which, in his judgment, a doctor was obliged
to discuss the risks of a proposed procedure. He indicated
that a doctor would normally be obliged to disclose 'the inherent implications' of a proposed operation, and that 'he
ought to warn of what may happen by misfortune however
well the operation is done, if there is a real risk of a misfortune inherent in the procedure'.[42] There was no indication
that the expert witnesses had spoken in these terms.

More recently, in *Reibl* v. *Hughes*,[43] the Supreme Court of
Canada rejected the view that the scope of the duty to disclose information about possible treatment is 'a matter
essentially of medical judgment, one to be determined by
the Court on the basis of expert medical evidence'.[44] The
Supreme Court held that the medical evidence was 'not determinative'.[45] In delivering the judgment of the court, Laskin
C.J.C. pointed out that to allow expert evidence to determine
what risks are material,[46] and hence (according to the current
Canadian doctrine) ought to be disclosed, would be 'to hand
over to the medical profession the entire question of the
scope of the duty'. He accepted that expert evidence was
relevant to findings as to the risks of surgery and other treatment, and that it would also have a bearing on their materi-
ality, although 'this is not a question that is to be concluded

[42] [1981] Q.B. 444D-E.

[43] (1980) 114 D.L.R. (3d) 1.

[44] *Reibl* v. *Hughes* (1977) 78 D.L.R. (3d) 35, 43 per Haines J. See also on
appeal to the Ontario Court of Appeal: (1978) 89 D.L.R. (3d) 112, 122.

[45] (1980) 114 D.L.R. (3d) 1, 12. Cf. *Sidaway* v. *Bethlem Royal Hospital*
[1982] 1 *Lancet* 808. For a discussion of *Reibl* v. *Hughes* and *Hopp* v. *Lepp*, see
E. Picard, 'Consent to Medical Treatment in Canada' (1981) 19 *Osgoode Hall Law
Journal* 140-51 and E. Picard, 'Patients, Doctors and the Supreme Court of
Canada (1981) 1 *Oxford Journal of Legal Studies* 441-6. See also M. A. Somerville, 'Structuring the Issues in Informed Consent' (1981) 26 *McGill Law Journal*
740-808.

[46] In the leading American case of *Canterbury* v. *Spence* (1972) 464 F. 2d
772, 787 it was agreed that a risk is material 'when a reasonable person, in what
the physician knows or should know to be the patient's position, would be likely
to attach significance to the risk or cluster of risks in deciding whether or not to
forego the proposed therapy'. In *Hopp* v. *Lepp* (1980) 112 D.L.R. (3d) 67, 80-1,
Laskin C.J.C. commented that 'this invites a finding of fact upon which expert
medical evidence of the judgment to be exercised would be admissible but not
determinative', and later explained that under this classification 'possible risks
whose consequences would be grave could well be regarded as material'. See,
further, *Reibl* v. *Hughes* (1980) 114 D.L.R. (3d) 1, 5; *White* v. *Turner* (1981)
120 D.L.R. (3d) 269, 283-6, 290.

on the basis of expert evidence alone'.[47] In an important passage, Laskin C.J.C. went on to say that:[48]

The issue under consideration is a different issue from that involved where the question is whether the doctor carried out his professional activities by applicable professional standards. What is under consideration here is the patient's right to know what risks are involved in undergoing or foregoing certain surgery or other treatment.

There is nothing especially 'medical' about the requirement that a doctor must obtain a patient's consent, and that he must sometimes disclose information to the patient before the patient decides whether to consent. These requirements are imposed, not in the interests of the patient's health, but in the interests of individual liberty. The basis 'is the right of a patient to decide what, if anything, should be done with his body'.[49]

Doctors involved in non-therapeutic experimentation do not make a practice of concealing the risks of the procedures from their patients. For the most part they are not convinced that, given the importance of their research, it is justifiable to omit to disclose information about any undesirable consequences which might ensue. But if there was a common and approved practice of non-disclosure, it is highly unlikely that judges would accept that evidence of such a practice conclusively established that a doctor was not in breach of the duty he owed to his patient. Similarly, if a doctor involved in renal transplantation failed to disclose the risks of a nephrectomy to a potential living donor, before obtaining his consent to the removal of one of his kidneys, a judge would be virtually certain to hold that the doctor was in breach of his duty of care to the donor, even if (which is not the case) the doctor could adduce evidence that his conduct was in accord with a common and professionally approved practice.[50]

[47] (1980) 114 D.L.R. (3d) 1, 13.
[48] Ibid. 13.
[49] *Hopp* v. *Lepp* (1980) 112 D.L.R. 67, 70 (S.C. Can.).
[50] See Edmund Davies L.J., 'The Patient's Right to Know the Truth' (1973) 66 *Proc. Roy. Soc. Med.* 533, 535. ('However eager the donor is to play out his self-sacrificial role, the surgeon is under a legal duty to make clear to him the risks involved. . . . He may not want the truth, but in this case the truth must be forced upon him. A man may declare himself ready to die for another, but the surgeon must never take him at his word.')

If a procedure is intended for the patient's benefit, it is difficult to balance the benefit to the patient's health which may result from his undergoing the treatment against the patient's interest in reaching an informed decision whether to accept the treatment. Evidence of the practice of doctors, and of the reasons for it, is certainly of great value. But the extent of a patient's right to be informed about a proposed procedure should not be equated with the issue of what tests are desirable, or what drugs should be prescribed, in a particular situation.

It is now commonly recognized that by no means all the practices and decisions of doctors are based simply on technical medical expertise.[51] This fact is likely to be reflected to a greater extent in judicial decisions, and judges are likely to become increasingly discriminating as to the circumstances in which evidence of a common and approved practice is treated as conclusive evidence of compliance with the required standard of care.

At present some English judges are likely to treat such evidence as conclusive, if the patient brings an action in which he challenges a doctor's failure to provide him with adequate information about a proposed procedure.[52] But it would be surprising, as well as regrettable, if in future the English courts did not play a more important role in protecting the interests of patients who wish to be able to reach an informed decision about whether to consent to medical procedures.

In some circumstances, a doctor will have to communicate information to the patient's advisers or to the person authorized to consent on his behalf, if the doctor is to fulfil the duty of care he owes the patient.[53] The relevant principles

[51] Cf. *Re D. (A Minor)* [1976] Fam. 185, 192B, per Heilbron J. ('a number of matters which were not in my view in reality matters of clinical judgment, but which were concerned, to a large extent, with grounds which were other than medical').

[52] See *Sidaway* v. *Bethlem Royal Hospital* [1982] 1 *Lancet* 808 (Skinner J.).

[53] Cf. *Steele* v. *Woods* (1959) 327 S.W. 2d 187, 198 per Justin Ruark J. (Missouri). ('Depending upon the circumstances of the case, the seriousness of the need, and the urgency of the situation, perhaps the time or interval of the patient's mental incapacity, the circumstances may require and make it his duty to communicate with and advise the husband or other members of the family who are available and competent to advise with or speak for the patient or take other steps to bring understanding of the need home to the patient.') See also *Lindsey C.C.* v. *Marshall* [1937] A.C. 97.

should be apparent from the discussion which follows, which focuses on the amount of information a doctor should communicate to the person on whom the procedure is to be performed, if he is to comply with his duty of care.

As has already been pointed out, a doctor will sometimes have to give more information about a proposed procedure if he is to avoid the possibility of liability in negligence than he must to avoid liability in battery.[54] Indeed, a doctor who will not be taking any part in the proposed procedure, and stands no risk of incurring liability in battery, may nevertheless be under a duty to disclose information about it.[55]

In examining the amount of information which a doctor must disclose, it is convenient to distinguish between those procedures which are intended to benefit the health of the patient and those which are not.

Procedures intended to benefit the patient's health

So pervasive is the common law emphasis on a person being able to decide for himself what is done to his own body that, even where the proposed procedure is for the benefit of the patient's health, the doctor will often be obliged to disclose more information about it than is necessary to avoid liability in battery. A doctor will sometimes be under a duty to disclose information even though he knows that the disclosure may lead the patient to come to a decision which will be to the detriment of his health. However, it is difficult to determine the circumstances in which a doctor is required to give additional information, and what information he must give on these occasions. These questions cannot be answered in the abstract. The situations which arise in practice are extremely varied, and a particular court's decision may be greatly influenced by the expert evidence adduced.

Half a century has now passed since a Canadian judge said that a doctor should deal honestly with his patient 'as to the necessity, character and importance of the operation and its

[54] *Chatterton* v. *Gerson* [1981] Q.B. 432, 442G. See also *Grewal* v. *National Hospital for Nervous Diseases, The Times,* 15 October 1982, per Dunn L.J.

[55] See *Smith* v. *Auckland Hospital Board* [1965] N.Z.L.R. 191. But see also *McLean* v. *Weir, Goff and Royal Inland Hospital* [1977] 5 W.W.R. 609, 612-13, *sub. nom. McLean* v. *Weir and Goff* [1980] 4 W.W.R. 330, 332; *Strachan* v. *Simpson* [1979] 5 W.W.R. 315, 337.

probable consequences and whether success might reasonably be expected to ameliorate or remove the trouble', but went on to emphasize that this does not involve warning the patient of dangers 'incident to, or possible in, any operation', nor the giving of details calculated 'to frighten or distress the patient'.[56] This statement still provides a good starting-point for a consideration of the amount of information a doctor should disclose, before obtaining consent to treatment. Yet even so general a statement[57] is of limited application, for an examination of the cases reveals that there are a number of factors which will affect the information a doctor should disclose.[58] These factors may be listed as follows:

1. *Patient's capacity to comprehend and reach a decision on issues involved.* Generally speaking, the greater the patient's capacity to comprehend the issues involved and come to a decision about them,[59] the greater will be the extent of the duty to disclose relevant information.[60] Conversely, the more restricted his capacity—whether by reason of his current medical condition,[61] limited intelligence or education,[62] or the complexity of the issues involved[63]—the less may be the extent of any duty to inform.[64]

2. *Extent to which patient wishes to be informed.* Many patients will indicate that they wish to leave all decisions to to the doctor, and in these cases the obligation to inform will generally be very different from that in which a patient asks

[56] *Kenny* v. *Lockwood* [1932] 1 D.L.R. 507, 525, per Hodgins J.A.

[57] For more recent general statements, see e.g. *Chatterton* v. *Gerson* [1981] Q.B. 432, 444D-E (quoted in part on p. 84, above); *Hopp* v. *Lepp* (1980) 112 D.L.R. (3d) 67, 81.

[58] For another account, see Speller, *Hospitals*, 182-7.

[59] See *Cryderman* v. *Ringrose* (1978) 89 D.L.R. (3d) 32, 41, 42.

[60] The information should be 'understandably communicated': see *Kelly* v. *Hazlett* (1976) 75 D.L.R. (3d) 536, 564.

[61] *Male* v. *Hopmans* (1965) 54 D.L.R. (2d) 592, 595, (1967) 64 D.L.R. (2d) 105, 113. See also *Daniels* v. *Heskin* [1954] I.R. 73, 87.

[62] See *Reibl* v. *Hughes* (1977) 78 D.L.R. (3d) 35, 42. See also *Daniels* v. *Heskin* [1954] I.R. 73, 87.

[63] See *Male* v. *Hopmans* (1965) 54 D.L.R. (2d) 592, 595, (1967) 64 D.L.R. (2d) 105, 113.

[64] But the fact that a patient has some difficulty with the English language is a reason for seeking to ensure that he understands the explanation, rather than explaining less: see *Reibl* v. *Hughes* (1980) 114 D.L.R. (3d) 1, 34.

for information about the proposed procedure, or any alternatives.[65] In general, the more a patient asks, the more the doctor should tell him.[66]

3. *Importance of the procedure.* Where the proposed procedure is thought to be essential for the patient's health,[67] the obligation to disclose information about, for example, the risks involved, will generally be much less than it is where the procedure in question is not essential.[68]

4. *Risks involved.* In the absence of other considerations, the greater the risks to the patient—both in terms of the likelihood of their occurring, and the seriousness of the consequences if they do[69]—which the doctor knows or ought to know, but which the patient cannot be expected to know, the greater will be the duty to disclose information about them.[70] Conversely, where the risks are particularly remote,[71] or of little consequence, or ones which the patient can be

[65] See *Reibl* v. *Hughes* (1980) 114 D.L.R. (3d) 1, 13; *Zimmer* v. *Ringrose* (1981) 124 D.L.R. (3d) 215, 221.

[66] *Smith* v. *Auckland Hospital Board* [1965] N.Z.L.R. 191, 197, 205-6, 212; *Hopp* v. *Lepp* (1980) 112 D.L.R. 67, 77, 81.

[67] As in *Bolam* v. *Friern Hospital Management Committee* [1957] 1 W.L.R. 582, 590.

[68] See *Gorback* v. *Ting, Ludwig and Victoria General Hospital* [1974] 5 W.W.R. 606, 609-10; *Kelly* v. *Hazlett* (1976) 75 D.L.R. (3d) 536, 565; *Wells* v. *Surrey Area Health Authority, The Times,* 29 July 1978, p. 3 (news report); *Reibl* v. *Hughes* (1980) 114 D.L.R. (3d) 1, 6, 34; *White* v. *Turner* (1981) 120 D.L.R. (3d) 269, 288-9. See also *Cryderman* v. *Ringrose* (1978) 89 D.L.R. (3d) 32, 41-2; *Zamparo* v. *Brisson* (1981) 120 D.L.R. (3d) 545.

[69] *Hopp* v. *Lepp* (1980) 112 D.L.R. (3d) 67, 80.

[70] *Marshall* v. *Lindsey C.C.* [1935] 1 K.B. 516, aff'd., *sub. nom. Lindsey C.C.* v. *Marshall* [1937] A.C. 97, 106-7, 115, 118, 121-2, 125; *Chatterton* v. *Gerson* [1981] Q.B. 432, 444D-E. See also *Murrin* v. *Janes* [1949] 4 D.L.R. 403, 405; *Halushka* v. *University of Saskatchewan* (1965) 53 D.L.R. (2d) 436, 443. Cf. *Crichton* v. *Hastings* (1972) 29 D.L.R. (3d) 692, 700-1. In *Chadwick* v. *Parsons* [1971] 2 Lloyds L.R. 49 (Q.B.), 322 (C.A.), liability in negligence was admitted in respect of a failure to warn the patient of what Salmon L.J. (ibid. 323) referred to as 'the serious risks which the operation carried with it'.

[71] As in *Bolam* v. *Friern Hospital Management Committee* [1957] 1 W.L.R. 582, 585, 589-90; *Chipps* v. *Peters* (1976, Ont.), unreported, noted in E. I. Picard, *Legal Liability of Doctors and Hospitals in Canada* (1978), 356; *McLean* v. *Weir, Goff and Royal Inland Hospital* [1977] 5 W.W.R. 609, 626; *sub. nom. McLean* v. *Weir and Goff* [1980] 4 W.W.R. 330; and in *Holmes* v. *Board of Hospital Trustees of City of London* (1977) 81 D.L.R. (3d) 67, 83. See also *Waters* v. *Park, The Times,* 4, 5, 6, and 15 July 1961; *O'Malley-Williams* v. *Board of Governors of the National Hospital for Nervous Diseases* [1975] 1 *Br. Med. J.* 635.

presumed to know,[72] the duty to disclose will be correspond-
ingly less.[73]

5. *Likely effect of information on patient.* In those rare cases
where information is likely to have a directly detrimental
effect on the patient's health,[74] a doctor will not normally be
in breach of his duty of care if he does not disclose this
information to the patient.[75] One exception may be where a
patient has gone to a doctor, not simply for treatment, but
for an assessment of his condition so that he can make financial and other arrangements for the future.[76] More difficult is
the situation in which the information is unlikely to have any
directly detrimental effect on the patient's health, but may
cause anxiety. Doctors sometimes shield patients from information on the ground that it would cause the patients to
worry, and the courts have not been unsympathetic to this
approach.[77] There is a danger that if too much weight is given
to this consideration it could abrogate what one New Zealand
judge has spoken of as the patient's 'right to decline operative
investigation or treatment however unreasonable or foolish
this may appear in the eyes of his medical advisers'.[78] It is not

[72] e.g. risks incidental to any operation: *Kenny* v. *Lockwood* [1932] 1 D.L.R.
507, 523, 525. See also *Murrin* v. *Janes* [1949] 4 D.L.R. 403, 406; *Hopp* v. *Lepp*
(1980) 112 D.L.R. (3d) 67, 77.

[73] In *Chatterton* v. *Gerson* [1981] Q.B. 432, 444D–E, Bristow J. spoke of a
duty to warn of any 'real risk of a misfortune inherent in the procedure'. For
another recent formulation, see *Hopp* v. *Lepp* (1980) 112 D.L.R. (3d) 67, 80–1.

[74] See generally *Hatcher* v. *Black*, *The Times*, 29, 30 June, 1 and 2 July 1954;
Daniels v. *Heskin* [1954] I.R. 73, 87.

[75] Cf. Mental Health Act 1959, s. 124(2) (h), (i).

[76] See generally Edmund Davies L.J., 'The Patient's Right to Know the Truth'
(1973) 66 *Proc. Roy. Soc. Med.* 533.

[77] See e.g. *Male* v. *Hopmans* (1965) 54 D.L.R. (2d) 592, 595, (1967) 64
D.L.R. (2d) 105, 113; *O'Malley-Williams* v. *Board of Governors of the National
Hospital for Nervous Diseases* [1975] 1 *Br. Med. J.* 635. See also *Chatterton* v.
Gerson [1981] Q.B. 432, 444E; *Hopp* v. *Lepp* (1980) 112 D.L.R. (3d) 67, 77;
Reibl v. *Hughes* (1980) 114 D.L.R. (3d) 1, 13, 34. But see Lawton L.J., 'Legal
Aspects of Iatrogenic Disorders: Discussion Paper' (1983) 76 *J. Roy. Soc. Med.*
289 ('I suspect that some doctors say nothing about risks because they are con-
fident that if they did their patients would not accept the treatment which they
are sure is required. The law would not accept this as a good reason for not telling
the patient what the risks were if he suffered from one of them.').

[78] *Smith* v. *Auckland Hospital Board* [1965] N.Z.L.R. 191, 219, per T. A.
Gresson J. See also *Lepp* v. *Hopp* (1979) 98 D.L.R. (3d) 464, 470, where Prowse J.
said 'Each patient is entitled to make his own decision even though it may not
accord with the decision knowledgeable members of the profession would make.
The patient has a right to be wrong.'

settled how much weight the courts will be prepared to give to the adverse effect of the information on the patient.[79] Where disclosure is unlikely to do more than cause anxiety a doctor would be unwise to rely on this factor alone. The patient's apprehension, or reluctance to consent to treatment, will sometimes be a reason for a doctor giving a more detailed explanation than usual of why the procedure is necessary.[80] Much will depend on the manner in which the doctor communicates the information. A doctor might be in breach of his duty of care if he discloses information (including information that he is required to disclose) in a way which causes needless alarm, and resultant injury to health.[81]

The problem in practice is that the various factors do not always point in the same direction. It is often necessary to determine which factor or combination of factors should, in the circumstances of the particular case, outweigh the others. Sometimes the problem is still more complex for there may be difficulties, not merely with how little information a doctor may give a patient, but with how much.

In some circumstances, a doctor might be in breach of his duty of care if he discloses certain information to a patient. This might be so if the information, however carefully communicated, was likely to cause grave harm to the patient's health. The situation is further complicated by the fact that the doctor may sometimes be obliged to disclose information if he is to avoid incurring liability under some other branch of the law. The law should never place a doctor in the dilemma of having to choose between giving information and risking liability in negligence, or of withholding it and risking liability in, say, battery.[82] For the most part the courts should be able

[79] Cf. *Waters* v. *Park, The Times*, 6 July 1961 (see also *The Times*, 4, 5, and 15 July 1961), where Havers J. is reported to have said, *in arguendo*, that *Hatcher* v. *Black* 'was a low watermark and he was not at all excited by it. His Lordship could not think of anything more damaging to the medical profession.' For a discussion of the extent to which information should be withheld in the 'best interests' of the patient, see G. Robertson, op. cit., n. 4, 120-2. See generally A. Buchanan, 'Medical Paternalism' (1978) 7 *Philosophy & Public Affairs* 370-90.

[80] *Hopp* v. *Lepp* (1980) 112 D.L.R. (3d) 67, 77. Cf. *Reibl* v. *Hughes* (1980) 114 D.L.R. (3d) 1, 13, 34.

[81] Cf. *Furniss* v. *Fitchett* [1958] N.Z.L.R. 396.

[82] Cf. J. C. Smith, 'Civil Law Concepts in the Criminal Law' [1972 B] *C.L.J.* 197, 208-10, 224.

to interpret the requirements of other branches of the law so that they do not conflict with the requirements of good medical practice. But quite apart from this, the reasonable medical practitioner is presumably free to disclose such information as he reasonably believes to be necessary to avoid criminal or tortious liability, even if but for this consideration he would have remained silent.

The communication of information which the doctor knows to be untrue raises special difficulties. A doctor would be wise to give no information rather than information which he knows to be untrue;[83] but when asked a specific question this option may not be open to him. Very occasionally he may be faced with the dilemma of having to give either an untrue answer or else a true answer which may cause harm to the patient's health.[84] The duty to answer carefully is not identical with a duty to answer truthfully,[85] and a doctor who gives an untrue answer will not necessarily be in breach of his duty of care. But although a doctor may sometimes be free to give an untrue answer,[86] it may be doubted whether he would ever be in breach of his duty of care for not doing so.[87]

Procedures not intended to benefit the patient's health

Where a medical procedure is not intended to benefit the health of the 'patient', there is no conflict between the patient's interest in self-determination and the patient's interest in health.[88] Here the doctor can only err by giving too little information, never by giving too much.[89] A doctor is likely to be in breach of his duty of care if he fails to make a full disclosure of all the factors that a reasonable person

[83] See generally *Chapman* v. *Rix*, *The Times*, 22 December 1960, per Lord Denning (dissenting).

[84] It could be argued that these were the only alternatives open to the doctor in *Hatcher* v. *Black*, *The Times*, 29, 30 June, 1 and 2 July 1954.

[85] *Smith* v. *Auckland Hospital Board* [1965] N.Z.L.R. 191, 197, 198, 219 (though cf. 215).

[86] See generally H. W. Smith, 'Therapeutic Privilege to Withhold Specific Diagnosis from Patient Sick with Serious or Fatal Illness' (1946) 19 *Tennessee Law Review* 349-57.

[87] Cf. Lord Denning, 'Medicine, Morals, and the Law' [1959] 2 *Br. Med. J.* 692.

[88] *Halushka* v. *University of Saskatchewan* (1965) 53 D.L.R. (2d) 436, 444. See also *Kelly* v. *Hazlett* (1976) 75 D.L.R. (3d) 536, 565; *Reibl* v. *Hughes* (1979) 89 D.L.R. (3d) 112, 127.

[89] See n. 50.

would wish to consider before deciding whether to consent.[90] Indeed, the doctor should disclose not merely what some hypothetical reasonable person would wish to know, and not merely what the doctor or the medical profession generally considers relevant, but also any other information which he has reason to believe that the particular person would wish to know before deciding whether to consent. At the same time, the doctor should seek to ensure that the patient understands the information disclosed.

C TORT OF DECEIT

Although often overlooked in this context, the tort of deceit may sometimes supplement the requirements of battery and of negligence, with regard to the information a doctor must disclose about a proposed procedure. This can best be illustrated by an examination of the facts of a well-known case involving a thyroidectomy.[91] There is a recognized risk to the voice in any thyroidectomy, but there were said to be special medical grounds for withholding this information from the patient. This was because knowledge of the risks would lead the patient to worry, which might stimulate the gland, and hence lessen the chance of the operation being a success. The patient alleged that when she asked whether there was any risk the doctor had assured her that there was none whatever, and that had he told her the truth she would not have undergone the operation, and her voice would not have been damaged. Assuming that the patient's account was correct, the patient would not have had any chance of recovering damages in battery unless she could establish that she did not consent to an operation of the same 'nature' as that which took place. She would not have had any chance of recovering damages in negligence unless she could establish that, despite the medical reasons for withholding the information, any reasonable medical practitioner would have given a

---

[90] Cf. *Halushka* v. *University of Saskatchewan* (1965) 53 D.L.R. (2d) 436. Hall J.A.'s view that the failure to disclose related only to 'trespass' (ibid. 446) was wrong; see now *Reibl* v. *Hughes* (1980) 114 D.L.R. (3d) 1; *Chatterton* v. *Gerson* [1981] Q.B. 432.

[91] *Hatcher* v. *Black*, *The Times*, 29, 30 June, 1 and 2 July 1954. An extract from the summing-up is printed in Denning, *The Discipline of Law* (1979), 242-4.

truthful answer to her question.[92] However, as the law stands at present, an action in deceit would have avoided these difficulties.

To recover damages in deceit the patient would need to establish that the doctor made a false representation of fact, knowing that it was false, or being reckless whether it was or not; that the representation was made with the intention that the patient should act upon it; and that the patient had so acted, and suffered harm in consequence.[93] A major obstacle to succeeding in an action in deceit often lies in the difficulty of proving that the person knew his representation to be false. If this difficulty were likely to arise in an 'informed consent' case, it could usually be avoided by bringing an action in negligence at the same time. To clear himself of the allegation of negligence the doctor would probably argue that it was good medical practice to conceal the risks—and hence admit that he knew of them.

Fact is often contrasted with opinion, and this raises the question of whether a doctor's statements about a proposed operation fall within the ambit of the tort. Some of the information will concern existing facts, such as the percentage of patients who are still living five years after the operation. There is no difficulty here. But there will also be statements of opinion about, for example, the likelihood of an operation being a success, given the patient's medical condition, and the techniques and drugs now available. It is with this category that the difficulties may seem to appear. However, they are

[92] The patient brought the action in negligence, and the trial judge, Denning L.J., appeared to favour the view that the doctor would not have been in breach of the required standard of care if he had concealed the risks. But the jury's verdict did not necessarily rest on acceptance of this view, for this was not the only matter in issue. This is evident from the following passage from the summing-up: 'But even if you think that [the doctor] did tell her that there was no risk, you would still have to ask yourselves: Was that deserving of censure? Was it negligence?—and, yet again, even if it was negligence, was she any the worse for it? Was there any damage which flowed from it, because beyond question one would have thought the only thing for this lady was to have the operation.' (*The Times* did not report the summing-up verbatim and the passage quoted does not appear in the substantial extract from the summing-up which Lord Denning included in *The Discipline of the Law* (1979). It appeared in a transcript provided by the Association of Official Shorthand Writers: see (1965) 5 *Med. Sci. Law* 171.)

[93] For the basic elements of the tort of deceit, see *Bradford Third Equitable Benefit Building Society* v. *Borders* [1941] 2 All. E.R. 205, 211.

mainly illusory, for as well as stating an opinion the doctor is representing that this is in fact his opinion.[94] If it is not his true opinion, and he is only giving it as such to induce the patient to undergo the operation, he has made a false representation of fact. On present indications it will not be any excuse that he did not intend the patient to suffer harm in consequence of the misrepresentation,[95] or even that he thought that only benefit would result.[96]

A representation may be implied by conduct. If a doctor acted in a way calculated to lead the patient to believe that a procedure was part of his treatment, when it was not, the doctor would have made a false representation of fact.[97] If the patient would not otherwise have permitted the doctor to carry out the procedure, and the patient suffered harm in consequence, the doctor could be liable in deceit.

II 'FREE' CONSENT

Writers on medical law sometimes state that consent must be 'freely given'. Discussion of this matter has often been confused by the assumption that principles concerning consent are the same in all contexts, and that because a very limited amount of pressure will render inoperative an employee's assumption of risk, the same amount of pressure will vitiate a patient's consent to medical treatment. The fallacy of the transplanted category[98] has, in the words of W. W. Cook, 'all

[94] See *Bisset* v. *Wilkinson* [1927] A.C. 177, 182.

[95] See *Derry* v. *Peek* (1889) 14 App. Cas. 337, 365, 374; *Bradford Third Equitable Benefit Building Society* v. *Borders* [1941] 2 All E.R. 205, 211. See also *Edgington* v. *Fitzmaurice* (1885) 29 Ch.D. 459, 481-2.

[96] See *Peek* v. *Gurney* (1873) L.R. 6 H.L. 377, 409-10; *Smith* v. *Chadwick* (1884) 9 App. Cas. 187, 201. None of the cases which support the view that motive is irrelevant were concerned with circumstances where the motive for the deception was the prevention of harm to the person deceived. But even if it is accepted that it is sometimes good medical practice to deceive a patient about a proposed operation, the courts may be reluctant to provide a new defence to the tort of deceit which would have the effect of leaving the deceived patient without compensation if he suffered harm in consequence. If the patient does not suffer harm in consequence of the misrepresentation, one of the essential elements of the tort is lacking.

[97] Cf. *R.* v. *Barnard* (1837) 7 C. & P. 784.

[98] The expression is taken from the title of the illuminating discussion of the issue by M. Hancock in (1959) 37 *Canadian Bar Review* 535-75.

the tenacity of original sin and must constantly be guarded against'.[99] Here, too, it is wrong to assume that the law of battery and the law of negligence will necessarily adopt an identical approach. Different areas of the law have different requirements, and conduct which suffices in one area may not suffice in another.

A TORT AND CRIME OF BATTERY

There are two ways in which an apparent consent may be held to be ineffective, for the purpose of the crime or tort of battery. If there is neither express assent nor express dissent, a court may draw a distinction between consent and sub-mission.[1] In this context submission is equated with acqui-escence, the absence of dissent, so that although 'every consent involves a submission . . . it by no means follows, that a mere submission requires a consent.[2] Mere submission is often indicative of consent,[3] but where it is shown that the person acquiesced because he did not realize what was in-volved,[4] or—less important in this context—for fear of the consequences of refusal,[5] the courts may find that the person did not consent. Although the distinction has more often been acted upon in criminal than in civil cases, there is no good reason why it should not be made with the tort, as well as the crime, of battery.[6]

---

[99] W. W. Cook, *The Logical and Legal Bases of the Conflict of Laws* (1942), 159.

[1] See e.g. *R.* v. *Case* (1850) 4 Cox C.C. 220, 223; *R.* v. *Wollaston* (1872) 12 Cox C.C. 180, 182. See also *R.* v. *Olugbajo* [1982] Q.B. 320, 332 (rape).

[2] *R.* v. *Day* (1841) 9 C. & P. 722, 724 (emphasis omitted), quoted with approval in *R.* v. *Olugbajo* [1982] 1 Q.B. 320, 332.

[3] *R.* v. *Sinclair* (1867) 13 Cox C.C. 28, 29 ('such absence of resistance as would reasonably imply consent'). See also *R.* v. *Day* (1841) 9 C. & P. 722, 724.

[4] See e.g. *R.* v. *Rosinki* (1824) 1 Mood. 19, 1 Lewin 11; *R.* v. *Case* (1850) 4 Cox C.C. 220; *R.* v. *Sinclair* (1867) 13 Cox C.C. 28; *R.* v. *Lock* (1872) L.R. 2 C.C.R. 10, 13; *Burrell* v. *Harmer* (1966) 116 *New L.J.* 1658. See also *R.* v. *Williams* [1923] 1 K.B. 340.

[5] *R.* v. *Day* (1841) 9 C. & P. 722, 724; *R.* v. *Woodhurst* (1870) 12 Cox C.C. 443, 444.

[6] The distinction was acted upon in *Agnew* v. *Jobson* (1877) 13 Cox C.C. 625 (tort), but not in *Latter* v. *Braddell* (1881) 50 L.J.Q.B. 448. In so far as the latter case suggests that something less than consent may be sufficient, it should not be followed. At one time a touching may have amounted to a battery only if it was 'against the will', rather than 'without the will' (i.e. 'without consent'), but nowadays the expression 'against the will' is generally treated as a synonym for 'without consent'.

The other means of dealing with cases where what could be regarded as consent was exacted under great pressure, is to invoke the principle that physical violence or threats of physical violence vitiate consent.[7] But it is clear that lesser forms of pressure will not of themselves vitiate consent.[8]

Consent is no less effective when it is unwillingly or reluctantly given; few patients would consent to major surgery if it were not for the force of surrounding circumstances, and the knowledge that health or even life may be in jeopardy if they do not consent. Financial inducements to consent to even non-therapeutic procedures would not vitiate consent.[9] Nor would the fact that the alternative to giving consent was a term of imprisonment,[10] or that there were psychological and social pressures to consent to, for example, the removal of a kidney for transplantation to a relative.[11]

B TORT OF NEGLIGENCE

There has been very little consideration of the amount of pressure a doctor may properly bring to bear on a patient, to induce him to consent, or of the circumstances in which a doctor may be obliged to shield a patient from undue pressure to consent. Nevertheless, it is possible to go a little beyond the mere statement that the doctor must do what any reasonable doctor would do in the circumstances.

[7] *Latter* v. *Braddell* (1881) 50 L.J.Q.B. 448.

[8] *Latter* v. *Braddell* (1881) 50 L.J.Q.B. 448 (non-therapeutic medical examination); *Li Hong Mi* v. *A.-G.* (1918) 13 H.K.L.R. 6, 44. Cf. *Conn* v. *David Spencer Ltd.* [1930] 1 D.L.R. 805 (false imprisonment).

[9] In *Halushka* v. *University of Saskatchewan* (1965) 53 D.L.R. (2d) 436 financial considerations had induced the student to consent to the experimental procedures. But it was not suggested that this vitiated his consent. For a discussion of this issue in relation to the analogous crime of rape, see *R.* v. *Arnold* [1947] 2 D.L.R. 438. Cf. *R.* v. *McCoy* [1953] 2 S.A. 4; *State* v. *Volschenk* [1968] 2 P.H., H.283.

[10] In *R.* v. *Severn*, *Daily Telegraph*, 25 April 1979, p. 21 (news report), a sex offender agreed to have a drug implanted into his thigh, rather than undergo a further term of imprisonment. There was reason to believe that the drug would control his libido. It was said that the implant would also make his breasts grow, but that these could be cut off later. (Consent to a specimen of blood being taken for testing is effective, even though consent would not have been given were it not for the fact that the consequence of refusal would be prosecution under the Road Traffic Act 1972, s. 8(7) (substituted by Transport Act 1981, s. 25(3), Sch. 8)).

[11] R. Ormrod, 'Medical Ethics' [1968] 2 *Br. Med. J.* 7, 9–10. See also *R.* v. *Landry* (1935) 64 C.C.C. 104.

A doctor will sometimes be justified in going to great lengths to persuade a patient to undergo a procedure which is in the best interests of the patient's health. With an unduly apprehensive patient, it might sometimes be bad medical practice not to do so.[12] But where the procedure is not intended for the benefit of a patient's health there is a stronger possibility of a doctor being in breach of his duty of care if he brings great pressure to bear on a patient, to induce him to consent. He may also be in breach of his duty of care if he does not attempt to shield his patient from undesirable pressures originating elsewhere. Official statements and codes on the subject of non-therapeutic experimentation often stress the need to obtain a 'free consent' or to prevent 'undue influence' being brought to bear on a patient.[13] These statements and codes could be admitted as evidence of the required standard of care in such cases.[14]

---

[12] But see *Wells* v. *Surrey Area Health Authority*, *The Times*, 29 July 1978, p. 3 (news report), which resulted from a woman being sterilized during the course of a Caesarean operation to bring about the birth of her third child. The patient was a Roman Catholic, who at the time of the operation was 35 years of age. She subsequently 'bitterly regretted the sterilization'. The possibility of sterilization was first raised when she was already in labour and 'in some state of exhaustion'. Croom-Johnson J. held that the patient understood the implications of the operation when she consented to it, and therefore dismissed her claim for 'assault'. But he awarded her damages of £3,000 on the ground that the hospital had been negligent in failing to give her proper advice about the operation. He urged the need for good counselling before taking 'this big and important step in a woman's life'. (See also 'Contraception by Female Sterilisation' (1980) 280 *Br. Med. J.* 1154, 1155.)

[13] See e.g. 'Responsibility in Investigations on Human Subjects', *Report of the Medical Research Council for the Year 1962–1963* (Cmnd. 2382; 1964), 21, 23 (Statement by the Medical Research Council); 'Experimental Research on Human Beings' [1963] 2 *Br. Med. J.* Suppl. 57 (Statement approved by Annual Representative Meeting of British Medical Association); 'Code of Ethics of the World Medical Association' [1964] 2 *Br. Med. J.* 177 ('Declaration of Helsinki'); 'Recommendations Guiding Medical Doctors in Biomedical Research Involving Human Subjects' [1976] 1 *Medical Journal of Australia* 206-7.

[14] *Furniss* v. *Fitchett* [1958] N.Z.L.R. 338, 405. See also *Qualcast (Wolverhampton) Ltd.* v. *Haynes* [1959] A.C. 743, 759.

MEDICAL PROCEDURES PERFORMED
WITHOUT CONSENT

> Every human being of adult years and sound mind
> has a right to determine what shall be done with his
> own body . . .
>
> Cardozo J., 1914[1]

In the absence of legally effective consent, a medical procedure
involving a bodily touching would often infringe the criminal
and the civil law.[2] However there are some circumstances in
which a doctor is legally justified in proceeding without consent. A statute may clearly authorize the performance of the
medical procedure in question.[3] This chapter deals with the
more common situation, where there is no clear statutory
authority for proceeding without consent.

It is widely accepted that a doctor is sometimes legally
justified in proceeding without consent, even though there is
no statute which expressly authorizes him to do so. English
judges have made extrajudicial statements to this effect,[4] and
doctors are constantly acting in the belief that this is so. But
there are very few English cases which are of assistance in
determining the circumstances in which a doctor is legally
justified in proceeding without consent—although there are

---

[1] *Schloendorff* v. *Society of New York Hospital* (1914) 105 N.E. 92, 93
(N.Y.).

[2] The crime and the tort that would most often be infringed are those which
are technically known as 'battery' (see ch. 2), and which are sometimes referred
to as criminal assault, and the tort of trespass to the person, respectively.

[3] Part VI of the Mental Health (Amendment) Act 1982 authorizes the treatment for mental disorder of patients who are liable to be detained under the
Mental Health Act, without (except in specified circumstances) the patients' consent being required. It does not apply to medical procedures performed for reasons
other than the treatment of mental disorder: in those cases the general legal
principles (discussed in this and other chapters of this book) will apply. For a
helpful account of the statutory provisions, see L. Gostin, 'A Review of the
Mental Health (Amendment) Act—III: The Legal Position of Patients While in
Hospital' (1982) 132 *New L.J.* 1199, 1199-1201.

[4] See e.g. Stephen, *Digest*, 148; Devlin, *Samples*, 91-3.

cases which indicate that the mere fact that a procedure is performed for the patient's benefit will not of itself justify a doctor in proceeding without consent.[5]

The justification, or justifications, discussed in this chapter will apply to the crime and the tort of battery and, in so far as medical procedures come within the range of other offences against the person, to those offences also.[6] There is no need to assume that there must be one comprehensive justification for the performance of medical procedures without consent, and in the absence of clear statutory authority. There may be a series of different, if overlapping, justifications with different theoretical bases.[7]

In considering the circumstances in which a doctor is legally justified in proceeding without consent, it is desirable to distinguish between those procedures which are intended to benefit the health of the patient, and those procedures which are not intended to have this effect.

I PROCEDURES INTENDED TO BENEFIT THE PATIENT'S HEALTH

In considering the circumstances in which a doctor is justified in proceeding without consent or express statutory authority, with the intention of benefiting the health of the patient, it is as well to distinguish between four main categories of cases. These categories cover most of the situations which arise in practice. For the purpose of these categories, it has been assumed that there is one person other than the patient who is authorized to consent 'on the patient's behalf'. In practice

[5] See e.g. *Cull* v. *Royal Surrey County Hospital and Butler* [1932] 1 *Br. Med. J.* 1195; *Devi* v. *West Midlands Regional Health Authority* [1980] C.L.Y. 687; and also *Odam* v. *Young* [1955] 2 *Br. Med. J.* 1453. Cases from other jurisdictions include *Boase* v. *Paul* [1931] 4 D.L.R. 435; *Mulloy* v. *Hop Sang* [1935] 1 W.W.R. 714; *Parmley* v. *Parmley and Yule* [1945] 4 D.L.R. 81, 89; *Stoffberg* v. *Elliott* [1923] C.P.D. 148; *Ex p. Dixie* [1950] 4 S.A. 748.

[6] For the purpose of the tort of negligence, the test would be whether a reasonable doctor would proceed without consent, in the circumstances in question.

[7] e.g. presumed consent; necessity; duty to act; right to prevent crime. For a discussion of some of these, see B. M. Hoggett, *Mental Health* (1976), 127; Glanville Williams, 'Necessity' [1978] *Crim. L.R.* 128, 132-4; Williams, *Textbook*, 568-9. See also P. D. G. Skegg, 'A Justification for Medical Procedures Performed Without Consent' (1974) 90 *L.Q.R.* 512, 512-14.

there will often be none, and there will sometimes be more than one.[8] However, any advantage which might accrue from a consideration of these variations would not outweigh the complications it would entail.

1. *Patient incapable of consenting, and not known to object to performance of the procedure. (Person authorized to consent on patient's behalf unavailable, and not known to object to performance of the procedure.)*

The argument for a doctor being justified in proceeding without consent is strongest in some of those cases where the patient is incapable of consenting, the person authorized to consent on his behalf is unavailable, and neither the patient nor that person is known to object to the performance of the procedure.[9] The range of procedures which a doctor is justified in performing without consent will vary according to the probable duration of the incapacity and unavailability.[10]

Short-term incapacity may result from the administration of a general anaesthetic, from heavy sedation, from the consumption of alcohol, or from other factors. In these cases, there is no question of a doctor being justified in doing everything that is in the interests of the patient's health,[11] for so broad a justification would create too great an inroad on the individual's interest in deciding what is done to his own body. But although it is generally accepted that a doctor is sometimes justified in proceeding without consent, there is no English case which is directly in point.[12] In the circumstances,

---

[8] See ch. 3, pt. II, esp. pp. 58–9, 72–3.

[9] Although, in delineating these categories, it has been convenient (in the interests of brevity) to use 'object' in the present tense, it is intended to embrace those cases where it is reasonably certain that if the person in question knew of the proposed procedure, and was capable of objecting, he would do so.

[10] This discussion will focus on cases of incapacity. But the same principles will be relevant to instances of short-term or long-term unavailability of any other person who could give a legally effective consent.

[11] See e.g. *Cull* v. *Royal Surrey County Hospital and Butler* [1932] 1 *Br. Med. J.* 1195; *Hamilton* v. *Birmingham Regional Hospital Board and Keates* [1969] 2 *Br. Med. J.* 456 (liability conceded).

[12] Nor are there any Australian or New Zealand cases which are particularly helpful—although see *Tate* v. *Fisher* (1875) 1 V.L.R. 244 (and see also *R.* v. *Loughnan* [1981] V.R. 443). A number of South African cases support the view that a doctor is sometimes justified in proceeding without consent: see *Stoffberg*

the English courts will almost certainly look to a line of Canadian decisions which have developed a justification for some medical interventions in the absence of consent.

One important decision was that of the Supreme Court of Nova Scotia in *Marshall* v. *Curry*.[13] During the course of an operation for the cure of a hernia, the doctor discovered that his patient had a grossly diseased left testicle. He was of the opinion that if the testicle was not removed it might become gangrenous, with the result that the pus might be absorbed into the circulation and a condition of blood poisoning set in. The patient was under a general anaesthetic at the time and, rather than wait until the patient's consent could be sought, the doctor went ahead and removed the diseased testicle. The patient brought an action in trespass, and the doctor's defence rested on the grounds that, if the testicle had not been removed, it would have been a menace to the health and life of the patient.[14] Chisholm C.J. ruled that 'where a great emergency which could not be anticipated arises' a doctor is justified in acting 'in order to save the life or preserve the health of the patient'.[15] He went on to find that the doctor had discovered conditions 'which neither party had anticipated, and which the defendant could not reasonably have foreseen' and that in removing the testicle the doctor had acted 'in the interest of his patient and for the protection of his health and possibly his life'.[16] He said that the removal 'was in that sense necessary', and considered that it would have been unreasonable to postpone the removal until a later date.[17] Accordingly, the doctor's action was held to be justified.

v. *Elliott* [1923] C.P.D. 148, 150; *Ex p. Dixie* [1950] 4 S.A. 748, 751; *Esterhuizen* v. *Administrator, Transvaal* [1957] 3 S.A. 710, 718, 721. In addition to the Canadian cases discussed below, see also the *dicta* in *Winn* v. *Alexander* [1940] 3 D.L.R. 778, 780; *Johnston* v. *Wellesley Hospital* (1970) 17 D.L.R. (3d) 139, 144; and *Schweizer* v. *Central Hospital* (1974) 53 D.L.R. (3d) 494, 507-8, 509. There was a passing reference to emergency situations in the judgments of Laskin C.J.C. in *Hopp* v. *Lepp* (1980) 112 D.L.R. (3d) 67, 70 and *Reibl* v. *Hughes* (1980) 114 D.L.R. (3d) 1, 10.

[13] [1933] 3 D.L.R. 260.
[14] The doctor's claim that the removal of the testicle was necessary in order to cure the hernia (see [1933] 3 D.L.R. 262) was not dealt with in the judgment.
[15] [1933] 3 D.L.R. 275. Chisholm C.J. purported to adopt the jurisprudence established in Quebec, as exemplified in *Parnell* v. *Springle* (1899) 5 Rev. de Jur. 74 and *Caron* v. *Gagnon* (1930) 68 Que. S.C. 155.
[16] [1933] 3 D.L.R. 275.   [17] Ibid. 275-6.

Subsequently, in *Murray* v. *McMurchy*,[18] the Supreme Court of British Columbia was faced with a similar case, but came to a different conclusion. In the course of a Caesarean section, the doctor discovered a number of fibroid tumours in the wall of the patient's uterus. He was concerned about the hazards of her having another pregnancy and, after consultation with the doctor who was assisting him, decided to tie the patient's Fallopian tubes. The patient subsequently brought an action in trespass. Macfarlane J. distinguished between the situation in which the operation was 'necessary in the sense that it would be, in the circumstances, unreasonable to postpone the operation until a later date' and the situation in which it was merely 'convenient' to perform the operation without waiting to obtain consent.[19] He said that if an operation is 'necessary as opposed to being convenient, for the protection of the life or even for the preservation of the health of the patient' a doctor is justified in proceeding without consent.[20] Despite the evidence of one specialist that the overwhelming majority of women would have been annoyed if the operation had not been performed immediately, the judge held that it would not have been unreasonable to postpone the operation until the patient's consent could be sought. The patient was awarded a substantial sum of damages.

The test applied in *Murray* v. *McMurchy* was influenced by the judgment of the Supreme Court of Canada in *Parmley* v. *Parmley and Yule*[21] as well as by *Marshall* v. *Curry*. In *Parmley* v. *Parmley and Yule* Estey J., with whom the rest of the court concurred, said that in circumstances of emergency great latitude may be given to a doctor. However, he said that, in the case in question, the fact that the patient was under the anaesthetic had provided a 'convenient, but not a necessary, opportunity' for proceeding without consent.[22]

The distinction between medical procedures which are 'necessary in the sense that it would be in the circumstances unreasonable to postpone' them, and medical procedures which are merely 'convenient', provides an adequate basis for

---

[18] [1949] 2 D.L.R. 442.   [19] Ibid. 444.
[20] Ibid. 443–4.   [21] [1945] 4 D.L.R. 81.
[22] [1945] 4 D.L.R. 81, 89. Cf. *Marshall* v. *Curry* [1933] 3 D.L.R. 260.

distinguishing between those cases where a doctor should be justified in proceeding without consent, and those where he should not be justified. However, it is possible to improve upon the terminology used by the Canadian courts. It would be better to avoid the strained and ambiguous use of 'necessary',[23] and state that a doctor is justified in proceeding without consent with any procedure which it would be unreasonable, as opposed to merely inconvenient, to postpone until consent could be sought.

There is a subtle but important difference between a test of whether it would be unreasonable to postpone an operation until a later date, and a test of whether it would be reasonable to proceed with it immediately. The latter test, which would probably be applicable in an action in negligence, is too broad for the purpose of the tort or the crime of battery. In some cases it would be reasonable to proceed with the operation immediately, and yet not unreasonable to postpone it until consent could be sought. The tort and the crime of battery safeguard an individual's interest in being able to determine for himself what is done to his own body, and the less extensive justification is therefore to be preferred. Under this justification a patient's health, let alone life, need never be put in jeopardy because of the impossibility of seeking consent. However, it would encourage a doctor to limit his intervention to that which could not reasonably be postponed.

The English courts may be expected to provide a justification at least as broad as the one advocated here.[24] But in view of the later cases, which have stressed that the inconvenience of postponing an operation is an insufficient reason for not doing so, *Marshall* v. *Curry* may well prove to be the 'high

[23] Cf. *Re Naylor Benzon Mining Co.* [1950] Ch. 567, 575.

[24] This formulation of the justification omits any reference to a requirement that the need for the procedure should not have been foreseen, or should not have been reasonably foreseeable. Emphasis was placed on this consideration in *Marshall* v. *Curry*, where the need for the procedure in question had not been reasonably foreseeable when the general anaesthetic had been administered. However such a restriction is pointless where the incapacity has not been induced by the doctor, or a member of the medical team. Even where it has been, it would be unsatisfactory for the doctor to be given the choice of either permitting the patient to suffer harm as a result of his not performing the operation, or else of performing it and risking liability in battery.

water' mark so far as operations without consent are concerned.[25] It is probably best explained in terms of the exceptional surrounding circumstances.[26]

There is a need for caution where a patient is not known to object to the performance of the procedure in question, but there is reason to believe that he might well do so. However, a patient's health should never be put in jeopardy because of the mere possibility that he might have refused consent; although in these cases a doctor should be particularly careful that he does nothing which could reasonably have been postponed until after consent had been sought.

The distinction between procedures which it would be unreasonable to postpone, and procedures which it would be merely inconvenient to postpone, is equally satisfactory with cases of long-term incapacity and unavailability. The longer the probable duration of the incapacity and unavailability, the broader will be the range of procedures which it would be unreasonable to postpone. If a patient is likely to be permanently incapable of consenting, and no one may consent on his behalf, a doctor should be justified in doing whatever good medical practice dictates should be done in the interests of the patient's health. But where the law provides for someone to be appointed to safeguard the patient's interests, or where the doctor could make use of statutory powers, it would be unwise to assume that a non-statutory justification will be available to a doctor for an indefinite period.[27] In

---

[25] In addition to the Canadian cases, discussed above, see also *Devi* v. *West Midlands Regional Health Authority* [1980] C.L.Y. 687. It cannot be assumed that *Boase* v. *Paul* [1931] 1 D.L.R. 562, [1931] 4 D.L.R. 435 would have been decided differently if the justification subsequently developed in the Canadian courts had been applied in that case. In *Boase* v. *Paul* a dentist had gone beyond the scope of a patient's consent and, while the patient was under a general anaesthetic, had extracted all his upper teeth. Mulock C.J.O. said that the diseased condition of the teeth was such as to 'imperil the plaintiff's health, if not his life, and called for their immediate removal' ([1931] 4 D.L.R. 435), but he did not consider that this justified their removal without consent.

[26] The patient was an unmarried man of 52 years of age, whose virility had been impaired, at the very least, following an accident more than a quarter of a century earlier. He had been told of the removal of the testicle a day or two after the operation, but he did not make any complaint until almost two and a half years later. The doctor was a surgeon of high standing, who over a number of years had done much to improve the patient's health.

[27] See B. M. Hoggett, *Mental Health* (1976), 128.

these circumstances it would sometimes be reasonable to postpone treatment until authorization could be obtained.

2. *Patient incapable of consenting, and not known to object to performance of the procedure. Person authorized to consent on patient's behalf available, but refuses to consent (or unavailable, but known to object to the performance of the procedure).*

If a patient is incapable of consenting, and time is available, consent must be sought from anyone else who is authorized to consent. If the patient has himself authorized someone to consent on his behalf, that person's refusal of consent should be given the same effect as a refusal of the patient himself.[28] However, in most cases the person authorized to consent will have received his authority from law, independently of the will of the patient.[29] If the postponement of the procedure will not result in avoidable suffering, or injury to the health of the patient, there can be no question of a doctor being justified in proceeding without consent. But in some cases the consequences of the refusal could be serious. For example, it is not unknown for parents who are Jehovah's Witnesses to refuse consent to a child being given a blood transfusion, even though without it the child will probably die. This situation raises all the important issues which arise when the person authorized by law refuses to consent; it is therefore proposed to concentrate on it.

In some cases there will be the possibility of consent or authorization being obtained from some other source.[30] Wardship proceedings can be pursued in the High Court, and the judge may then authorize the procedure.[31] Alternatively, if

[28] Assuming, of course, that the authority to give or withhold consent extends to the procedure or circumstances in question.

[29] See ch. 3, pt. II, esp. pp. 58-9, 72-3.

[30] As to the replacement of persons who have been appointed guardians of mentally disordered persons under the Mental Health Act 1959, see s. 42(3) of that Act (as amended by the Mental Health (Amendment) Act, 1982, s. 65(1), Sch. 3).

[31] See e.g. *Re B. (A Minor) (Wardship: Medical Treatment)* [1981] 1 W.L.R. 1421; see also N. V. Lowe and R. A. H. White, *Wards of Court* (1979), 108. An account of some of the advantages of wardship proceedings, especially since the simplification of procedure in 1971, is given in Ormrod, 'Ethics', 25-6. But he makes no mention of the expense of such proceedings.

the child's health is being avoidably impaired or neglected, and the child is in need of care it is otherwise unlikely to receive, a juvenile court can commit the child into the care of a local authority.[32] The local authority can then give legally effective consent.[33] In emergency cases, a juvenile court has been known to sit in a hospital and make such an order, so that a doctor could obtain an effective consent.[34] But hospital authorities have been officially advised against making use of this possibility. They have been told to rely 'on the clinical judgment of the consultants concerned after full discussion with the parents'.[35] This makes it all the more important to ascertain the extent of any justification which may be available to the doctor.

It could, of course, be argued that there is no need for any justification. If criminal proceedings were brought as a result of a doctor overriding a parent's refusal of consent, and thereby saving a child's life, the courts could be relied on to make an order of absolute discharge.[36] The medical defence societies have assured doctors of their full support in such cases,[37] and in civil proceedings any award of damages would be unlikely to be more than nominal. However, these considerations do not do away with the need for a justification. Once it is accepted that a doctor should act in a particular manner then, in the absence of a good reason to the contrary, the law should provide a justification. In some cases the

[32] Children and Young Persons Act 1969, ss. 1(2), 20(1). For further details as to the conditions of the exercise of this power, see generally ss. 1, 2, and 20. In some cases it may be appropriate to seek a place of safety order under s. 28 of the Children and Young Persons Act 1969.

[33] Children and Young Persons Act 1969, s. 24(2). Wardship proceedings cannot be used to review a local authority's exercise of discretionary power under a care order: *A.* v. *Liverpool City Council* [1982] A.C. 363.

[34] See e.g. A. C. Fairburn and A. W. Tredinnick, 'Babies Removed from their Parents at Birth: 160 Statutory Care Actions' (1980) 280 *Br. Med. J.* 987, 988-9.

[35] See (1961) 637 Parl. Deb. H.C. *97* (Mr Enoch Powell, MP, Minister of Health); Ministry of Health Circular F/P9/1B, dated 14 April 1967. Similar advice has been given to local authorities: see Home Office Circular No. 63/1968, dated 5 March 1968. (The text of these circulars is printed in *Clarke Hall and Morrison's Law relating to Children and Young Persons* (9th edn., 1977, edd. M. Booth and B. Harris), 1118-19.)

[36] Powers of Criminal Courts Act 1973, s. 7(1).

[37] See e.g. S. Cochrane Shanks, reported in [1961] 1 *Br. Med. J.* Suppl. *292*; J. Leahy Taylor, Letter, 'Thou shalt not strive officiously', (1982) 285 *Br. Med. J.* 1743.

difficulties of providing a justification which permits the
approved conduct, but not other conduct also, may count
against doing so. But this factor can only be determined after
the possible justifications have been examined. The case for
providing a justification is here supported by other considerations. One is that because of their uncertainty about the law,
some doctors have been hesitant to act, with the result that
lives have been lost which could otherwise have been saved.[38]
Another is that very occasionally the doctor's intervention
may not have the desired effect, and may even hasten the
patient's death. It would be unreasonable to require a doctor
to risk incurring liability in these cases.

Doctors have frequently proceeded without consent where
parents have refused consent. The courts have yet to deal
with this situation, but Ormrod L.J. has said, extrajudicially,
that where parents have religious or cultural objections 'to
various forms of treatment, such as blood transfusion or
operation', the doctor 'is entitled to act on his clinical judgment of the child's best interests'. But he added that the
doctor would be unwise to follow this course 'except in
urgent cases'.[39]

The Children and Young Persons Act 1933 provides a clear
indication of what should be the policy of the law in this
area. It makes it an offence for someone who has attained the
age of sixteen years, and has the custody, charge, or care of a
child under that age, wilfully to neglect the child in a manner
likely to cause unnecessary suffering or injury to health.[40]
There are therefore circumstances in which a parent will be
guilty of a criminal offence if he prevents a child from receiving necessary medical treatment.[41] The child's physical welfare

[38] For examples, see *Taylor's Principles and Practice of Medical Jurisprudence*
(12th edn., 1965, ed. K. Simpson), vol. i, 67; Note, 'Parent's Refusal of Consent'
[1960] 1 *Br. Med. J.* 1371.

[39] Ormrod, 'Ethics', 25.

[40] Children and Young Persons Act 1933, s. 1(1). See also s. 1(2) (a), by virtue of which a parent or other person legally liable to maintain someone under
the age of sixteen years is deemed to have neglected him in a manner likely to
cause injury to health if he fails to provide adequate medical aid or, if being unable otherwise to provide it, fails to take steps to procure its provision under the
relevant enactments. For an account of statutory antecedents of s. 1(2), see *R.* v.
Sheppard [1981] A.C. 394, 402.

[41] See e.g. *Oakey* v. *Jackson* [1914] 1 K.B. 216, 219, 220.

is clearly the paramount consideration. But it is not the only consideration, and an adequate justification must take account of a parent's legitimate interest in what is done to his child, and by whom.

A doctor should not be justified in proceeding without consent wherever failure to treat would cause 'unnecessary suffering or injury to health',[42] for this would enable a doctor to bypass the parent altogether in a great many circumstances. But a justification which was restricted to circumstances in which the parent was risking criminal liability by wilfully neglecting the child, in a manner likely to cause unnecessary suffering or injury to its health, would not be adequate. It would not apply to cases where the parent's neglect was not wilful,[43] yet the need for treatment was no less urgent.

The test suggested by the Canadian cases already discussed, whereby a doctor will be justified in proceeding with procedures which it is unreasonable to postpone, could be adopted in this context. But its application would not be the same as it would be where the person authorized to consent was unavailable, but not known to object to the procedure in question. In this context, a doctor should be justified in proceeding without consent where three conditions are present. First, that in the circumstances it is not reasonable, or in the time available practicable, to take action so that someone else is empowered to authorize the performance of the procedure. Secondly, that the procedure is necessary to save the life of the child, to prevent permanent injury to its health, or to prevent prolonged pain and suffering.[44] And thirdly, that despite the making of all reasonable efforts to obtain consent, consent has been unreasonably refused.[45] The concept of unreasonable refusal of consent is one which the courts apply in similar contexts.[46] For example, they sometimes have to determine whether a parent is guilty of

---

[42] Cf. Children and Young Persons Act 1933, s. 1.

[43] See *R.* v. *Sheppard* [1981] A.C. 394.

[44] Cf. Health Amendment Act 1961 (N.Z.), s. 2. For another formulation, see S. R. Speller, *Law of Doctor and Patient* (1973), 30, and generally ibid. 31-5.

[45] Or, where the person authorized to consent is unavailable, but is known to object to the procedure in question, it would have been unreasonable for that person to have withheld consent.

[46] But see *R.* v. *Blaue* [1975] 1 W.L.R. 1411, 1415.

wilful neglect by unreasonably refusing to permit an operation on a child,[47] and whether a plaintiff's damages should be reduced on the grounds of unreasonable refusal to undergo medical treatment.[48]

This discussion has focused on the situation where a parent refuses to consent to medical procedures to be performed on a child.[49] However, the justification should be equally applicable if ever someone else is authorized by law to consent to medical procedures on another, and refuses to do so.

3. Patient capable of consenting, but refuses to do so. (Person authorized to consent on patient's behalf unavailable.)

In all but the most exceptional circumstances, a doctor may not carry out treatment involving the bodily touching of a patient who is capable of consenting, if the patient's consent has not been sought, or if the patient has refused to give consent. The fact that, without the treatment, the patient's health will suffer will not of itself justify a doctor in overriding the patient's refusal. Indeed, in many circumstances, even the certainty that the patient will die if treatment is not given will not justify a doctor in proceeding without consent.

However, there is at least one exception to the general rule that consent is required. Where someone has done something in an apparent attempt to kill himself,[50] doctors will often be justified in taking action to avert the consequences of that

[47] See *Oakey* v. *Johnson* [1914] 1 K.B. 216, 219; Children and Young Persons Act 1933, s. 1.

[48] See A. H. Hudson, 'Refusal of Medical Treatment' (1983) 3 *Legal Studies* 50-9; *Selvanayagam* v. *University of West Indies* [1983] 1 All E.R. 824, 826-7. See also e.g. *Lane* v. *Willis* [1972] 1 W.L.R. 326 (action stayed because of unreasonable refusal of plaintiff to submit to a medical examination); Mental Health Act 1959, s. 52(3) (unreasonable objection to the making of an application for admission for treatment, discussed in *W.* v. *L.* [1974] Q.B. 711). The factors which some moral philosophers take into account, when distinguishing between 'ordinary' and 'extraordinary' means of preserving life (see pp. 143-6), could sometimes be of assistance in determining whether a refusal of medical treatment was unreasonable.

[49] See Glanville Williams, 'Necessity', [1978] *Crim. L.R.* 128, 133-4 for a discussion of some possible grounds of justification.

[50] What is said of such cases should also be applicable to those cases where the need for treatment results from an act of some other person, done in compliance with a suicide pact. S. 3 of the Criminal Law Act 1967 could provide a basis for intervention in the latter circumstances.

action. Prior to the abolition of the offence of suicide,[51] there was no difficulty in explaining the legal basis for a doctor acting to prevent a person from attempting to commit suicide, or to avoid death resulting from such an attempt. Suicide was a felony, so the doctor was simply exercising the general liberty to prevent a felony.[52] Doctors were not only free to prevent someone from committing suicide; they were sometimes under a duty to do so.[53] However, since the enactment of the Suicide Act 1961 it has continued to be accepted that doctors are sometimes free—sometimes, indeed, under a duty[54]—to prevent patients from committing suicide.

In some cases, the person who has apparently attempted to commit suicide will be suffering from a mental disorder which prevents the giving or withholding of consent. But in many cases the person will have a sufficient understanding to give, or withhold, consent.[55] This is so, even though the act will often result from a passing impulse or temporary depression, rather than from a rational and fixed decision. If

---

[51] Suicide Act 1961, s. 1.

[52] See *R.* v. *Duffy* [1967] 1 Q.B. 63, 67.

[53] See *Thorne* v. *Northern Group Hospital Management Committee* (1964) 108 *Sol. J.* 484, *The Times*, 6 June 1964. The death which gave rise to this litigation occurred in 1960, when suicide was still an offence. But the reports do not suggest that the duty of care and supervision was in any way dependent on that fact.

[54] *Selfe* v. *Ilford and District Hospital Management Committee* (1970) 114 *Sol. J.* 935, *The Times*, 26 November 1970, [1970] 4 *Br. Med. J.* 754. In *Hyde* v. *Tameside Area Health Authority*, *The Times*, 16 April 1981, [1981] 1 *Lancet* 1062, (1981) 282 *Br. Med. J.* 1716-17, the plaintiff had attempted to commit suicide while a patient in hospital. He became a tetraplegic in consequence of the attempt, and Anthony Lincoln J. awarded him damages of £200,000. The Court of Appeal allowed the defendant's appeal, Lord Denning M.R., Watkins L.J., and O'Connor L.J., all agreeing that on the evidence no breach of duty had been established. No member of the court suggested that there was never a duty to prevent suicide, although Lord Denning M.R. was of the view that on grounds of public policy the personal representatives of someone who had committed suicide, or the person himself if his attempt does not succeed, should not be permitted to claim damages. The other members of the court did not express such a view. See also *Hôpital Notre-Dame* v. *Dame Villemure* [1970] Que. S.C. 538, revsd. *sub. nom. Villemure* v. *L'Hopital Notre-Dame* (1972) 31 D.L.R. (3d) 454; *Haines* v. *Bellissimo* (1977) 82 D.L.R. (3d) 215.

[55] If the patient agreed to treatment, it would invariably be accepted that he was capable of giving a legally effective consent. On suicide and attempted suicide, see generally *Suicidology* (1976, ed. E. S. Shneidman); H. G. Morgan, *Death Wishes?* (1979); W. H. Trethowan, 'Suicide and Attempted Suicide' [1979] 2 *Br. Med. J.* 319-20.

restrained and given assistance, the majority are glad that their action did not result in death.[56] Hence, even if it is accepted that a person should not be prevented from carrying out a calm and reasoned decision to terminate his own life,[57] there is an overwhelming case for intervention where there is reason to believe that, if given help, the person will be glad he did not kill, or seriously injure, himself. Doctors are constantly intervening in these circumstances and there can be little doubt that, were their conduct to be questioned, the courts would hold it justified.[58]

Where the need for life-saving treatment does not result from any act of the patient taken with a view to ending his own life,[59] it is normally accepted that a doctor is bound by

[56] This is true of many survivors of serious suicide attempts, as well as of para-suicides. See R. Fox, 'Attempted Suicide' and 'Suicide' in *Dict. Med. Ethics* at 31 and 425, respectively.

[57] The Suicide Act 1961 did not provide a legally-protected right to kill one-self, but it would now be open to a court to adopt the view that there is such a right, in at least some circumstances. However in *Hyde* v. *Tameside Area Health Authority* (see n. 54) Lord Denning M.R. was of the view that, although suicide was no longer a crime, it was still 'unlawful'. Some means of committing suicide certainly involve a crime: see e.g. *Bryan* v. *Mott* (1975) 62 Cr. App. R. 71 (cf. *R.* v. *Norton* [1977] *Crim. L.R.* 478); *R.* v. *Criminal Injuries Compensation Board, ex p. Clowes* [1977] 3 All E.R. 854; *R.* v. *Criminal Injuries Compensation Board, ex p. Parsons, The Times,* 25 November 1982 (C.A.) (Offences against the Person Act 1861, s. 34); and see also Homicide Act 1957, s. 4. *Quaere,* whether suicide, or attempted suicide, infringes s. 18 of the Offences against the Person Act 1861 (or any common law offence of maim). S. 18 makes it an offence 'un-lawfully and maliciously' to cause grievous bodily harm 'to any person' (with intent to do some grievous bodily harm 'to any person'), whereas adjoining offences are phrased in terms of 'any other person' (see ss. 20, 23, 24). (But see *R.* v. *Arthur* [1968] 1 Q.B. 810, esp. 813. Cf. *R.* v. *Pardoe* (1894) 17 Cox C.C. 715. On the greater including the lesser, see e.g. *R.* v. *Woodburne and Coke* (1722) 16 St. Tr. 53, 81.) Even where suicide does involve the commission of a crime, it does not follow that there is always a statutory right to prevent it: s. 3 of the Criminal Law Act 1967 permits only the use of such force 'as is reasonable in the circumstances' in the prevention of crime.

[58] Cf. Viscount Kilmuir L.C. in (1961) 229 Parl. Deb. H.L. 544. See also cases cited in nn. 53, 54 above; G. Zellick, 'The Forcible Feeding of Prisoners: An Examination of the Legality of Enforced Therapy' [1976] *Public Law* 153, 171–2; Williams, *Textbook*, 570–1.

[59] Whatever may once have been the case, a consideration of this matter is not assisted by an examination of the extent to which the refusal of life-saving treat-ment would have amounted to the felony of suicide. The considerations which are relevant when a Jehovah's Witness refuses a blood transfusion necessary to save life, or a patient decides he would rather die at home instead of undergoing major surgery which could prolong his life for a few months, are very different from those which arise with most attempted suicides.

the patient's refusal of consent. Hence in *R. v. Blaue*,[60] where
the assailant's victim was a Jehovah's Witness who refused to
consent to the blood transfusion that was necessary to save
her life, there was no suggestion that the doctor would have
been justified in overriding her refusal of consent. In one case
a patient recovered nominal damages from a doctor who performed a life-saving operation on her, despite her refusal of
consent.[61] Such conduct would often amount to a criminal
assault, and there would be the possibility of obtaining an
injunction restraining further treatment.

The general principle is well stated in the words of the
famous American judge, quoted at the beginning of this
chapter. Unfortunately, there are a handful of cases in which
the English courts appear to have lost sight of the principle.
Early this century, in *Leigh v. Gladstone*,[62] a prisoner who
had been forcibly fed brought an action for damages. Lord
Alverstone C.J. said that it was the duty of the prison offi-
cials, not merely under the rules but also apart from the
rules, to preserve the health and life of the prisoners. He
appeared to assume that if there was a duty to provide life-
sustaining food and treatment, there was also a power to administer it without consent.[63] The same assumption seems to
have been made in a number of recent prosecutions for manslaughter.[64] The best known of these is *R. v. Stone*.[65] The
deceased, who lived with the defendants, suffered from an-
orexia nervosa. She made it clear that she did not want any

[60] [1975] 1 W.L.R. 1411. Blaue was the assailant who was convicted of manslaughter, but acquitted of murder by reason of his diminished responsibility.

[61] *Anon.*, noted in D. J. A. Kerr, *Forensic Medicine* (1935), 71.

[62] (1909) 26 T.L.R. 139. (This case was cited by Edmund Davies L.J. in
Southwark London Borough Council v. *Williams* [1971] 1 Ch. 734, 736.)

[63] There was no suggestion that the hunger strike amounted to an attempt to
commit suicide, or that the duty to preserve health and life was in any way dependent on the liberty to prevent the felony of suicide. For an excellent discussion of
Leigh v. Gladstone, and forced feeding generally, see G. Zellick, op. cit., 153–87.
See also P. D. G. Skegg, 'A Justification for Medical Procedures Performed Without Consent' (1974) 90 *L.Q.R.* 512, 525–6, and generally, M. Brazier, 'Prison
Doctors and their Involuntary Patients' [1982] *Public Law* 282, 292–6.

[64] *R.* v. *Stone* [1977] Q.B. 354; *R.* v. *Wilkinson, The Times*, 19 April 1978,
p. 5 (news report) (application for leave to appeal against conviction rejected by
Court of Appeal); *R.* v. *Smith* [1979] *Crim. L.R.* 251. See also *R.* v. *Bonnyman*
(1942) 28 Cr. App. R. 131. But see *R.* v. *Cowan* [1955] V.L.R. 18, 22, and also
R. v. *Sidney* (1912) 5 D.L.R. 256, 261.

[65] [1977] Q.B. 354.

medical assistance, and there was no reason to believe that
she would have consented to medical treatment. The jury
found that the defendants had assumed a duty of care for the
deceased, and that a failure to fulfil this duty resulted in the
death.[66] In upholding the conviction for manslaughter, the
Court of Appeal appears to have assumed that it was open to
the defendants, or to a doctor, to disregard the wishes of the
'victim'. But in this and the other prosecutions there does not
appear to have been any consideration of what a coroner
once spoke of as 'an absolute principle that a person of full
age and consciousness is entitled to refuse treatment by a
doctor'.[67]

It does not follow from the fact that a doctor, or anyone
else, is under a duty to provide medical treatment (or food)
that there is an entitlement—much less, an obligation—to
administer that treatment (or food) irrespective of the views
of the patient. The doctor who was responsible for the victim
in *R.* v. *Blaue* undoubtedly owed her a duty of care, and in
the circumstances would have been in breach of that duty if
he had not given her the opportunity of having a blood
transfusion. But there was no suggestion that he was therefore obliged, or even permitted, to administer it without
consent.

[66] It is undoubtedly desirable that a doctor be summoned in these circumstances, both to provide independent evidence that the deceased was refusing
medical treatment, and to ensure that the patient is informed of the treatment
which is available, and the consequences if it is not administered. In some cases
there will be a statutory power to take some action: see e.g. National Assistance
Act 1948, s. 47 (the operation of which is discussed by J. A. M. Gray, 'Section
47' (1981) 7 *Journal of Medical Ethics* 146-9). But unless it is clear that, had a
doctor been summoned, the patient would have consented to life-saving treatment, or that such treatment could lawfully have been imposed in the absence
of consent, a failure to summon a doctor should not give rise to liability in
homicide.

[67] *The Times*, 6 January 1967, p. 10. See also N. O'Bryan (a Judge of the
Supreme Court of Victoria), 'The Consent of the Patient to Surgical and Medical
Procedures' (1961) 8 *Proceedings of the Medico-Legal Society of Victoria* 138;
Stephen, *Digest*, 148; *Stoffberg* v. *Elliott* [1923] C.P.D. 148; *Masny* v. *Carter-
Halls-Aldinger Co.* [1929] 3 W.W.R. 741, 745. In *R.* v. *Smith* [1979] *Crim. L.R.*
251 Griffiths J. did at least recognize that the wishes of the deceased might be
relevant. But he left it to the jury 'to balance the weight that it is right to give to
his wife's wish to avoid calling in a doctor against her capacity to make rational
decisions', and added 'If she does not appear too ill it may be reasonable to abide
by her wishes. On the other hand, if she appeared desperately ill then whatever
she may say it may be right to override.' See [1979] *Crim. L.R.* 252-3.

If, from the fact that a doctor had a duty of care to a patient, it followed that he was entitled to administer necessary treatment without consent, the right to refuse treatment would be severely curtailed. Although some cases appear to have proceeded on the assumption that there is such an entitlement, the courts are unlikely to adopt expressly so undesirable a doctrine. For the most part doctors should not administer even life-saving treatment if the patient refuses consent and no one else is authorized to give it.[68]

There is, however, one situation where, despite the absence of any act taken with the intention of committing suicide, it is desirable that a doctor should administer some treatment even if consent is not forthcoming. This is in the special case of the acutely ill or depressed patient, who may have a sufficient understanding to give consent, but whose current condition predisposes him to refuse it. It is typified by the patient suffering from a kidney disease who demanded to be taken off dialysis. After her health improved, she said 'Don't listen to me, that's my uraemia talking, not me. I want to stay on the programme.'[69] The rationale for intervention is the same as that which is widely accepted in relation to attempted suicides:[70] the likelihood that, if restored to a better condition, the patient will be glad to go on living. Hence, if there are grounds for believing that if a patient is given medication, or some relatively minor treatment, the patient would subsequently consent to life-saving treatment, a doctor should in the last resort take action to restore the patient to a condition in which he can make a rational decision.

A court could provide a justification which applied to a doctor who took action in such circumstances.[71] But it would

[68] See generally I. Kennedy, 'The Legal Effect of Requests by the Terminally ill and Aged not to receive further Treatment from Doctors' [1976] *Crim. L.R.* 217–32. Three possible exceptions are discussed, but rejected, in P. D. G. Skegg, op. cit., 526–9.

[69] J. Hamburger and J. Crosnier, 'Moral and Ethical Problems in Transplantation' in *Human Transplantation* (1968, edd. F. T. Rapaport and J. Dausset), 37, 39. Cf. *McFarland* v. *Stewart* (1900) 19 N.Z.L.R. 22.

[70] Cf. Glanville Williams, 'Euthanasia' (1973) 41 *Med.-Leg. J.* 14, 26–9, esp. 27.

[71] If it is accepted that doctors should act in these circumstances, despite the patient's refusal of consent, it can be argued that it is better openly to admit what is being done, than act on the fiction that the patient is incapable of giving or withholding consent.

be very difficult to set acceptable limits to such a justification, and there would be the danger of its existence being
exploited by doctors so that they could go ahead whenever
they considered the patient's refusal of consent to be unreasonable. A court might therefore be reluctant to provide a
justification to cover these cases. Instead, a doctor may be
left to act in the knowledge that the patient will probably be
grateful for his intervention, and that it is extremely unlikely
that legal proceedings will be instituted.

In the overwhelming majority of cases, a doctor would not
be justified in administering any treatment to a patient who
is capable of consenting, but refuses to do so.

4. *Patient incapable of consenting, but known to object to performance of the procedure. (Person authorized to consent on patient's behalf unavailable.)*

Sometimes a patient who has refused to consent to the procedure in question will become incapable either of giving or
of withholding consent. It has been suggested that once this
happens a doctor is no longer bound by the earlier refusal of
consent, but may proceed in the same way as he can if the
patient is not known to object.[72] However, such an approach
would give no weight to the patient's interest in deciding for
himself what is done to his own body. If the patient has
foreseen the circumstances which have since arisen and there
is no reason to believe that he would have changed his
mind if still capable of doing so, the doctor should only be
justified in proceeding to the same extent as he could if the
patient were still capable of consenting. But if these conditions are not present, a doctor should be justified in proceeding to the same extent as he can in other cases where a
patient is incapable of consenting.[73]

---

[72] W. C. J. Meredith, *Malpractice Liability of Doctors and Hospitals* (1956),
155. See also L. E. Rozovsky, *Canadian Hospital Law* (1974), 39–40; Speller,
Hospitals, 192, n. 1.
[73] As to which, see category 1, above.

II PROCEDURES NOT INTENDED TO BENEFIT
THE PATIENT'S HEALTH

Some writers suggest that there is a general doctrine of necessity whereby a greater countervailing benefit to the actor, to
some other person, or to the public at large, may justify what
would otherwise be a tort or a crime. It has, for example,
been said that any lesser crime than homicide is justified by
the preservation of life.[74] If this were so, a doctor might
sometimes be justified in proceeding without consent to
remove a kidney from a living person, to transplant it into
someone who would otherwise die of kidney failure.[75] But
although the 'necessity' to save life, or to prevent serious
injury to health, may sometimes justify acts which would
otherwise constitute a battery,[76] it is extremely unlikely that
a doctor will be held to be justified in performing, without
consent, any surgical procedure not intended for the benefit
of the patient. It is just possible to envisage cases in which a
court might grant an absolute discharge if criminal proceedings were brought. One such case might be where a patient
with a rare blood group will die if his blood is not 'topped
up', and the only way of obtaining the blood is to remove it
from someone who is unable to consent. But even in a case
such as this, it would be unreasonable for the person to be
unable to obtain compensation for any harm or loss he
suffered.

[74] See e.g. G. H. Gordon, *Criminal Law of Scotland* (2nd edn., 1978), 422.

[75] Cf. J. Harris, 'The Survival Lottery' (1975) 50 *Philosophy* 81–7.

[76] A doctor would be justified in pushing past someone who was seeking to
prevent his gaining access to a patient, to administer life-saving treatment. See
Carter v. *Thomas* [1893] 1 Q.B. 673, 678–9. See also *Humphries* v. *Connor*
(1864) 17 Ir. C.L.R. 1; *Thomas* v. *Sawkins* [1935] 2 K.B. 249.

PART III
THE END OF LIFE

6

DRUGS HASTENING DEATH

I will give no deadly medicine to anyone if asked, nor
suggest any such counsel . . .

Hippocratic Oath

If a doctor prescribes or administers a drug which accelerates
a patient's death, he comes within the potential scope of the
law of homicide.[1] But such conduct would not always amount
to murder or manslaughter—or, for that matter, any other
criminal offence.[2] In some circumstances the doctor's conduct
might not be regarded as a legally recognized cause of death.
Even if it were so regarded, the doctor would not usually
have the fault element of murder or manslaughter.

This chapter begins with an examination of the general
principles of the law of homicide, as they relate to the administration of drugs (and other medical acts) which may
have the effect of hastening death. It then discusses the application of these principles to the administration of pain-
relieving drugs, which sometimes have the incidental effect
of hastening death. The circumstances in which a doctor
might incur liability in consequence of an omission to act will
be discussed in the next chapter, and chapter 8 will contain a
discussion of the special case of the termination of artificial
ventilation.

---

[1] See generally *R.* v. *Packard* (1841) Car. & M. 236, 245-6; *R.* v. *Plummer*
(1844) 1 Car. & K. 600, 605; *R.* v. *Murton* (1862) 3 F. & F. 492, 501; *R.* v. *Cook*
(1898) 62 J.P. 712; *R.* v. *Instan* [1893] 1 Q.B. 450, 454. Judges have sometimes
spoken in terms of whether death was caused or accelerated by the conduct in
question. See e.g. *R.* v. *Webb* (1834) 2 Lewin 196, 212; *R.* v. *Plummer*, above,
607; *R.* v. *Morby* (1882) 8 Q.B.D. 571, 575; *R.* v. *Senior* [1899] 1 Q.B. 283, 285.
See also *R.* v. *Crook* (1859) 1 F. & F. 521, 523 ('produced or accelerated').

[2] For other offences which could sometimes apply to the prescription or administration of drugs which hasten death, see Offences against the Person Act
1861, ss. 18, 23, 24; Suicide Act 1961, s. 2.

I GENERAL PRINCIPLES

External elements

Murder and manslaughter have the same external elements;[3] the difference between them lies in their different fault elements. Their external elements involve causing the death of a fully-born human being.[4]

Only acts 'but for which' death would not have occurred when it did, can be regarded as a cause of death for the purpose of the law of homicide. But by no means all 'but for' causes are regarded as imputable causes. The act may be treated as simply part of the history[5]—as a doctor's act would be if a patient were knocked down and killed when crossing a road, which the patient would not have been doing but for the doctor's request that he attend the surgery.

There is no need for the act to be the sole, or even the main, cause of death. For the purpose of the law of homicide it is sufficient if the act is a cause, provided it is a cause 'outside the de minimis range, and effectively bearing upon the acceleration of the moment of the victim's death'.[6] If a policeman were to question a dying man about the identity of his assailant, and thereby hasten very slightly the moment of the man's death, his act could be disregarded under the de minimis principle.[7] But if someone were to administer a lethal blow, or poison, to someone whose death was imminent, that person would nevertheless be regarded as having caused the death.

Fault element

A person who intends to kill, or who has no substantial doubt that his act will kill, has the fault element for murder. If

[3] For what is meant by 'external elements', see ch. 1, n. 13.

[4] See generally Smith and Hogan, 270-84; Williams, *Textbook*, 325-48.

[5] *R. v. Smith* [1959] 2 Q.B. 35, 43. Cf. *R. v. Pagett, The Times*, 4 February 1983. See also *R. v. Jordan* (1956) 40 Cr. App. R. 152 (as to which, see now *R. v. Smith*, above, 43-4; *R. v. Blaue* [1975] 1 W.L.R. 1411, 1414-15; *R. v. Malcherek* [1981] 1 W.L.R. 690, 696). As to the 'year and a day' rule, see *R. v. Dyson* [1908] 2 K.B. 454.

[6] *R. v. Cato* [1976] 1 W.L.R. 110, 116. See also ibid. 117; *R. v. Malcherek* [1981] 1 W.L.R. 690, 696; *R. v. Pagett, The Times*, 4 February 1983.

[7] On the limited application of the maxim *de minimis non curat lex* in English criminal law, see Williams, *Textbook*, 573-6.

a doctor gave an injection for the purpose of hastening death, or if he administered a drug which he knew would have this effect, he would therefore be guilty of murder if the patient died in consequence.

An intention to cause really serious bodily harm is also— in at least most circumstances—a sufficient fault element for murder.[8] The possible exception is where it would be lawful intentionally to cause such harm. If a person intentionally causes serious bodily harm in the course of using reasonable force in self-defence, no problem would arise if he were regarded as having the fault element of murder. A well-established justification would be available to him. But where a doctor intentionally causes serious bodily harm by performing an operation to which consent has been given, and for which there is a good reason, there could be difficulties if the doctor were regarded as having the fault element for murder. Rather than provide a separate justification, it might be convenient to say that as it was lawful for the doctor to intend to cause serious bodily harm in these circumstances, he is not to be regarded as having the fault element for murder.[9] But where—as is usually the case—it is unlawful intentionally to cause serious bodily harm, a person may be convicted of murder if he acts with this intention, and thereby hastens death. There is no need to prove that he knew that his act would endanger life.

In the leading case of _R_. v. _Hyam_[10] the trial judge directed the jury that a person could be convicted of murder if, when doing the act which led to the death, that person knew that it was 'highly probable' that death or serious bodily harm would result. The House of Lords dismissed the defendant's appeal, but in the course of doing so raised the possibility of a defendant being convicted of murder even though he did not desire that death or really serious bodily harm should ensue, and even though he did not believe that death or really serious bodily harm was 'highly probable'.[11] Lord Hailsham

---

[8] _R_. v. _Cunningham_ [1982] A.C. 566. On 'really serious' as a synonym for 'grievous' in this context, see _D.P.P._ v. _Smith_ [1961] A.C. 290, 334. On the meaning of 'bodily harm', see pp. 30-1, above.

[9] Cf. _R_. v. _Hyam_ [1975] A.C. 55, 77D-79C.

[10] [1974] Q.B. 99, [1975] A.C. 55.

[11] This fault element is distinct from the one which is suggested by a passage

and Lord Cross both delivered speeches which indicated that in their opinion it was unnecessary for the trial judge to have inserted the word 'highly', before 'probable', in his direction to the jury.[12] Viscount Dilhorne also quoted, without any hint of disagreement, formulations which used the words 'probably' and 'likely'.[13] And although Lord Diplock and Lord Kilbrandon both dissented,[14] they delivered speeches which supported the view that a person could be regarded as having the fault element of murder if he knew that death was a 'likely' consequence of his act.[15]

Doctors rarely take action believing that it is highly probable that their act will hasten death. However there are occasions on which doctors do something believing that it is highly probable that really serious bodily harm will ensue—and others when they believe that death or really serious bodily harm is a 'probable' or 'likely' consequence.[16] If it is accepted that a doctor would not have the fault element of murder if he acted lawfully in intentionally causing really serious bodily harm, it would follow that he would not have

in *D.P.P.* v. *Smith* [1961] A.C. 290, discussed in Smith and Hogan 289–91.

[12] [1975] A.C. 76G–77B, 77E–F, 78C per Lord Hailsham, 97C per Lord Cross. See also *R.* v. *Cunningham* [1982] A.C. 566, 575G.

[13] [1975] A.C. 81. There was not necessarily any inconsistency between these statements and his subsequent comment that 'the doing of the act with the knowledge that certain consequences are highly probable . . . has been recognised as amounting to malice aforethought' for at least one hundred years (ibid. 82D). The trial judge had directed the jury in terms of high probability, rather than probability, so it was not necessary to go beyond this to decide the appeal.

[14] On the point at issue, see now *R.* v. *Cunningham* [1982] A.C. 566.

[15] [1975] A.C. 86E–F, 86H–87A per Lord Diplock; 98B–C per Lord Kilbrandon ('and was indifferent whether that consequence followed or not'). On the interpretation of Lord Diplock's speech in *R.* v. *Hyam*, see *R.* v. *Cunningham* [1982] A.C. 566, 575C–D ('endanger life').

[16] In everyday speech, something is not normally described as 'probable' if it is thought that there is a less-than-even chance of its occurring. But Lord Hailsham and Lord Cross also used terms which can be applied where there is a much less-than-even chance of something happening. See [1975] A.C. at 79B–D ('serious risk') (and also 76F) per Lord Hailsham; and 96F,H ('may well') per Lord Cross. And in other contexts, the term 'likely' (which was used by Lord Diplock and Lord Kilbrandon; see n. 15, above) has been used in an extensive sense. See e.g. *R.* v. *Larkin* [1943] K.B. 174, *R.* v. *Church* [1966] 1 Q.B. 59, *D.P.P.* v. *Newbury* [1977] A.C. 500 ('likely', 'serious risk', and 'dangerous' used interchangeably in discussions of unlawful act manslaughter); and also *R.* v. *Sheppard* [1981] A.C. 394, 405C. Cf. *Parkin* v. *Norman* [1983] 1 Q.B. 92, 101E–F, 103H–104A. On foresight of probability and foresight of possibility, see also *La Fontaine* v. *R.* (1976) 136 C.L.R. 62. Cf. *R.* v. *Gush* [1980] 2 N.Z.L.R. 92.

the fault element of murder simply because he believed that really serious bodily harm was a probable, or highly probable, consequence of his otherwise lawful conduct. But what of the case where a doctor intervenes, believing that it is probable—even highly probable—that his conduct will hasten the patient's death? This discussion will focus on cases of high probability; if it becomes apparent that a doctor would not be guilty of murder whenever he knew that death was the 'highly probable' consequence of his conduct, it will follow that he would not be guilty of murder simply because he knew that death was, in some sense, 'probable' or 'likely'.

If a patient had a very serious heart condition, doctors might consider it most unlikely that the patient would live for another year if he did not have a heart transplant. They might believe that if he had a transplant it was probable—even highly probable—that he would die earlier than if he did not have one, but that there would be a significant possibility that the transplant would be a success. If it was, the patient would live a fuller and longer life than if he did not have a transplant. If the patient consented to the operation being performed in these circumstances, and the doctors went ahead, would they have the fault element of murder?

In *R. v. Hyam*, there was no need for their Lordships to consider whether there were any exceptions to the general rule that a person would have the fault element for murder if, when he did an act which caused death, he believed that it was highly probable that the act would hasten death.[17] Nevertheless Lord Hailsham did discuss the example of a surgeon who performs a heart transplant in the hope of saving a patient's life, although he recognizes that there is at least a high degree of probability that it will hasten death.[18] He said that his own opinion corresponded with that of the Commissioners on the Criminal Law, when they said that it ought to

[17] That being so, the silence of four of the Law Lords should not be interpreted as implying that they would disagree with Lord Hailsham's qualification concerning absence of lawful excuse. Their judgments may be compared with some of those dealing with recklessness where on the facts it was clear that the risk was an unreasonable one, and judges did not mention that the taking of a reasonable risk would not be reckless. See e.g. *R. v. Briggs* [1977] 1 W.L.R. 605, *R. v. Parker* [1977] 1 W.L.R. 600. Cf. *R. v. Stephenson* [1979] Q.B. 695, 703F. On the interpretation of 'reckless', see now *R. v. Caldwell* [1982] A.C. 341.

[18] See [1975] A.C. 74E–F, 77C,G.

make no difference in point of legal distinction whether death results from a direct intention to kill, or from wilfully doing an act of which death is the probable consequence. Lord Hailsham went on to say that the heart surgeon 'exposes his patient to the risk, but does everything he can to save his life, regarding his actions as the best or only means of securing the patient's survival'. He said that the surgeon 'is, therefore, not exposing his patient to the risk without lawful excuse or regardless of the consequences'.[19] In Lord Hailsham's view, a person would not be guilty of murder if he had a lawful excuse for exposing the deceased to the risk of death.[20] He said that the transplant surgeon would not be liable even if he foresaw as a high degree of probability that he would hasten death.[21] Lord Hailsham made a number of references to the concept of 'lawful excuse';[22] but there was no suggestion that there would be a lawful excuse only where the conduct came within the scope of some established defence or justification.[23]

There is very little danger of a judge taking the view that a doctor would be guilty of murder whenever he performed an act which hastened death, knowing that it was probable, or highly probable, that it would have this effect. The doctor would not be guilty where the risk was a reasonable one—or, to put it another way, where there was a 'lawful excuse' for exposing the patient to that risk.

Just as there is only one crime of murder, although it can be committed with one of several fault elements, so there is only one crime of manslaughter. But it is customary to speak of different varieties of manslaughter, according to the fault element in question. The two varieties which are most likely to be of importance in a medical context are 'unlawful act' (or

[19] See [1975] A.C. 77G.

[20] See ibid. 79B–C for Lord Hailsham's final propositions. (In this context, there is no need to examine Lord Hailsham's statement that the act must be 'aimed at someone', and be deliberate.)

[21] See also Criminal Law Revision Committee, Fourteenth Report, *Offences against the Person* (Cmnd. 7844; 1980), para. 8 ('Even where the person acting knows that there is a high probability that his act will cause death, it is not necessarily an unlawful act. He may be a surgeon acting in circumstances which make it reasonable to take even this grave risk.'). See also ibid., para. 119.

[22] See [1975] A.C. 77D–79C.

[23] As to which, see e.g. Smith and Hogan, 322–31.

constructive) manslaughter, and negligent (or reckless) manslaughter.

'Unlawful act' manslaughter encompasses those instances
where death is caused by an unlawful act,[24] which any reasonable person would recognize as involving the danger of at
least some harm.[25] Hence, if a doctor carried out a risky non-
therapeutic experimental procedure, knowing that legally
effective consent had not been given, he would have the fault
element for unlawful act manslaughter. If his conduct resulted
in the patient's death the doctor would be guilty of unlawful
act manslaughter, even though he did not believe that there
was any risk of death, and even though he performed the
procedure with the greatest care and competence.

Negligent manslaughter occurs where death is brought
about by the defendant's gross negligence.[26] A defendant can
be convicted even though he was not aware that there was
any risk to the deceased, but the negligence must be so
serious that the jury regard it as sufficient to warrant a conviction of manslaughter. Where death resulted from a doctor's
extreme carelessness in prescribing a drug, the doctor could
be regarded as guilty of negligent manslaughter.

Where death results from a lawful act, performed without
negligence, it can be described as a case of lawful homicide.

Defences?

None of the established defences to murder and manslaughter
is likely to be applicable to the conduct of a doctor in prescribing or administering a drug, or performing any other act
in the course of medical practice. Does it therefore follow
that if a doctor administers a drug to a patient, for the purpose
of ending that patient's life, he would in all circumstances be
guilty of murder? It is as well to examine several possible
'defences'. They concern the consent of the patient or a

---

[24] *R.* v. *Lamb* [1967] 2 Q.B. 981. The act must be unlawful for some reason
other than that it is negligently performed: see *Andrews* v. *D.P.P.* [1937] A.C. 583.

[25] *R.* v. *Church* [1966] 1 Q.B. 59, 70; *D.P.P.* v. *Newbury* [1977] A.C. 500,
507; *D.P.P. for Jamaica* v. *Daley* [1980] A.C. 237, 246.

[26] *R.* v. *Bateman* (1925) 19 Cr. App. R. 8 (a case involving a doctor); *Andrews*
v. *D.P.P.* [1937] A.C. 583. On principle, negligence as to death (or, at the very
least, serious bodily harm) should be required as a prerequisite to conviction; but
see *R.* v. *Stone* [1977] Q.B. 354, 363. See generally Smith and Hogan, 316-20.

relative, the medical condition of the patient, and the doctor's exemplary motive, professional qualifications, and compliance with medical ethics.

The presence or absence of consent would sometimes be of crucial importance in determining whether a person was guilty of murder, or of manslaughter. If a patient died in consequence of an operation to remove his kidney, for the purpose of transplanting it into someone who was in need of it, a doctor would not be guilty of murder if the patient had consented to the operation. But if he knew that consent had not been given, the doctor would be guilty of murder, for he would have intended to cause really serious bodily harm when it was unlawful to do so. Similarly, if a patient died in consequence of a dangerous but medically desirable procedure which was intended to benefit that patient's health, the doctor would not incur criminal liability if the patient had consented to the procedure. But if the doctor knew that legally effective consent had not been given, and that the circumstances were not such that he was justified in going ahead without consent, the doctor might be guilty of unlawful act manslaughter.

Although the presence or absence of consent will affect liability for murder and manslaughter, one thing is clear: consent to being killed is no defence to a charge of murder or manslaughter.[27] Even if the patient pleaded with the doctor to end his life, this would not provide the doctor with a defence in law. And, just as a patient's consent to being killed would not provide a doctor with a defence, nor would the consent of a relative, or anyone else.

The fact that a patient would be very severely handicapped if he were to live, or would find life a burden, does not affect the general principle that it is murder to kill a person by doing some positive act,[28] with the intention of hastening

---

[27] J. F. Stephen, *History of the Criminal Law of England* (1883), vol. iii, p. 16; *H.M. Advocate* v. *Rutherford* [1947] J.C. 1, 5–6; Criminal Law Revision Committee, Fourteenth Report, *Offences against the Person* (Cmnd. 7844; 1980), para. 126; and see also *R.* v. *Croft* [1944] 1 K.B. 295. But see Homicide Act 1957, s. 4 (killing in pursuance of a suicide pact).

[28] Where there is an intentional omission to prolong life, the patient's medical condition is often of crucial importance in determining a doctor's criminal (and civil) liability: see ch. 7, esp. pp. 149–53.

death.[29] There were several statements to this effect in
Farquharson J.'s direction to the jury in *R.* v. *Arthur*.[30] He
said that it was an important principle in law that 'However
serious the case may be; however much the dis-advantage of a
mongol or, indeed, any other handicapped child, no doctor
has the right to kill it.'[31] There was, he said, no special power,
facility, or licence to kill children who are handicapped or
seriously disadvantaged in any irreversible way.[32] *R.* v. *Arthur*
resulted from the death of a newly-born child, but what was
said on this matter is equally applicable to other patients.

As the consent of the patient or others, or the patient's
medical condition, will not provide a doctor with a defence if
he administers a drug for the purpose of ending the patient's
life, it is as well to consider whether the doctor's exemplary
motive, medical qualifications, or compliance with medical
ethics, would provide him with a defence.

A doctor's reason for acting will sometimes affect his
liability under the law of homicide. If a patient died in consequence of a very risky operation performed in the hope of
saving the patient's life, the doctor would not normally be
guilty of murder. But if death resulted from the doctor performing an identical operation on a healthy person, for the
sake of an unnecessary research project, he would be liable.
However, it is clear that the motive of alleviating suffering
will not provide a legal justification for a doctor who intentionally administers what he knows to be a lethal dose of a
drug. In *R.* v. *Arthur* Farquharson J. said that it was accepted

[29] However, in cases of 'mercy killing' by relatives it has become customary
to accept a plea of diminished responsibility, and a conviction for manslaughter
ensues. See Lawton L.J., 'Mercy Killing: The Judicial Dilemma' (1979) 72 *J. Roy.
Soc. Med.* 460–1; Roger Leng, 'Mercy Killing and the CLRC' (1982) 132 *New L.J.*
76–8.

[30] *R.* v. *Arthur* (1981) 283 *Br. Med. J.* 1340, [1981] 2 *Lancet* 1101. The
pages cited in footnotes in this and the next two chapters are to the official
transcript of Farquharson J.'s summing-up to the jury, in the Leicester Crown
Court, on 3, 4, and 5 November 1981. Some information about the trial is to be
found in *A.-G.* v. *English* [1983] A.C. 116 (prosecution for contempt of court,
following publication of newspaper article during the trial). Extracts from the
summing-up were printed in (1981) 78 *Law Society Gazette* 1341.

[31] Transcript, 16F.

[32] Transcript, 17A. Farquharson J. was directing his comments to the 'doing
of an act, a positive act', rather than an omission to do something that would
enable a patient to live. See 17D.

that the doctor had acted from the highest of motives, but directed the jury that 'however noble his motives were . . . that is irrelevant to the question of your deciding what his intent was'.[33] He said that:[34]

> It may be that somebody faced with an ageing relative who was suffering from an incurably painful disease, from the best motive in the world, decides to put a pillow over the poor soul's head so that he or she dies. That would mean that there was then an intent to kill by putting a pillow over the head. The motive, of course, would have been the kindest and the best.

If a doctor acts with the intention of bringing about the death of a patient, the fact that he was acting to alleviate suffering, or for some other exemplary motive, would not at present provide him with a defence to a charge of murder.[35]

In some circumstances the fact that a person has particular medical qualifications will affect that person's liability for murder or manslaughter. If a patient died in the course of a heart transplant operation, performed by a doctor with appropriate qualifications and experience, the doctor would not normally be liable. But if the operation were performed by a layman it would be very difficult to resist the conclusion that he exposed the patient to an unjustified risk, and that he was grossly negligent in attempting the operation. However, the fact that someone was medically qualified would make no difference if he administered a drug—or took any other action—for the purpose of hastening the death of a patient. In the few cases in which doctors have been prosecuted for murder or attempted murder in consequence of things done in the course of medical practice, trial judges have stressed that the law does not place doctors in any special position. In *R. v. Adams*[36] Devlin J. said that the law was the same for all: there was not any special defence for medical men. And in *R. v. Arthur* Farquharson J. said there 'is no special law . . . that places doctors in a separate category and gives them extra protection over the rest of us'.[37] They are, he said, 'given no special power . . . to commit an act which causes death'.[38]

---

[33] Transcript, 26C–D.   [34] Transcript, 26D–E.
[35] See *R.* v. *Hyam* [1975] A.C. 55, 73. See generally Williams, *Sanctity*, 283–4.
[36] *The Times*, 9 April 1957. See n. 52, below.
[37] Transcript, 16G.   [38] Transcript, 16H.

Even if a doctor acted in compliance with statements on medical ethics propounded by the British Medical Association, or any other organization, this would not of itself provide a doctor with a defence if he administered a drug—or did any other act[39]—for the purpose of hastening the death of a patient. In *R.* v. *Arthur* Farquharson J. commented that it was customary for a profession to agree on rules of conduct for its members but instructed the jury that 'that does not mean that any profession can set out a code of ethics and say that the law must accept it and take notice of it. It may be that in any particular feature the ethic is wrong.'[40] He said that 'whatever a profession may evolve as a system of standards of ethics, cannot stand on its own, and cannot survive if it is in conflict with the law'.[41] It would therefore be open to a jury to find a doctor guilty of murder even though they believed that he acted in accordance with the ethical standards currently accepted by the medical profession.

The conclusion must be that neither the consent of the patient or anyone else, nor the condition of the patient, nor the doctor's exemplary motive, professional qualifications, or compliance with accepted standards of medical ethics, would provide any defence for a doctor who prescribed or administered a drug—or did any other act—for the purpose of hastening the death of the patient.

II PAIN-KILLING DRUGS

It is widely accepted that if there was no other way to assuage pain, a doctor would be morally justified in administering a pain-killing drug to a patient whose death was imminent, even if he believed that the drug might have the incidental effect of hastening death.[42] But would the doctor be guilty of

---

[39] As to omissions, see ch. 7, esp. pp. 142-3, 146-7. [40] Transcript, 17E–G.

[41] Transcript, 82A. But Farquharson J. went on to say that he imagined that the jury 'would think long and hard' before concluding that eminent doctors 'have evolved standards which amounted to committing a crime' (Transcript, 82B–C).

[42] This view is accepted by leading opponents of active euthanasia: see e.g. Pope Pius XII, allocution to the Italian Society for the Science of Anaesthetics, 24 February 1957, (1957) 49 *Acta Apostolicae Sedis* 129–47; Archbishop Donald Coggan, 'On Dying and Dying Well: Moral and Spiritual Aspects' (1977) 70 *Proc. Roy. Soc. Med.* 75, 76.

murder if the drug did hasten death? The question seems preposterous. That it can be asked results from the possibility that any act which hastens death may be regarded as a cause of death,[43] and also from the fact that a person can be convicted of murder even though he did not desire to hasten death, and was not substantially certain that his conduct would have this effect.[44]

It is overwhelmingly unlikely that a doctor will be prosecuted as a result of his prescribing or administering a drug in these circumstances.[45] Were there to be a prosecution, there would be no danger of the jury convicting the doctor, whatever the content of the judge's summing-up. But there would in fact be more than one way in which a judge could avoid directing the jury that a doctor would be guilty of murder or manslaughter if he administered a pain-killing drug to a patient whose death was imminent, in the belief that the drug might well hasten death. The different possibilities will now be examined.[46]

Fault element

If a doctor prescribed a pain-killing drug for the purpose of hastening the death of the patient, he would have the fault element for murder. But what of the case where he simply believed that it might well have this effect?

The speeches in the House of Lords in *R.* v. *Hyam* raised the possibility of someone being guilty of murder because he knew that it was 'probable' or 'likely' (rather than highly probable, or substantially certain) that his act would hasten death. Given the facts of that case, there was no need for their Lordships to consider risk-taking in medical practice. But, as has already been mentioned, Lord Hailsham did discuss the imaginary case of a surgeon who performed a heart transplant, believing that there was a high degree of probability

---

[43] See cases cited in n. 1, above.

[44] See *R.* v. *Hyam* [1975] A.C. 55.

[45] Assuming, that is, that the patient was not opposed to the administration of the drug, and was not given a greater quantity of it than could reasonably be regarded as necessary to relieve pain.

[46] As the discussion of an important case on causation leads on to the question of whether there is a special defence, the fault element will be considered first and then the external elements and possible defences.

that his conduct would hasten death. Lord Hailsham said that the surgeon would not be liable when—as in his example—there was a lawful excuse for the conduct. If the courts give effect to some of the statements in *R. v. Hyam* which support a very broad fault element for murder, they can be expected to accept that the general statements must be qualified in this way.[47]

In the example given by Lord Hailsham, the reason why the surgeon was justified in exposing his patient to the risk was that he regarded his actions 'as the best or only means of securing the patient's survival'. Even if length of life were the sole relevant consideration, it could be argued that doctors would sometimes be justified in prescribing or administering pain-killing drugs which may hasten death. Such drugs can have the effect of prolonging life, by improving the patient's capacity to sleep and eat.[48] However, there is no reason to believe that length of life is the sole consideration. A slight risk of death is inherent in many operations which are performed to remedy conditions which do not themselves endanger life. Where death is imminent, much greater risks are justifiable to reduce or extinguish pain.

There is not the least doubt that it would be accepted that, if there was no other clearly preferable way of relieving the pain of a patient whose death was imminent, a doctor could properly prescribe or administer a drug for that purpose—even though he believed that the drug might hasten death.[49] As such risk-taking would be regarded as justifiable, it would come within the 'lawful excuse' exception in Lord Hailsham's broad formulation of the fault element for murder. Even if it were highly probable that the drug would hasten death, the doctor should not be regarded as having a fault element sufficient for conviction of murder.

In this context, manslaughter is more straightforward than murder. Unless the doctor acted in a way in which no reasonable doctor would act, he would not have the fault element

[47] See pp. 125-6, above.

[48] See generally R. G. Twycross, 'Euthanasia—A Physician's Viewpoint' (1982) 8 *Journal of Medical Ethics* 86, 88.

[49] It is assumed that the patient would not be known to have been opposed to the administration of the drug.

for negligent manslaughter. And provided the doctor was not committing some non-fatal offence, he would not have the fault element for unlawful act manslaughter.

External elements

It would often be extremely difficult to prove that a pain-killing drug did hasten death. Sometimes such drugs will prolong life, by reducing the debilitating effects of severe pain,[50] and patients can die of pneumonia whether or not they have been given drugs that sometimes lead to respiratory complications.

Even if it were apparent that the administration of the pain-killing drug did accelerate death,[51] there is a strong possibility that the doctor's conduct would not be regarded as a cause of death, for the purpose of the law of homicide. In relation to most deaths there are innumerable acts but for which death would not have occurred. The issue of whether a particular 'but for' cause is also an 'imputable' cause, is often left to the jury as a matter of common sense. But sometimes judges propound principles which lead to the conclusion that particular conduct should, or should not, be regarded as a cause for legal purposes. Both approaches played a part in the summing-up of Devlin J. (as he then was) in *R. v. Adams*,[52] the leading English case in which a judge has discussed the legal implications of the administration of pain-killing drugs which may hasten death.

---

[50] See R. G. Twycross, 'Euthanasia', in *Dict. Med. Ethics* 164, 165; Linacre Report, 58-9.

[51] Where death does result, it will usually be because the drug depresses respiration, which may lead to the patient contracting pneumonia. A doctor has suggested to me that it is the decision to administer or withhold antibiotics that is crucial. Where the doctor is under a duty to administer antibiotics and omits to do so, his omission may be regarded as a cause of death if it is apparent that, had the antibiotic been administered, death would not have resulted. But if he is under no duty to administer antibiotics, his omission to do so will not break any chain of causation between the administration of the pain-killing drug and the patient's death. Furthermore, a patient may die of pneumonia, even though an antibiotic has been administered.

[52] *The Times*, 9 April 1957. For a detailed account of this case, see Sybille Bedford, *The Best We Can Do* (1958). For a briefer account, see H. Palmer, 'Dr. Adams' Trial for Murder' [1957] *Crim. L.R.* 365-77. For the relevant portion of Devlin J.'s summing-up, see Sybille Bedford, above, 220-1; Williams, *Sanctity*, 289.

In *R.* v. *Adams* Devlin J. told the jury that cause 'means what you twelve men and women sitting as a jury in the jury box would regard in a common-sense way as the cause'. He gave the example of a doctor who did or omitted to do something, because of which death occurred 'at eleven o'clock instead of twelve o'clock, or even on Monday instead of Tuesday'. He said:[53]

[N]o people of common sense would say 'Oh, the doctor caused her death.' They would say the cause of her death was the illness or the injury, or whatever it was, which brought her into hospital, and the proper medical treatment that is administered and that has an *incidental* effect of determining the exact moment of death, or may have, is not the cause of death in any sensible use of the term.

But he also said that:

If the first purpose of medicine, the restoration of health, can no longer be achieved there is still much for a doctor to do, and he is *entitled* to do all that is *proper* and necessary to relieve pain and suffering, even if the measures he takes may *incidentally* shorten life.

He repeated the second statement in the course of a lecture three years later, when he went on to say that 'proper medical treatment consequent upon illness or injury plays no part in legal causation'; and that 'to relieve the pains of death is undoubtedly proper medical treatment'.[54]

The principle that 'proper medical treatment . . . plays no part in legal causation' would lead to a satisfactory result in relation to the administration of pain-relieving drugs to a patient whose death was imminent. Although the courts would have the last word on the propriety of the treatment, there could here be no doubt what their view would

---

[53] Emphasis added. Cf. *R.* v. *Burdee* (1916) 86 L.J. K.B. 871, 871–2 per Darling J.

[54] The text of the lecture, which was delivered before the Medical Society of London, is included in Devlin, *Samples*, 83–103. The relevant passage is at p. 95. Parts of Devlin J.'s summing-up in *R.* v. *Adams* could be regarded as giving effect to the *de minimis* principle. See, for example, the passage in which he indicated that a doctor who is aiding the sick and dying does not have 'to calculate in minutes, or even in hours, and perhaps not in days or weeks, the effect on a patient's life of the medicines which he administers or else be in peril of a charge of murder'. But he also said that 'no doctor, nor any man, no more in the case of the dying than of the healthy, has the right deliberately to cut the thread of life'.

be.[55] In the course of his summing-up in *R.* v. *Arthur*, Farquharson J. mentioned the example of someone suffering from 'the agonies of terminal cancer' whose doctor gave increasing dosages of a drug to relieve pain. The judge said that there comes a point when 'the amount of those doses are such that in themselves they will kill off the patient, but he is driven to it on medical grounds'. He said that in such a case the jury would undoubtedly say 'that could never be murder. That was a proper practise of medicine.'[56]

There are objections to the adoption of a general principle whereby nothing which could be described as proper medical treatment could be regarded as a cause for legal purposes.[57] But in view of the lead given by Devlin J. in *R.* v. *Adams* it is likely that, in any future case involving the prescription or administration of a drug to relieve the pains of death, a judge would be prepared to manipulate the concept of causation to avoid the conclusion that the doctor's act was in law a cause of death.[58]

Lord Devlin's approach has been criticized on the ground that it obscures the value-judgment involved,[59] something that can also be said of other cases on causation. But to deal with such conduct without openly providing a defence for an

---

[55] But there is no similar consensus that it would be proper to administer pain-killing drugs which may lead to the death of a patient who would otherwise be expected to live for years. Some risk would sometimes be justifiable, but not nearly as great a risk as in those cases where death is imminent in any event. Professor Glanville Williams's argument which leads to the conclusion that 'a physician may give any amount of drug necessary to deaden pain, even though he knows that that amount will bring about speedy or indeed immediate death' (Williams, *Sanctity*, 288) goes beyond *Adams*, and the current consensus.

[56] Transcript, 19C-E. See also Law Reform Commission of Canada, *Euthanasia, Aiding Suicide and Cessation of Treatment* (Working Paper 28, 1982), p. 70.

[57] See pp. 167-8.

[58] For a different interpretation of Devlin J.'s direction to the jury in *R.* v. *Adams*, see Helen Benyon, 'Doctors as Murderers' [1982] *Crim. L.R.* 17, 18. The Director of Public Prosecutions has recently made it clear that he has no intention of challenging the law laid down in Devlin J.'s direction to the jury in *Adams*. See *Daily Telegraph*, 3 March 1982, p. 10; J. D. J. Havard, Letter, 'The legal threat to medicine' (1982) 284 *Br. Med. J.* 900.

[59] See Williams, *Textbook*, 532 (but see 329); and see also Williams, *Sanctity*, 290; cf. Devlin, *Samples*, 95, esp. n. 1. (Professor Glanville Williams accepts that following *Adams* a doctor who administers a pain-killing drug in the circumstances specified will not risk liability in homicide. See e.g. Glanville Williams, 'Euthanasia and Abortion' (1966) 38 *University of Colorado Law Review* 178, 183; Glanville Williams, 'Euthanasia' (1973) 41 *Med.-Leg. J.* 14, 15.)

intentional killing is in keeping with the conventional moral analysis of such conduct. For although the law rarely distinguishes between consequences which are desired, and consequences which are undesired but foreseen as substantially certain, such a distinction is commonly made when evaluating the morality of a particular course of conduct.[60] Away from the law, 'intended' consequences are often distinguished from 'foreseen but unintended' ones. The latter are not discounted entirely, but it is widely accepted that there are some circumstances in which it is morally justifiable to pursue a course of action which will result in a foreseen but undesired consequence, when it would be wrong to seek to bring about that consequence.[61] The distinction is by no means universally accepted, and would not be suitable for general legal use. However, the great majority of doctors appear to share the widely-held view that, as Lord Jowitt L.C. once accepted,[62] there is a real distinction between using drugs to alleviate pain, even though it can be foreseen that life may be shortened, and administering drugs for the purpose of shortening life. The former would not generally be regarded as an intentional killing.

As English law rarely distinguishes between consequences which are desired, and those which are undesired but foreseen as substantially certain, the courts sometimes manipulate the concept of causation, to avoid the conclusion that someone who foresaw that certain consequences would result from his act is necessarily legally responsible for them.[63] By

[60] See H. L. A. Hart, *Punishment and Responsibility* (1968), 120 ('outside the law a merely foreseen, though unwanted, outcome is not usually considered as intended, and this is so in big matters as well as small').

[61] For an account of the principle of 'double effect', and the context in which it operates, see 'The Principle of Respect for Human Life', *Linacre Papers* (No. 1, 1978), 2-13. The principle is there stated in these terms: 'Doing an action that has a bad effect is permissible if the action is good in itself, the intention is solely to produce the good effect, the good effect is not achieved through the bad effect, and there is sufficient reason to permit the bad effect.' (Ibid. 10.) For a bibliography see Jonathan Glover, *Causing Death and Saving Lives* (1977), 303-4. See also Germain Grisez, 'Against Consequentialism' (1978) 23 *American Journal of Jurisprudence* 21-72.

[62] See (1950) 169 Parl. Deb. H.L. 593.

[63] See e.g. *Beatty* v. *Gillbanks* (1882) 9 Q.B.D. 308 (lawful acts not to be regarded as the cause of unlawful acts of others). Cf. *Wise* v. *Dunning* [1902] 1 K.B. 167.

so doing they not only reach a conclusion which is more in accord with the conventional analysis of the situation than one in which a person is regarded as having intentionally caused the undesired event, but they also avoid the task of providing an appropriate defence. Of course, the conventional moral analysis may change. But even then, a judge might well choose to follow the approach favoured in *R.* v. *Adams*, rather than seek to provide a new defence.[64]

Defences?

It has been suggested that a defence of necessity might sometimes be available to a doctor who administered a pain-killing drug, knowing that it would hasten death.[65] In practice the issue is unlikely to arise. Doctors who administer pain-killing drugs do not normally have the fault element for murder or manslaughter, and even if they did the courts could avoid the conclusion that the doctor's act was in law a cause of death. This is just as well, for recent cases indicate that English courts are extremely reluctant to provide a defence of necessity.[66] Were occasion to arise, there might be a slightly greater willingness to provide a more specific justification, which in this context could have the same effect as a general doctrine of necessity. In *R.* v. *Adams* Devlin J. denied that there was any special defence open to a doctor in these circumstances.[67]

---

[64] This would almost certainly be the case if legislation gave effect to the Law Commission's recommendations that there should be a statutory provision abolishing any defence of necessity that might be available at common law, and that any statutory defence of necessity should not extend to the crime of murder: see *Criminal Law: Report on Defences of General Application* (Law Com. No. 83, 1977), pp. 27–32.

[65] Williams, *Sanctity*, 284, 286–8, 290; Williams, *Textbook*, 533; E. Garth Moore, 'The Common Law Doctrine of Necessity', in *Decisions about Life and Death* (Church Information Office, 1965), 49, 50 (but see the chapter drafted by him in *On Dying Well* (Church Information Office, 1975), 51, 58).

[66] See e.g. *Buckoke* v. *Greater London Council* [1971] Ch. 655, 668. This reluctance is likely to be even greater in relation to the law of homicide. *Buckoke* v. *Greater London Council* was not cited to the court in *Johnson* v. *Phillips* [1976] 1 W.L.R. 65, where the existence of a defence (presumably of necessity) appears to have been assumed: but see Glanville Williams, 'Necessity' [1978] *Crim. L.R.* 128, 131 ('It perhaps says something about the attitude of the bench to legal defences that this solitary decision represents an acceptance of necessity as a reason not for acquitting but for convicting.'). Cf. *R.* v. *Loughnan* [1981] V.R. 443.

[67] See also Devlin, *Samples*, 93 ('This direction was not . . . given on the basis that the relief of pain justified an act that would otherwise be murder in law.').

However his statement that 'If the first purpose of medicine, the restoration of health, can no longer be achieved ... [the doctor] is entitled to do all that is proper and necessary to relieve pain and suffering, even if the measures he takes may incidentally shorten life' might be used by a judge who wished to provide a specific justification.

A concluding remark

A doctor's freedom to prescribe pain-killing drugs is not unlimited. If a patient died in consequence of a doctor prescribing larger quantities of an analgesic than could reasonably be believed to be necessary to relieve pain, the doctor could sometimes be guilty of manslaughter or—if he had an appropriate fault element—murder. If the doctor prescribed a drug which he knew to be likely to hasten death, when he knew that a much safer but equally effective alternative was available, he could be guilty of murder if the patient died in consequence. But if a doctor avoided such pitfalls, he would not risk liability for murder or manslaughter if he prescribed a drug to relieve 'the pains of death', although he knew that the drug might well hasten death.

7

ALLOWING TO DIE

> I am satisfied that the law relating to murder . . . is
> the same now as it was before the trial [of Dr Arthur];
> that it is the same irrespective of the age of the victim;
> and that it is the same irrespective of the wishes of
> the parents or any other person having a duty of care
> to the victim. I am also satisfied that a person who
> has a duty of care may be guilty of murder . . . by
> omitting to fulfil that duty, as much as by commit-
> ting any positive act.
>
> Sir Michael Havers A.-G., 1982[1]

This chapter contains a discussion of the circumstances in
which a doctor would be guilty of murder or manslaughter
if he omitted to provide treatment which would save or
prolong a patient's life.

To simplify the discussion, three assumptions will be
made. The first is that there is already a doctor–patient
relationship between the doctor and the person in question.[2]
The second is that the means of prolonging life are available,
and the doctor could employ them without conflict with his
duty to other patients. The third is that it is apparent that, if
'life-prolonging' treatment were provided, the patient's death
could be postponed or averted.[3]

---

[1] (1982) 19 Parl. Deb. H.C. (6th ser.) *349*. The Attorney-General said that he
was also satisfied that the law relating to attempted murder was the same as it was
before the trial of Dr Arthur, and that a person may be guilty of attempted
murder by omitting to fulfil a duty of care. Although the trial judge's summing-
up could hardly be taken to have changed the law on attempted murder, the
phrase 'does an act' in s. 1(1) of the Criminal Attempts Act 1981 could be taken
to exclude the possibility of attempted murder being committed by omission: see
generally Ian Dennis, 'The Criminal Attempts Act 1981' [1982] *Crim. L.R.*
5, 7–8.

[2] See generally Lord Nathan, *Medical Negligence* (1957), 36–40. See also
Barnett v. *Chelsea and Kensington Hospital Management Committee* [1969] 1
Q.B. 428.

[3] There are many circumstances in which it could not be established that a
patient's life could have been prolonged, even if the doctor had done all that it
was within his power to do.

I OMISSIONS: THE GENERAL PRINCIPLES

In the law of homicide, there is an important distinction between acts and omissions.[4] Where a person is not under any duty to act, recognized by the law of homicide, his omission to save or prolong life will not be regarded as a cause of death.[5] It is only where there is a duty to act[6] that an omission to act in that way will be given the same effect as an act, for the purpose of the external elements of homicide. In such cases, the omission may be regarded as a cause of death if, but for the omission, death would have been postponed.

Murder, and the form of manslaughter known as negligent manslaughter, can both be committed by omission as well as by act.[7] The fault element remains the same, whether death is hastened by an act, or by an omission to fulfil a duty to act. If a doctor withheld treatment for the purpose of hastening the patient's death, he would have the fault element for murder.[8] If a doctor was not aware that death or really serious

[4] For discussions of whether there is a morally significant difference between acts and omissions, see e.g. Jonathan Glover, *Causing Death and Saving Lives* (1977), 92–112; Philippa Foot, 'Euthanasia' (1977) 6 *Philosophy & Public Affairs* 85, 100–5, reprinted in *Ethical Issues Relating to Life and Death* (1979, ed. J. Ladd), 14, 28–32; [A. J. L. Gormally] 'Is there a morally significant difference between killing and letting die?' *Linacre Papers* (No. 2, 1978).

[5] The distinction between acts and omissions is sometimes expressed in terms of acts of commission and acts of omission; e.g. *R.* v. *Lowe* [1973] Q.B. 702, 709.

[6] See generally P. R. Glazebrook, 'Criminal Omissions: The Duty Requirement in Offences against the Person' (1960) 76 *L.Q.R.* 386–411; Criminal Law Revision Committee, Fourteenth Report, *Offences against the Person* (Cmnd. 7844; 1980), pp. 108–10. See also *R.* v. *Miller* [1983] 2 W.L.R. 539, [1983] 1 All E.R. 978, esp. 981c-d per Lord Diplock.

[7] But 'unlawful act' manslaughter cannot at present be committed by omission: see *R.* v. *Lowe* [1973] Q.B. 702 (but see Editorial, 'Homicide by Neglect' [1976] *Crim. L.R.* 529, 530–1).

[8] For a discussion of the fault element for murder, see pp. 122–6, 132–3, above. On murder by omission, see e.g. *R.* v. *Marriott* (1838) 8 Car. & P. 425, 433; *R.* v. *Bubb and Hook* (1850) 14 J.P. 562; *R.* v. *Lowe* (1850) 3 Car. & K. 123, 124; *R.* v. *Hughes* (1857) Dears. & Bell 248, 250; *R.* v. *Conde* (1867) 10 Cox C.C. 547, 549; *R.* v. *Handley* (1874) 13 Cox C.C. 79, 80–1; *R.* v. *Gibbins and Proctor* (1918) 13 Cr. App. R. 134, 138, 140. See also *R.* v. *White* (1871) L.R. 1 C.C.R. 311, 314; Infanticide Act 1938, s. 1(1); Homicide Act 1957, s. 2(1). In *R.* v. *Arthur* (1981; see ch. 6, n. 30) Farquharson J. placed great emphasis on the distinction between acts and omissions (see, e.g. Transcript, 12B, 17C-D, 20A-D, 87H-88A; but see also 27H-28B). The cases cited above are evidence of the long-accepted view that murder can be committed by omission, and Farquharson J.'s statements should not be interpreted as indicating his rejection of that view. Until a very late stage of the trial the prosecution had focused on the doctor's act

bodily harm would result from his omission to act, he would nevertheless have a sufficient fault element for manslaughter if his omission could be characterized as grossly negligent.[9]

II THE CRUCIAL TEST

Despite Lord Hailsham's claim that 'The law, at the moment, is perfectly plain: if you have got a living body, you have got to keep it alive, if you can',[10] it would be wrong to assume that a doctor is always obliged to take steps to prolong a patient's life. Doctors are sometimes free—sometimes, indeed, required—to allow a patient to die. It is therefore necessary to ascertain the test that the courts will apply, to determine whether a doctor is in breach of his duty of care if he omits to prolong a patient's life.

There is reason to believe that the crucial test is whether, in the same circumstances, all reasonable doctors would have kept the patient alive. But before discussing this test it is desirable to consider an alternative test, which the courts might be urged to adopt. It is based on the moralists' distinction between ordinary and extraordinary means of preserving life.

'Ordinary' and 'extraordinary' means

It might be argued that, when caring for a patient, a doctor is obliged to employ ordinary means of preserving life, but is not obliged to use extraordinary means. The distinction between ordinary and extraordinary means of preserving life has been developed by moral theologians to distinguish measures which, in their view, a person is morally obliged to take to preserve his own life, from those measures which he is

in prescribing the drug, rather than on his omission to ensure that John Pearson received food, or was treated if he contracted pneumonia. It seems that in view of the way in which the prosecution approached the case, the judge considered it unnecessary to direct the jury as to the circumstances in which murder—and hence attempted murder—could be committed by omission.

[9] *R.* v. *Bateman* (1925) 19 Cr. App. R. 8; *R.* v. *Stone* [1977] Q.B. 354. See also *R.* v. *Bourne* [1939] 1 K.B. 687, 693, and ch. 6, n. 26.

[10] The statement was made in the course of a discussion which was broadcast on BBC Radio 4. See 'Life after Brain Death—the Uses of the Neomort' (1976) 96 *The Listener* 14, 15 (8 July 1976).

not normally morally obliged to take.[11] In a medical context, they regard 'ordinary' means as 'all medicines, treatments, and operations, which offer a reasonable hope of benefit for the patient and which can be obtained and used without excessive expense, pain, or other inconvenience', whereas 'extraordinary' means are regarded, on this view, as 'all medicines, treatments and operations which cannot be obtained or used without excessive expense, pain or other inconvenience, or which, if used, would not offer a reasonable hope of benefit'.[12]

It is only in comparatively recent times that the distinction between 'ordinary' and 'extraordinary' means has been used in the context of providing, rather than seeking or submitting to, medical treatment.[13] Here, the issues are still more complicated. Even if it were accepted that a doctor is normally under a duty to employ ordinary means of preserving life, but not usually under a duty to employ extraordinary means, the views of the patient might sometimes be of crucial importance in determining the doctor's obligations.[14] For example, a refusal of consent could be held to release a doctor from any obligation to provide even ordinary means, whereas a request or undertaking could sometimes be held to create an obligation to provide extraordinary means. Nevertheless there are many occasions on which these and similar complications do not arise, and where a court could still take the view that a doctor was obliged to employ ordinary, but not extraordinary, means of preserving life.

The fact that it is sometimes difficult to decide whether a procedure should, in the circumstances, be regarded as an

[11] See generally [A. J. L. Gormally], 'Ordinary and Extraordinary Means of Prolonging Life', *Linacre Papers* (No. 3, 1979), esp. 7-10.

[12] G. Kelly, *Medico-Moral Problems* (1958), 129. See also Pope Pius XII, Address of 24 November 1957 to doctors (1957) 49 *Acta Apostolicae Sedis* 1027-33, esp. 1030, 1032; G. R. Dunstan, 'Life, Prolongation of: Ordinary and Extraordinary Means' in *Dict. Med. Ethics* 266-8.

[13] See [A. J. L. Gormally], 'Ordinary and Extraordinary Means of Prolonging Life', op. cit., 10-11.

[14] The views of the patient are sometimes of importance in relation to the initial issue of whether the means should be regarded as 'ordinary' or 'extraordinary', in the circumstances in question. Weight is sometimes given to factors such as 'psychological repugnance', which may result in a procedure being considered extraordinary, rather than ordinary, in relation to a particular patient.

ordinary or extraordinary means of preserving life, is not a
good reason for refusing to employ the distinction. Difficulties of classification will occur with any test.[15] Nor is it a
valid objection that the classification will sometimes change
with time, or even with different circumstances at the same
time. In this field, flexibility is highly desirable.

Nevertheless, there are several reasons why it is undesirable that the courts should openly invoke the moralists'
distinction between ordinary and extraordinary means of
preserving life, when determining whether a doctor was in
breach of his duty in withholding treatment that would prolong life. One is that the distinction is easily misunderstood,
for doctors also speak of 'ordinary' treatment, which they
contrast with heroic, unusual, or 'extraordinary' treatment.[16]
In doing so, they use the terms in a descriptive rather than a
normative sense,[17] to refer to conventional, established treatment; a new procedure not yet in general use would not be
regarded as 'ordinary', even though it involved no excessive
expense, pain, or other inconvenience and offered a reasonable hope of benefit. When doctors distinguish between
ordinary and extraordinary procedures they rarely take
account of the personal and other non-medical considerations
which play a part in the moralists' distinction. It is desirable
to avoid terminology which invites such confusion, and
which has led to the misapprehension that there is alleged to
be a moral obligation to accept (and, some would add,
provide) usual, but not unusual, treatment.

Another reason for declining to adopt the distinction
between ordinary and extraordinary means is that the distinction has been developed by Roman Catholic moral
theologians, and remains closely identified with that tradition. For a judge to adopt it expressly in the course of
determining cases which involve persons who disown that

---

[15] Cf. Williams, *Sanctity*, 291 ('if life has become a burden to the patient');
Glanville Williams, 'Euthanasia' (1973) 41 *Med.-Leg. J.* 14, 21 ('no sufficient
probability of the patient being restored to a reasonably full life'); Williams,
Textbook, 237 ('whether life has or will have any value for the patient').

[16] See generally Paul Ramsey, *The Patient as Person* (1970), 118–24.

[17] For the moralists, 'ordinary' procedures are by definition obligatory, so an
element of circularity can enter into the discussion. They do not regard what is
medically ordinary as always obligatory.

tradition, and who do not share some of the assumptions which lie behind the distinction,[18] would cause needless resentment and controversy.[19] Moreover, the most recent Roman Catholic discussions and pronouncements have themselves sought to draw the distinction in language other than 'ordinary' or 'extraordinary', in order to avoid confusion with medical usage. Instead, they have said that treatment which is disproportionately burdensome, or futile, is not obligatory.[20]

The 'reasonable doctor' test

The courts are likely to accept that a doctor should only be regarded as in breach of his duty, if he omits to save or prolong life, if in the same circumstances all reasonable doctors would have sought to save or prolong life. This test would be applicable in a civil action for negligence,[21] and therefore already plays a part in the context of negligent manslaughter.[22]

A test phrased in terms of reasonableness is more in line with accepted legal terminology than one expressed in terms of ordinary and extraordinary means of prolonging life. The test of whether all reasonable doctors would, in the circumstances, have prolonged life provides a limit to the intervention of the law of homicide in these cases.[23] It is not enough that some reasonable doctors would have prolonged life: a doctor will not be convicted unless the jury accepts that, in

[18] For an account of these assumptions, see [A. J. L. Gormally], 'Ordinary and Extraordinary Means of Prolonging Life', op. cit., n. 11, 7–8. Of course, the assumptions which lie behind some of the other possible tests (see e.g. n. 15) would also be vigorously disputed by many persons.

[19] Cf. G. Grisez and J. M. Boyle, *Life and Death with Liberty and Justice* (1979), 257, 495 n. 28.

[20] See Linacre Report, 45–53, esp. 46–9; and see also Sacred Congregation of the Doctrine of the Faith, 'Iura et Bona' (Declaration on Euthanasia) (1980) 72 *Acta Apostolicae Sedis* 542–52.

[21] It is unlikely that a doctor would be held to be under a duty to prolong life when he would not have to take such action to comply with his duty of care under the tort of negligence. But the test suggested in the text above can also take account of any obligation placed on a doctor by s. 1 of the Children and Young Persons Act 1933, as well as contractual obligations, or other undertakings. (For an analysis which stresses the doctor's contractual duties, see Helen Benyon, 'Doctors as Murderers' [1982] *Crim. L.R.* 17, 23–8. See also n. 49, below.)

[22] See e.g. *R.* v. *Bateman* (1925) 19 Cr. App. R. 8, 13.

[23] Such a limit is highly desirable, given the consequence of holding that a doctor was in breach of his duty in intentionally allowing a patient to die.

the circumstances, all reasonable doctors would do so.[24]
Many of the considerations which lie behind the distinction
between ordinary and extraordinary means can be taken into
account, but so too can other considerations.[25] The test does
not ossify one set of views as to the circumstances in which it
is permissible to withhold treatment. It accommodates
changes in medical conditions and ethical opinion, and does
not commit the courts to any one approach to these matters.

In deciding whether a doctor had failed to do what any
reasonable doctor would do in the same circumstances,
evidence of common and approved practice is of very great
importance.[26] But the question whether a patient should be
enabled to live, or allowed to die, is not simply a technical
medical one.[27] Expert evidence will be essential in deciding
what could have been achieved by treating the patient, and at
what cost in pain and suffering. But, on the question of
whether the doctor was in breach of his duty of care in allowing the patient to die, evidence of a professional consensus
should not be treated as conclusive.[28]

---

[24] Similarly, a doctor should not be regarded as having neglected a child, contrary to s. 1 of the Children and Young Persons Act 1933, if in the circumstances
at least some other reasonable doctors would also have omitted to provide life-
prolonging treatment. (A doctor should only be considered to have failed to provide 'adequate . . . medical aid' if he failed to provide what any reasonable doctor
would provide in the circumstances.) A person should certainly not be convicted
in consequence of an intentional omission to prolong the life of a child, if the
overwhelming consensus of medical and other opinion is that in view of the pain
and suffering, or cost, or demand on a scarce resource, such action is unwarranted.
A person should not be said to have neglected to do what no reasonable person
would expect him to do. But on the interpretation of s. 1, see generally *R. v.
Sheppard* [1981] A.C. 394.

[25] For a suggestion that another distinction is fundamental, see R. G. Twycross, 'Euthanasia', in *Dict. Med. Ethics*, 164. This is the distinction between
acute and terminal illness. Twycross states that the two are 'distinct pathophysio-
logical entities', and that what is appropriate to the former (e.g. gastric tubes,
intravenous infusions, antibiotics, respirators, cardiac resuscitation) is often in-
appropriate with the latter, where it is not a matter of assisting the patient through
a critical period with the hope of recovery of health. The tort of negligence and
the law of homicide can take account of this distinction.

[26] See pp. 82–6.

[27] Cf. *Re D. (A Minor) (Wardship: Sterilisation)* [1976] Fam. 185, 192B per
Heilbron J. ('a number of matters which were not in my view in reality matters
of clinical judgment, but which were concerned, to a large extent, with grounds
which were other than medical').

[28] Such evidence may leave the jury with a misleading impression: contrast
the impression left by the expert witnesses called by the defence in *R. v. Arthur*

In a prosecution for murder or manslaughter it would be for the jury, rather than the judge, to determine whether a doctor had omitted to do what any reasonable doctor would do in the circumstances. But this does not mean that the views of the judge would be of no importance. A judge would often be in a position to influence the jury, and in some cases his ruling upon whether a doctor was legally free to save the patient's life could be of crucial importance. Where the doctor is not free to proceed without consent, he can scarcely be regarded as being obliged to do so. Hence a judge could properly direct a jury that on certain assumptions the doctor would have committed a criminal offence by treating the patient, and that therefore it could not be said that all reasonable doctors would have taken such action.

III APPLICATION OF THE TEST

By considering separately some of the different circumstances which may occur, it is possible to go a little beyond the bare statement that a doctor will be in breach of his duty if he omits to do what all reasonable doctors would do in the circumstances. It is possible to get some idea of how the test will apply in different circumstances. The categories to be discussed do not encompass all the situations which occur. But they do raise at least most of the important issues, and the discussion should give some indication of how other situations might be dealt with.

The discussion will proceed on the assumption that the doctor is aware that, if he does not act, the patient will die earlier than he would otherwise have done. The doctor would therefore have a state of mind which would suffice for conviction of murder, if the other elements of the offence were

with the poll of consultant paediatricians and paediatric surgeons, conducted by the BBC Panorama team, and summarized by Ian Kennedy, 'Reflections on the Arthur trial', *New Society*, 7 January 1982, pp. 13, 14 (600 questionnaires sent out; 340 replies received by 7 November 1981, of which 280 were fully completed. Some 90 per cent of the respondents indicated that they would give normal care to an otherwise healthy Down's syndrome baby which had been rejected by its parents. Eight per cent said they would simply feed and care for the child, but not give active medical treatment if the child contracted a potentially fatal illness. None of the respondents would have done what Dr Arthur did).

present.[29] The important issue would then be whether the doctor would be in breach of his duty of care in omitting to prolong the patient's life.

For the purpose of this discussion, the term 'life-prolonging treatment' will be used to refer to all measures that could reasonably be expected to counteract causes and conditions which would otherwise soon result in the patient's death. Such measures will range from the provision of artificial ventilation to prolong the life of a dying person for a day or two, to the removal of a diseased appendix from a young patient, after which the patient may be expected to live for half a century or more. The term 'provide' will be used to comprehend cases where the doctor will be under a duty to arrange for life-prolonging treatment to be provided, or give advice on how to obtain such treatment, as well as those where he must employ or administer it himself.

1. *Where consent to life-prolonging treatment would be forthcoming if required, but the doctor has not agreed to provide it.*

Concentration on controversial cases involving new-born children suffering from spina bifida, or Down's syndrome, can obscure the fact that there is virtual unanimity that in a great number of circumstances any reasonable doctor would take steps to prolong his patient's life. If a normally healthy patient is suffering from appendicitis, or pneumonia, or respiratory difficulties resulting from an asthmatic attack, his doctor would usually be obliged to ensure that his patient had the opportunity of receiving the necessary treatment. If the doctor did nothing, knowing that the patient would die in consequence, the doctor would normally be in breach of his duty of care. He would have omitted to do what any

---

[29] In theory it would sometimes be easier to establish the elements of murder than of manslaughter in such a case. This is because at present unlawful act manslaughter requires an act of commission (see n. 7), and before a jury can find someone guilty of negligent manslaughter they must agree that there is a high degree of negligence, such as is often characterized as 'reckless' or 'gross'. A jury might not always be prepared to accept that a doctor was grossly negligent, even if they accepted that he was aware of the consequence of his omission to fulfil a duty to prolong life. But in practice a jury would probably be less unwilling to find a doctor guilty of manslaughter than of murder.

reasonable doctor would do in the circumstances, and in law his conduct could amount to murder if death ensued.[30]

Although it is accepted that in a great many circumstances a doctor should not allow a patient to die (assuming, for the moment, that there is no problem about obtaining consent), it is also generally agreed that a doctor is not always obliged to take all possible steps to prolong a patient's life. The dictum 'Thou shalt not kill; but needst not strive / Officiously to keep alive'[31] is commonly quoted with approval in a medical context, even by those who are strongly opposed to 'active euthanasia'. Where doctors persist in prolonging life long after any hope of recovery is past, their conduct is often criticized.

In examining the legal duty of a doctor to prolong a patient's life, the difficulty does not lie in agreeing that a doctor is often obliged to prolong the life of his patient, but is sometimes free to omit to do so. It lies in deciding in what circumstances a doctor is free to allow his patient to die. In any prosecution it would be for the jury to decide whether a doctor had failed to do what any reasonable doctor would do in the circumstances. But juries would sometimes be influenced by what was said by the judge in his summing-up, so it is worth looking at recent cases for indications of likely judicial attitudes.

In *Lim v. Camden and Islington Area Health Authority*[32] a patient (herself a doctor) suffered a cardiac arrest after a minor gynaecological operation. Although her breathing and heartbeat were eventually restored, her brain had by then

---

[30] In some circumstances an omission to provide treatment would amount to an offence under s. 1 of the Children and Young Persons Act 1933. But an omission to provide treatment should not lead to liability under that section if some reasonable parents, or some reasonable doctors, would also omit to provide treatment in the same circumstances, despite having knowledge of all the relevant facts (see n. 24). *Quaere*, whether a doctor who omitted to provide care for a new-born child would ever commit an offence under s. 27 of the Offences against the Person Act 1861 (abandoning child under the age of two years, thereby endangering the child's life).

[31] These words appeared originally in A. H. Clough's ironical poem, 'The Latest Decalogue'. It seems that he intended to satirize the way in which people were allowed to die because of lack of food and medical care. The words have come to be quoted, in a different context, to support the distinction Clough questioned.

[32] [1979] Q.B. 196, [1980] A.C. 174.

suffered severe and irreversible damage. At times she had
some memory of the past, could understand a little, read a
little, and speak a little. At other times 'she would lapse into
a depressed, withdrawn, non-responsive, non-communicative
and even non-co-operative behaviour not unlike a child of a
few years old'.[33] The health authority accepted liability for
negligence, and the only issue before the courts was the
quantum of damages. However in the course of his judgment
Lord Denning M.R. implied that a doctor was not always
obliged to persist in efforts to resuscitate a patient, following a cardiac arrest.[34] In this case twenty-five minutes had
elapsed before the patient's breathing was restored to normal,
and she was brought back to what Lord Denning M.R.
described as 'a life which is not worth living'.[35] He said that
after an accident such as occurred in this case, those concerned are faced with an agonizing decision: 'is she to be kept
alive? Or is she to be allowed to die? Is the thread of life to
be maintained to the utmost reach of science? Or should it be
let fall and nature take its inevitable course?' In such circumstances, he said, 'those about her should say: "For mercy's
sake, let the end come now".'[36] The implication of this and
other passages[37] in Lord Denning's judgment was that in
some circumstances doctors could properly omit to take
action which would result in a patient living for a very considerable time, but in a state of 'living death'.[38]

In *Re B. (A Minor)*[39] the court had to decide whether an

[33] [1979] Q.B. 227.

[34] The other two judgments in the Court of Appeal did not touch upon this
issue, and it was not mentioned in judgments in the House of Lords. But Bristow J.
was reported to have said, during the course of the original trial, that 'One of the
questions that arises is whether it was really wise to bring her back to life in the
intensive care unit. Doctors are in an intolerable dilemma.' *The Times*, 23 November 1977, p. 4 (news report). See also Lord Scarman, 'Legal Liability and Medicine'
(1981) 74 *J. Roy. Soc. Med.* 11, 14–15.

[35] [1979] 1 Q.B. 216A.   [36] Ibid. 216G–H.

[37] See ibid. 214E, 216A. See also *Whitehouse* v. *Jordan* [1980] 1 All E.R.
650, 654j per Lord Denning M.R. ('Seeing this boy's present condition, most
would say: "What a pity they did not let him die." ')

[38] [1979] 1 Q.B. 214E, 219A per Lord Denning M.R. The expression was also
used by Bristow J.: see ibid. 205A.

[39] *Re B. (A Minor) (Wardship: Medical Treatment)* [1981] 1 W.L.R. 1421
(C.A.). For a consideration of possible implications of this case, see Glanville
Williams, 'Down's Syndrome and the Duty to Preserve Life' (1981) 131 *New L.J.*
1020–1.

operation, to relieve an intestinal blockage, should be performed on a new-born child suffering from Down's syndrome,
who had been made a ward of court. If the operation was not
performed the child would die within a matter of days. If it
was performed, and was successful, the child would probably
live for twenty or thirty years—although in a seriously
handicapped state.[40] Templeman L.J. said that the decision
for the court was:[41]

whether the life of this child is demonstrably going to be so awful that
in effect the child must be condemned to die, or whether the life of this
child is still so imponderable that it would be wrong for her to be condemned to die.

He decided that the operation should be performed,[42] although he accepted that there might be cases where the life
of a child was 'so bound to be full of pain and suffering' that
a court might be driven to a different conclusion.[43] The other
judge, Dunn L.J., agreed with Templeman L.J., and said that
here there was 'no evidence that this child's short life is likely
to be an intolerable one'.[44]

Lim and *Re B.* were not, of course, criminal cases and it
would be a mistake to exaggerate the importance, in a criminal
context, of anything said in these cases. It would also be
erroneous to suppose that there are no other circumstances in
which a doctor could properly omit to prolong the life of a
patient. Nevertheless the statements quoted[45] do provide a
necessary corrective to the extrajudicial statement of Lord
Hailsham's,[46] quoted earlier in this chapter. They support
the view that in some circumstances a doctor may omit
to take steps to prevent a patient from dying, and that such

[40] For the view of the Law Reform Commission of Canada, see its Working
Paper 28, *Euthanasia, Aiding Suicide and Cessation of Treatment* (1982), p. 60
('In the Commission's view this child should be treated for the [obstruction]. To
abandon the child and allow him to die of starvation is unacceptable and contrary
to the norms of criminal law.').

[41] [1981] 1 W.L.R. 1424B.

[42] Booth J. apparently reached the same conclusion in a similar case, less than
a year later. See *Human Concern*, Summer 1982, p. 1.

[43] See [1981] 1 W.L.R. 1424B-E. But see *McKay* v. *Essex Area Health
Authority* [1982] Q.B. 1166, 1180E, 1188C-E.

[44] [1981] 1 W.L.R. 1424H.

[45] See also Ormrod, 'Ethics', 29-30.

[46] See n. 10, above.

circumstances are not restricted to those in which death is inevitable within the near future in any event.

There may have been a time when a judge would have encouraged a jury to take the view that a doctor would be acting improperly in failing to operate on any child suffering from spina bifida, when by doing so he could prolong the child's life. But it is now most unlikely that a judge would encourage a jury to come to the conclusion that a doctor was guilty of murder or manslaughter in omitting to operate, to prevent the death of a child who could be regarded as a particularly severe case of spina bifida.[47] Even in the situation which was before the court in *Re B.*, it is far from certain that a judge would seek to direct a jury in a way which could result in a doctor being convicted of murder or manslaughter, as a consequence of his omission to operate to save the life of the child.[48]

2. *Where the doctor has agreed to provide additional life-prolonging treatment.*

In some circumstances, a doctor who has agreed to provide particular life-prolonging treatment may be under a duty to give that treatment, although if it were not for that undertaking he would have been free to omit to do so.

Having expressly agreed to provide particular treatment, there are circumstances where any reasonable doctor would comply with that undertaking.[49] Furthermore, a doctor who

[47] See generally, 'The Ethics of Selective Treatment of Spina Bifida' [1975] 1 *Lancet* 85–8; Editorial, 'Withholding Treatment in Infancy' (1981) 282 *Br. Med. J.* 925–6; Editorial, 'The Right to Live and the Right to Die' (1981) 283 *Br. Med. J.* 569–70; *The Times*, 13 August 1981, p. 1. See also J. Lorber, Letter to the Editor, *The Times*, 17 August 1981.

[48] Some indication of the likely attitude of a jury may be gauged from the results of a survey conducted by Market and Opinion Research International ('MORI') in September 1981. Of the 1953 adults who were interviewed, 46 per cent thought that everything possible should be done to help a severely handicapped baby to live, whereas 23 per cent thought a severely handicapped baby should be given a quick and painless death. But 86 per cent of those interviewed were of the opinion that a doctor should not be found guilty of murder if, with the parent's agreement, he sees to it that a severely handicapped baby dies. Only 7 per cent were of the opinion that the doctor should be convicted of murder in these circumstances (the other 7 per cent being 'don't knows'). See *The Times*, 9 November 1981, p. 1; 10 November 1981, p. 3. See also *The Times*, 26 March 1982, p. 5; 'Public Opinion and Severe Neonatal Handicap' [1982] 1 *Lancet* 811.

[49] In practice a doctor will not give an express undertaking that he will do all

has started on a particular course of action will often be obliged to complete it, or to arrange for someone else to do so. For example, having commenced a major operation a doctor cannot omit to finish it (without ensuring that someone will take over from him), even if he would not have been in breach of his duty if he had not operated in the first place. Nor will the completion of the operation always extinguish his obligation. There will often be an obligation to arrange for the continuing care or treatment of the patient. For example, having transplanted an organ into a patient, a doctor is not free to omit to take steps to ensure that the patient is provided with drugs to prevent his body 'rejecting' the transplanted organ. There are circumstances in which an omission to do so could result in criminal liability.

The fact that a doctor has commenced a particular course of life-prolonging treatment will not always oblige him to continue with it indefinitely, simply because it is prolonging the patient's life.[50] Many patients with cardiac or respiratory arrest are now provided with artificial ventilation in the hope that they will recover. If it becomes apparent that the patient's brain is damaged to an extent that precludes a return to consciousness, a doctor will not be regarded as in breach of his duty if he omits to continue artificial ventilation, even though he knows that, if it is not continued, the patient will die. In such cases the initial provision of artificial ventilation will not be considered to give rise to a continuing obligation. A judge would not encourage a jury to adopt the view that in such

that he can to prolong the patient's life indefinitely, even if it is established that there is no prospect of a return to consciousness. But even if a doctor had contracted to prolong the patient's life in such circumstances, it may be argued that such an undertaking would be socially undesirable, and that whatever the position in the law of contract such an undertaking should not affect the tort of ngeligence, much less the law of homicide. In the nineteenth century, criminal liability for omissions was sometimes founded (at least in theory) on the breach of certain contractual duties. However, these instances were encompassed in the broader rule laid down in, for example, *R.* v. *Nicholls* (1874) 13 Cox C.C. 75, 76, and accepted in *R.* v. *Hall* (1919) 26 Cox C.C. 525, 529. References to contract continued to be made in some cases (e.g. *R.* v. *Pittwood* (1902) 19 T.L.R. 37, 38), although these cases can be explained on other grounds.

[50] In some circumstances artificial ventilation could be regarded as having been provided on the condition that it would be withdrawn if the ventilator was later required for another patient, who had a better chance of recovery.

circumstances all reasonable doctors would continue with artificial ventilation.[51]

3. *Where the patient refuses consent to life-prolonging treatment (and no one else is able to give a legally effective consent).*

To what extent does a patient's refusal of consent to treatment affect the duty of a doctor to provide life-prolonging treatment which he would have been under a duty to provide, if consent had been forthcoming? In answering this question, it is desirable to consider separately the situation where the need for treatment results from an attempt to commit suicide, and that where the need for life-prolonging treatment does not result from action taken by the patient, with the intention of ending his own life.[52]

Where a patient has attempted to commit suicide, a doctor will normally be legally justified in taking action to avert the consequences of that attempt.[53] But is he under a duty to take such action? There are circumstances in which the court might well take the view that a doctor was obliged to save the patient's life.[54] If the doctor responsible for a patient following an apparently typical 'suicide attempt' omitted to take steps to save the patient's life, because he believed all such patients should be left to die, or because he disliked the patient, it could be said that he behaved in a way in which no reasonable doctor would behave. If he withheld treatment with the intention that the patient should die, it is not beyond the bounds of possibility that he would be regarded as guilty of murder.

It is, however, undesirable that a doctor should always be obliged to take steps to prevent a patient from committing

---

[51] In *R.* v. *Malcherek* [1981] 1 W.L.R. 690 (see esp. 697) there was no hint of judicial criticism of the doctor's conduct in omitting to provide further artificial ventilation. For an account of the case, see pp. 195-7, below.

[52] In this discussion, all references to attempts to commit suicide, or to acts taken by the patient with the intention of ending his own life, should be taken to include apparent attempts to commit suicide, and also cases where the patient was a passive partner in a suicide pact.   [53] See pp. 110-12.

[54] Cf. *Selfe* v. *Ilford and District Hospital Management Committee, The Times,* 26 November 1970; *Hyde* v. *Tameside Area Health Authority, The Times,* 16 April 1981 (as to which, see ch. 5, n. 54). See also *McFarland* v. *Stewart* (1900) 19 N.Z.L.R. 22.

suicide, or to avert the consequences of such an attempt, There are circumstances in which reasonable doctors will disagree as to whether a patient should be prevented from giving effect to, for example, a long-standing well-considered decision to end his own life. Such cases may be rare,[55] but it is undesirable that a doctor should risk liability in homicide if he omits to intervene in such a case, even if he is entitled to intervene.

Where the need for treatment does not result from some act of the patient's, taken with the intention of ending his own life, a doctor is rarely if ever entitled to override a patient's wishes.[56] As the doctor is not entitled to administer treatment against the patient's wishes, there is clearly no question of his being under a duty to do so.[57] Hence in *R.* v. *Blaue*[58]—where a Jehovah's Witness refused to consent to a blood transfusion even though she knew that she would die without one—there was no hint of criticism of the doctor who respected her wishes.[59] Had she been willing to consent, the doctor would have been under a duty to provide a blood transfusion to save her life. As she refused consent the doctor was not entitled, much less obliged, to do so.[60]

Where the patient is suffering from a remediable condition which predisposes him to refuse consent, and there is reason to believe that if restored to a better condition the patient will be glad to go on living, it is just possible that a court would hold that a doctor is justified in overriding a patient's refusal of consent.[61] But even if a doctor was entitled to proceed in such circumstances, it could not be said that all reasonable doctors would do so. Therefore failure to proceed should not give rise to criminal liability.

Except in some cases of attempted suicide, an adult patient's

[55] See J. H. Brown, Letter, 'Is suicide ever rational?' [1981] 1 *Lancet* 660–1.
[56] See pp. 112–16.
[57] He may, however, be under a duty to inform the patient of the likely consequences of his refusal.
[58] [1975] 1 W.L.R. 1411.
[59] Blaue was the original assailant, who was indicted for murder. Had there been grounds for criticizing the doctor's omission to act, Blaue's counsel could have been expected to suggest that the doctor's conduct contributed to a break in the chain of causation between Blaue's acts and the girl's death.
[60] This point appears to have been overlooked in *R.* v. *Stone* [1977] Q.B. 354—although see National Assistance Act 1948, s. 47.
[61] See pp. 115–16.

refusal of consent releases a doctor from any obligation he would otherwise be under, to save the patient's life. The doctor will not be in breach of his duty in allowing the patient to die.

4. *Where neither parent is willing to consent to life-prolonging treatment of the child, and the child is incapable of giving consent.*

In a great many circumstances, the parents' refusal of consent will release a doctor from an obligation to provide particular medical treatment for the child. But when life is in immediate peril there is an important distinction between an adult patient who refuses consent, and a child who is incapable of consenting, and whose parents refuse consent. In the case of an adult, a doctor is rarely entitled to proceed without consent. Where he is not entitled to proceed, there is obviously no question of his being under a duty to do so. But in the case of a child whose life is in immediate peril and whose parents refuse consent to life-saving treatment, a doctor will often be legally justified in proceeding despite the parents' objection to treatment.[62] However, it is one thing to say that a doctor is in law free to act, despite the parents' objections; it is quite another to say that he is under a duty to do so. The issue here is duty, not entitlement.[63]

In the case of a reasonably normal child whose life is in immediate peril, the parents' wish that the child be allowed to die will not release a doctor from an obligation he would otherwise be under, to save the child's life. Granted that a doctor is free to act, it is inconceivable that a court would accept that the parents' objection to a doctor taking any steps to assist a normal child to breathe at birth, or while in hospital following a severe attack of asthma, would release a doctor from any obligation he would otherwise be under, to save the child's life. In such circumstances, any reasonable doctor would act to save his patient's life.

[62] See pp. 106–10. In some circumstances, a doctor may be under a duty to ensure that the appropriate authority is informed that parental consent is not forthcoming, so legal proceedings can be taken to enable someone else to grant consent, or to authorize performance of the procedure.

[63] On omissions to treat children, see generally A. R. Holder, *Legal Issues in Pediatrics and Adolescent Medicine* (1977), ch. 4.

The mere fact that a child has some handicap does not mean that the child's doctor is free to allow the child to die because the parents object to the child being enabled to live. Consider the case of a young child who is in a doctor's care in hospital, but who has a club-foot, or is a spastic. If the child's diseased appendix bursts, and the child's life is in immediate peril, the parents' wish that the child be allowed to die would not release the doctor from his obligation to his patient. There is little danger of a judge or jury adopting the view that in this circumstance some reasonable doctors would let the child die.

But what of the child who is severely handicapped?[64] If the parents' objections will not release a doctor from an obligation he would otherwise be under, to save the life of a mildly handicapped child, will they nevertheless be decisive if the child's handicap can be regarded as severe? The issue here is not whether a doctor is ever free to omit to prolong the life of a severely handicapped child. There is every reason to believe that there are circumstances in which he may omit to do so.[65] The issue is whether the parents' objections release a doctor from any duty he would otherwise be under, to save the child's life.[66]

Many doctors are of the opinion that if a child—at any rate, a newly-born child—is severely handicapped, a doctor should not prolong the child's life if the parents do not wish the child to be kept alive.[67] This approach is open to criticism.

[64] See generally J. A. Robertson, 'Involuntary Euthanasia of Defective Newborns: A Legal Analysis' (1975) 27 *Stanford Law Review* 213–69.

[65] See category 1, above. To give one extreme example, it is agreed that if a child is born an anencephalic a doctor is not obliged to take steps to keep the child alive.

[66] Liability for omissions was barely discussed in *R.* v. *Arthur* (see n. 8, above). Furthermore the defence submitted that there was no intention to accelerate death. (For a convincing critique of the view that the course of conduct which gave rise to that case should not be regarded as an attempt to hasten death, but simply as a holding operation, see *REGINA* v. *ARTHUR: A verdict on the Judge's summing-up in the trial of Dr. Leonard Arthur, November 1981* (LIFE, 1982), pp. [7]-[12].)

[67] British Medical Association, *Handbook of Medical Ethics* (rev. edn., 1981), 32; 'Management of Handicapped Babies' (1981) 282 *Br. Med. J.* 1001 (Statement by President of British Paediatric Association); 'Comments arising from Court of Appeal Decision on Baby with Down's Syndrome' (1981) 283 *Br. Med. J.* 567. See also T. McKeown, Letter to the Editor, *The Times*, 17 August 1981; but see H. C. McLaren, Letter to the Editor, *The Times*, 22 August 1981.

A doctor's primary obligation is to the child, not to the parents.[68] Parents may act for good, bad, or mixed motives, and even where their motives are above suspicion their judgment should not be beyond question.[69]

It is undesirable that the parents' wishes should be regarded —in isolation from all other factors—as a substantial or conclusive reason for omitting to save the patient's life, in cases where, but for those wishes, any reasonable doctor would have enabled his patient to live.[70] But if a doctor was prosecuted for allowing a severely handicapped child to die in these circumstances, prominent members of the medical profession would almost certainly give evidence in his favour. In practice, most judges would then be very loath to say anything that would encourage a jury to take the view that the doctor behaved in a way in which no reasonable doctor would behave. Furthermore, whatever the content of the judge's summing-up, it is most unlikely that a jury would convict a doctor in these circumstances. The division of opinion on this issue is such that it is highly unlikely that any jury would reach a unanimous, or even a sufficient majority, verdict, in a trial involving a doctor who complied with parental wishes by omitting to save the life of a newly-born but severely handicapped child.

However, if a doctor omitted to perform a simple life-saving operation on an older severely handicapped child, simply because his parents did not wish him to live, a jury might adopt the view that the child's doctor had omitted to do what any reasonable doctor would do in the circumstances.

[68] Cf. Ormrod, 'Ethics', 29–30 ('Physicians . . . should consider the quality of life they are able to preserve and the consequences of interfering with the natural progress of life towards its end. But the responsibility is theirs and theirs alone. It cannot be shared with relatives, although in appropriate cases it may be explained to them or discussed in general terms.'). See also Lord Edmund-Davies, reported in the *Guardian*, 6 November 1981, p. 10 ('It is not the Law of the land that doctors may decide to shorten a life by a single day. It is not the right of parents to determine the matter. They may make martyrs of themselves; they cannot make martyrs of their children.').

[69] Cf. *Re B. (A Minor)* [1981] 1 W.L.R. 1421.

[70] Nor should it be assumed that life in an institution is 'intolerable', and a fate worse than death. But see generally Glanville Williams, 'Down's Syndrome and the Doctor's Responsibility' (1981) 131 *New L.J.* 1040–1.

8

THE TERMINATION OF
ARTIFICIAL VENTILATION

The victim died on October 8, 1979, when, in view
of the fact that he was virtually already dead, the
breathing machine on which he had been placed on
October 5 was finally switched off.

Lord Hailsham L.C., 1981[1]

The issue to be considered in this chapter is whether there is
any way in which an English court could avoid the conclusion that a doctor would be guilty of murder if, knowing that
death would ensue, he turned off[2] an artificial ventilator in
circumstances in which it was widely regarded as good
medical practice to do so.[3]

In numerical terms, the issue is much less significant than
it was a decade or more ago. Then, as now, doctors sometimes
terminated artificial ventilation once it was established that a
patient's brain had irreversibly ceased to function.[4] Death

---

[1] *R.* v. *Cunningham* [1982] A.C. 566, 573.

[2] 'Turning off' a ventilator is not the only way of stopping artificial ventilation. The expression will be used in this chapter to refer to anything a doctor may
do to terminate artificial ventilation. Except where the context requires otherwise,
'terminate' and 'withdraw' will be used to refer to the permanent termination or
withdrawal of artificial ventilation.

[3] For the view that in English law such conduct amounts to murder, see D. W.
Elliott, 'When is the Moment of Death?' (1964) 4 *Med. Sci. Law* 77, 78. See also
Zelman Cowen, 'Organ Transplantation—The Legal Issues' (1969) 6 *University
of Queensland Law Journal* (2), 3, 9; L. Kushnir, 'Bridging the Gap: The Dis-
crepancy Between the Medical and Legal Definitions of Death' (1976) 34 *University of Toronto Faculty of Law Review* 199, 209.

[4] See e.g. R. Y. Calne, *Renal Transplantation* (2nd edn., 1967), 152 ('In cases
with cerebral damage who have been managed with a tracheostomy and artificial
respiration, if there is no evidence of brain recovery, after a given period of time,
it is customary to disconnect the machine and allow the patient to die.'); W. S.
Peart, Letter to the Editor, *The Times*, 3 June 1969 ('Doctors regularly turn off
respirators which are maintaining patients who have a normal heartbeat. They do
this because they have arrived at a decision that conscious life is no longer possible
with the condition present. . . . Since there is no spontaneous respiration . . . the
heart will then stop beating . . . and death follows.'). See also M. F. A. Woodruff,

was certified as having occurred after ventilation had ceased and the heart had stopped beating. Nowadays, however, such patients are commonly regarded as having died before artificial ventilation has been terminated and the heart has stopped beating. In these cases, doctors now speak of 'ceasing to ventilate a corpse', rather than of 'allowing the patient to die'. Were a doctor to be prosecuted for terminating artificial ventilation in such circumstances, it would now be open to an English court to accept that the patient was already dead. There would no longer be any need to consider whether there was some other way of avoiding the conclusion that the doctor's conduct was a cause of death, for the purpose of the law of homicide.[5]

Even if there were not at present any circumstances in which it could be regarded as good medical practice to terminate artificial ventilation, with the knowledge that this would hasten death, there might be such circumstances in the future. It would therefore be as well to consider whether there were any means by which the courts could avoid the conclusion that such conduct amounted to murder. But there are already, in fact, circumstances in which some doctors do terminate the artificial ventilation of still-living patients, although they know that the patients are likely to die earlier than they would if artificial ventilation were continued. The artificial ventilation of severely handicapped brain-damaged neonates, for example, is sometimes terminated irrespective of any determination of brain death.[6] In some cases, after surgery for the resection of a considerable length of infarcted bowel, a patient fails to establish adequate spontaneous respiration. The patient will be put on a ventilator, but sometimes the patient's condition will deteriorate, with multiple organ failure and metabolic

'Advances in Transplantation Surgery' (1968) 201 *Practitioner* 676, 678; D. L. Crosby, Letter, 'Determination of Death' [1970] 1 *Lancet* 1287–8; Editorial, 'Donors for Organ Grafting' [1972] 1 *Br. Med. J.* 582; J. D. Briggs and D. N. H. Hamilton, 'Kidney Transplantation' (1976) 34 *Health Bulletin* 192, 195; D. W. Evans and L. C. Lum, Letter, 'Brain Death' [1980] 2 *Lancet* 1022.

[5] For a fuller account of the developments outlined in this paragraph, see pp. 190–8.

[6] R. O. Robinson, 'Brain Death in Children' (1981) 56 *Archives of Disease in Childhood* 657, 658.

derangement. If it becomes apparent that the patient will not survive long in any event, some doctors terminate artificial ventilation, rather than prolong the process of dying.[7] Patients whose brain-stem function has not irreversibly ceased, but who are in an irreversible non-cognitive condition, are usually able to breathe spontaneously. But there is widespread agreement that, if such a patient is unable to breathe spontaneously,[8] a doctor should not be obliged to provide, or continue with, artificial ventilation.[9]

If a doctor terminated artificial ventilation in circumstances in which it could be regarded as good medical practice to do so, it is highly unlikely that he would be prosecuted for murder, or for any other criminal offence.[10] It is even more unlikely that a jury would convict the doctor, whatever the judge said in the course of his summing-up. Nevertheless, it is desirable to ascertain whether, in the absence of statutory reform, a judge could avoid directing the jury that a doctor would always be guilty of murder if he turned off an artificial ventilator, knowing that the patient was likely to die earlier than if artificial ventilation had been continued.

If a doctor knows that his conduct will hasten the patient's death, he has the fault element for murder.[11] To avoid the conclusion that the doctor was guilty of murder it would

[7] This example was given by Dr John Searle, in the course of a discussion with John Guille, published under the title 'To Care Intensively?' in *Nucleus*, July 1978, pp. 22-5. Dr Searle said of this case, 'If we conclude that there is no reasonable chance that the patient will survive, intensive care medicine is withdrawn. This may involve turning off the ventilator or sometimes simply ventilating the patient on air instead of an air-oxygen mixture.'

[8] The litigation concerning Karen Quinlan was conducted in the belief that she was in this condition. See *In the Matter of Karen Quinlan* (1976) 355 A. 2d 647, esp. 653-6 (N.J.).

[9] This was evident from the widespread discussion of the case of Karen Quinlan. See e.g. Editorial, *The Times*, 2 April 1976.

[10] There do not appear to have been any such prosecutions in England, or in common law jurisdictions elsewhere in the Commonwealth.

[11] For an account of the fault element of murder, see Smith and Hogan, 285-91; Williams, *Textbook*, 208-17, and see also pp. 122-6, above. A doctor who turns off a ventilator which is maintaining a ventilator-dependent patient would by no means always have the fault element for murder. He may believe that the patient will now be able to breathe spontaneously. (For an argument that morally a doctor who withdraws artificial ventilation may not intend to hasten death, even though he believes that this will be the consequence, see [A. J. L. Gormally], 'Is there a morally significant difference between killing and letting die?', *Linacre Papers* (No. 2, 1978), pp. 13-14.)

therefore be necessary to demonstrate that the doctor's conduct was not to be regarded as a cause of death, for the purpose of the law of homicide, or that there was some defence available to the doctor. There is no established defence which clearly applies to such conduct, and most judges would be extremely reluctant to recognize a new defence to what could be regarded as intentional killing. They would probably be less reluctant to manipulate the law concerning causation, in order to achieve a desired result.

Before examining the ways in which judges might be able to avoid the conclusion that a doctor would always be guilty of murder if he turned off an artificial ventilator, with the knowledge that death would ensue, two preliminary points should be made. One is that there are circumstances in which a doctor would undoubtedly be guilty of murder if he turned off a ventilator, knowing that death would ensue. He would certainly be guilty of murder if the patient had respiratory difficulties following an allergic reaction, and the doctor knew that the patient wished to go on living, and was likely to make a full recovery. The second preliminary point is that no special difficulties would arise if a doctor simply omitted to do something to enable artificial ventilation to continue. If he omitted to do something, his omission would not be regarded as a cause of death unless he was under a legal duty to continue to provide artificial ventilation.[12] For the lawyer, the special problem that arises when a doctor turns off a ventilator which is maintaining a ventilator-dependent patient is that the doctor's conduct could be regarded as an act hastening death.

In many cases a doctor will terminate artificial ventilation to see whether the patient is now able to breathe spontaneously. He will not believe that his conduct will probably hasten death. If the patient is still unable to breathe satisfactorily, but is not brain dead, the doctor would often be under a legal duty to recommence artificial ventilation.[13] If he omitted to

[12] See ch. 7, esp. pp. 142-3.

[13] If the patient was still alive, but the doctor was not under any duty to recommence artificial ventilation, the law would not take cognizance of his omission. But in that event the question would arise whether his conduct in turning off the ventilator was a cause of death. Much of the discussion in this chapter would apply to that situation, which also raises issues about the fault element for

restore artificial ventilation, when under a duty to do so, his omission would count as a cause of death, for the purpose of the law of homicide. This chapter is directed towards the exceptional case where, at the time the doctor turns off the ventilator, he is aware that the patient will die earlier than he would if artificial ventilation were continued.

I ACT CAUSING DEATH?

If a doctor turned off a ventilator which was maintaining a ventilator-dependent patient, in circumstances in which it could be regarded as a good medical practice to do so, there are two ways in which a court might be able to avoid the conclusion that the doctor's conduct was a cause of death, for the purpose of the law of homicide. One would be to accept that the doctor's conduct in terminating artificial ventilation was an act, but to deny that it was for legal purposes a cause of death. The other would be to regard the doctor's conduct as an omission to provide further artificial ventilation, rather than as an act hastening death. If in the circumstances there was no duty to provide further artificial ventilation, the doctor's conduct would not count in law as a cause of death.

If a doctor terminates the artificial ventilation of a ventilator-dependent patient, his conduct is on the face of it an act which causes death to occur at the time when it does. If it is an act, it is certainly a 'but for' cause. But would it have to be regarded as an imputable cause?[14] Sometimes any acceleration of death would be so trifling that it could be disregarded under the *de minimis* principle. In other cases a more general doctrine would be required. One possibility is suggested by Lord Devlin's statement that 'proper medical treatment consequent upon illness or injury plays no part in legal causation'.[15] This principle is consistent with the well-established principle that if death results from proper medical

murder (some of which are discussed in ch. 6). Cf. Ian Kennedy, *Unmasking of Medicine* (1981), 157–8.

[14] See p. 122, above.

[15] Devlin, *Samples*, 95. The application of this principle to the administration of pain-relieving drugs is discussed at pp. 135–8, above.

treatment necessitated by an injury, the person responsible for the injury can be held to have caused the death.[16] Of course the termination of artificial ventilation is not on a par with the relief of 'the pains of death', which was what Lord Devlin was discussing when he stated that proper medical treatment plays no part in legal causation. Although the relief of 'the pains of death' and the termination of artificial ventilation have both led to patients dying earlier than they would otherwise have done, the former can more easily be described as medical treatment. However, there is no need to treat Lord Devlin's formulation as if it were a statute. If it were broadened very slightly, so that for 'proper medical treatment' one substituted 'medical practice considered proper in the circumstances' it would provide a principle that could be applied to the termination of artificial ventilation. In many circumstances it would undoubtedly be improper to terminate artificial ventilation, and if a doctor did so his conduct would be regarded as a cause of death. But if the doctor terminated artificial ventilation in circumstances in which the court accepted that it was proper to do so, the doctor's conduct would not be regarded as a cause of death.

In the past decade there have been several occasions on which courts have accepted that doctors have acted properly in terminating the artificial ventilation of severely brain-damaged patients, whom the judges assumed were still alive when artificial ventilation was terminated. The cases involved the prosecution of persons whose conduct led to the patients being in a ventilator-dependent state. In the Scottish case of *Finlayson* v. *H.M. Advocate*[17] the Lord Justice-General (Emslie) stated that it 'certainly cannot be said that the act of disconnecting the machine was an unwarrantable act'. He held that it did not break the chain of causation.[18] In *R.* v. *Malcherek*, *R.* v. *Steel*[19] the English Court of Appeal (Criminal Division) also held that the discontinuance of treatment did not break the chain of causation between the

---

[16] See *R.* v. *Jordan* (1956) 40 Cr. App. R. 152, 157; *R.* v. *Smith* [1959] 2 Q.B. 35, 42–3; and also *R.* v. *Evans and Gardiner (No. 2)* [1976] V.R. 523.

[17] *Finlayson* v. *H.M. Advocate* [1978] S.L.T. (Notes) 60.

[18] Ibid. 61.

[19] [1981] 1 W.L.R. 690.

initial injuries and the deaths.[20] The judgment of the court, which was delivered by Lord Lane C.J., continued:[21]

Although it is unnecessary to go further than that for the purpose of deciding the present point, we wish to add this thought. Whatever the strict logic of the matter may be, it is perhaps somewhat bizarre to suggest, as counsel have impliedly done, that where a doctor tries his conscientious best to save the life of a patient brought to hospital in extremis, skilfully using sophisticated methods, drugs and machinery to do so, but fails in his attempt and therefore discontinues treatment, he can be said to have caused the death of the patient.

The unwillingness to regard the doctor's conduct as a cause of death is of interest in this context. One way of avoiding the conclusion that the doctor's conduct was a cause of death would be to accept the principle that a medical practice considered proper in the circumstances plays no part in legal causation.

This principle, however, is open to more than one criticism.[22] One is that it fudges the issues, that it is a matter of 'playing with language'.[23] But it is not unusual for the courts to manipulate the concept of causation to achieve a desired result, and a willingness to do so would be preferable to holding a doctor guilty of murder if he terminated artificial ventilation in circumstances in which he would have been free to have omitted to continue it. If a judge is unable or unwilling to provide a justification for what could be considered an intentional killing, yet does not wish to see the conduct regarded as murder, the possibility of his achieving the desired end by manipulating principles relating to causation should not be ruled out—as Devlin J.'s direction to the jury in *R.* v. *Adams*[24] demonstrates.

A second objection to acceptance of the principle that a proper medical practice plays no part in legal causation is that such a principle might be applied in other contexts to

---

[20] See also *R.* v. *Kitching and Adams* [1976] 6 W.W.R. 697, esp. 714–15 (Man. C.A.).

[21] [1981] 1 W.L.R. 697.

[22] See Roger Leng, Note, 'Death and the Criminal Law' (1982) 45 *M.L.R.* 206, 208.

[23] Cf. Williams, *Textbook*, Suppl. (1979), p. [9].

[24] *The Times*, 9 April 1957; Williams, *Sanctity*, 289; discussed on pp. 135–8, above.

enable doctors to bring about deaths in circumstances that would not meet with widespread approval. It might, it could be objected, enable doctors to pursue a programme of active euthanasia of handicapped children or geriatric patients. Medical opinion about the termination of life in these contexts might change in the future, just as it has done in the recent past in relation to abortion. Although the courts would be the final arbiter of whether a particular practice was a proper one, they might prove unwilling or incompetent to exercise an independent judgment about the propriety of a particular practice. Doctors might then be free to bring about the death of patients in circumstances which would not meet with general approval. There would be no need for a statute on the subject: as a result of manipulation of the concept of causation, the doctor's conduct would not be regarded as a cause of death, so there would be nothing which required legal justification.

The fact that acceptance of a principle might have unacceptable repercussions is not necessarily a reason for rejecting it. Much depends upon the likelihood of the unacceptable repercussions developing, and whether there are other ways of achieving the desired objective. English judges would be likely to be cautious about invoking the principle that a medical practice considered proper in the circumstances plays no part in legal causation. It is unlikely, for example, that judges would seek to manipulate the concept of causation in order to give effect to their views on 'mercy killing'. They would accept that this is a matter about which, as Lord Devlin has said, 'It could not give satisfaction to the public if a solution were to be found by the use of the blunt instrument of a decision in a particular case, which depended on the composition of the court.'[25] The controversial issue of 'mercy killing' is in striking contrast with some instances of the termination of artificial ventilation. It has been widely accepted that doctors may properly terminate the artificial ventilation of severely brain-damaged ventilator-dependent patients. Many of these patients can now be regarded as dead before artificial ventilation is finally terminated, but a similar

[25] Lord Devlin, *The Judge* (1979), 10.

consensus may develop about the propriety of terminating artificial ventilation in other circumstances, if it has not already done so. Where there is such a consensus, a decision in a particular case could 'give satisfaction'.

It is possible to exaggerate the danger of adopting the principle that a medical practice considered proper in the circumstances plays no part in legal causation.[26] Nevertheless, it is sufficiently serious to encourage a search for other ways of avoiding the conclusion that a doctor would always be guilty of murder in withdrawing artificial ventilation from a patient whom he knew to be dependent upon it.

II AN OMISSION?

Another way of avoiding the conclusion that a doctor would always be guilty of murder, in terminating the artificial ventilation of a patient whom he knew to be dependent upon it, would be to classify the doctor's conduct as an omission, rather than as an act.[27]

If a patient who is dependent on artificial ventilation is being moved from, say, one ward to another, artificial ventilation will often be provided by means of a self-inflating ambu bag, which the doctor squeezes at the same rate as normal breathing and thereby forces air into the patient's lungs.[28] If a doctor stops squeezing the bag, and hence ventilating the patient, his conduct would undoubtedly be regarded as an omission—just as it would be if he had been providing mouth-to-mouth resuscitation and stopped doing so. Being an omission, the doctor's conduct would only count in law as a cause of death where there was a duty to continue to provide

[26] The danger could be reduced if, when accepting the principle, the courts specified the circumstances in which it would apply. Two circumstances where the principle might work satisfactorily are the administration of pain-relieving drugs to patients whose deaths are already imminent, and the withdrawal of life-support measures from patients who have no prospect of a return to consciousness.

[27] This approach was criticized by I. M. Kennedy, 'Switching Off Life Support Machines: The Legal Implications' [1977] *Crim. L.R.* 443, 444–5. But see the reply by Professor Glanville Williams, Letter, 'Switching Off Life Support Machines' [1977] *Crim. L.R.* 635. See also Helen Benyon, 'Doctors as Murderers' [1982] *Crim. L.R.* 17, 19–23, esp. 20–1.

[28] See also M. G. Harries, 'Mechanical Aids to Ventilation for Use in the Field' [1979] 2 *Br. Med. J.* 426, 427.

artificial ventilation in these circumstances. Where there was no such duty, the law of homicide would not take cognizance of his omission.

If mechanical ventilators were equipped with a device which would automatically switch off the ventilator after twelve hours, if it were not reset for another twelve, it would rarely be necessary to turn off a ventilator. The question therefore arises whether, in the absence of so simple a device, the courts are obliged to regard the withdrawal of artificial ventilation as an act, rather than as an omission—and therefore to adopt a different analysis from that which would be appropriate if a doctor ceased squeezing an ambu bag, or omitted to replace a gas cylinder on a gas-powered ventilator.[29]

If the presence or absence of a relevant muscular contraction always determined whether conduct was to be regarded as an act,[30] there would be no point in exploring the possibility of a doctor's conduct in turning off a ventilator being regarded as an omission, for legal purposes. But the physical movement test is not always conclusive. There are circumstances in which conduct is commonly classified as an omission, even though it involves some willed muscular contraction. For example, a doctor is not regarded as committing an act causing death if he writes 'Nursing care only' on his patient's chart, or instructs a nurse to desist from any attempt to resuscitate a severely brain-damaged child, although the child's life could otherwise have been prolonged. The doctor's conduct is regarded, as a whole, as an omission to provide such means.[31] This being so, it would only constitute a cause of death, for the purpose of the law of homicide, if there was a duty to provide treatment, or resuscitation, in the circumstances in question.

In the unlikely event of a doctor being prosecuted for terminating artificial ventilation, in circumstances in which it

[29] For an account of such a ventilator, see A. R. Aitkenhead, M. I. Willis, and W. H. Barnes, 'An Economical Mobile Intensive Care Unit' (1980) 280 *Br. Med. J.* 1219-21.

[30] See O. W. Holmes, *The Common Law* (1882), 54.

[31] A striking feature of the debate about *R.* v. *Arthur* (1981) (p. 129, n. 30, and generally chs. 6, 7) was the virtually unquestioned acceptance of the view that, even if a doctor has instructed nurses not to take action to prolong life, his conduct is to be analysed as an omission, rather than as an act.

could be regarded as good medical practice to do so, a judge
might simply leave the jury to decide, virtually unaided,
whether the doctor's conduct should be regarded as an act
causing death, or as an omission to prolong life. He might
follow the example of Farquharson J. who said, in the course
of his summing-up in *R. v. Arthur*:[32]

> it has become very clear, you may think, that it is a very difficult area
> to decide precisely where a doctor is doing an act, a positive act, or
> allowing a course of events or a set of circumstances to ensue, and
> really this awful problem is now being placed on your shoulders.

But a judge might wish to give the jury some guidance on
how the distinction between acts and omissions should be
drawn in this context. It is therefore appropriate to examine
two approaches which have been suggested. Neither is entirely
satisfactory in its original form; but both could be developed
to provide a test which would enable a jury to conclude that,
in at least some cases, a doctor's conduct in terminating
artificial ventilation is to be regarded as an omission, rather
than as an act.

One approach

It was Professor G. P. Fletcher who first proposed that a
doctor's conduct in turning off a ventilator could sometimes
be regarded as an omission, with the consequence that the
doctor responsible for the patient would not incur liability
in homicide when he was not under a duty to provide artificial ventilation.[33]

Fletcher's approach gave considerable weight to current
linguistic usage.[34] He sought to build on the popular distinction

---

[32] Transcript, 17C-D. But see also ibid. 19-20, where Farquharson J. did
imply that the doctor's conduct 'in setting out that course of management,
prescribing that drug' did not necessarily have to be regarded as 'in the nature
of a positive act'.

[33] G. P. Fletcher, 'Prolonging Life' (1967) 42 *Washington Law Review* 999–
1016, reprinted in slightly abbreviated and amended form as 'Prolonging Life:
Some Legal Considerations' in *Euthanasia and the Right to Death* (1969, ed. A. B.
Downing), 71-84. (It is the later, revised version that will be cited in this chapter.)
See also G. P. Fletcher, 'Legal Aspects of the Decision Not to Prolong Life'
(1968) 203 *J.A.M.A.* 65-8.

[34] The past tense is adopted in this account of Professor Fletcher's views, for
he proposed a different approach in his *Rethinking Criminal Law* (1978), ch. 8,

between causing and permitting death. He recognized that some omissions may be said to cause death, so the distinction between causing and permitting death could not serve as the basis of a distinction between acts and omissions. But he suggested that 'permitting harm to occur should be sufficient for classification as an omission'.[35]

Fletcher asked 'Is turning off the respirator an instance of causing death or permitting death to occur?' and gave this answer:[36]

If the patient is beyond recovery and on the verge of death, one balks at saying that the activity causes death. It is far more natural to speak of the case as one of permitting death to occur. It is significant that we are inclined to refer to the respirator as a means for prolonging life; we would not speak of insulin shots for a diabetic in the same way. The use of the term 'prolongation of life' builds on the same perception of reality that prompts us to say that turning off the respirator is an activity permitting death to occur, rather than causing death. And that basic perception is that using the respirator interferes artificially in the pattern of events.

He went on to say:

Of course, the perception of the natural and of the artificial is a function of time and culture. What may seem artificial today, may be a matter of course in ten years. Nonetheless, one *does* perceive many uses of the respirator today as artificial prolongations of life. And that perception of artificiality should be enough to determine the legal classification of the case. Because we are prompted to refer to the activity of turning off the respirator as activity permitting death to occur, rather than causing death, we may classify the case as an omission, rather than as an act.

Fletcher's reliance on a distinction between 'natural' and

esp. 606-10, 622-5. He there suggests that the distinction between acts and omissions should be replaced by a distinction between killing and letting die. This is not simply a reformulation of the traditional distinction; his category of 'killing' includes some omissions. But the distinction between acts and omissions is so fundamental to the English law of homicide that it would not be open to a court to replace it with another distinction. Fletcher's original attempt to work within the traditional categories is therefore of more importance, for the purpose of this discussion, than his subsequent proposal for their replacement by new categories.

[35] G. P. Fletcher, 'Prolonging Life: Some Legal Considerations', op. cit., 82. For a fuller account of the steps by which Fletcher reached that conclusion, and a critique thereof, see P. D. G. Skegg, 'The Termination of Life-Support Measures and the Law of Murder' (1978) 41 *M.L.R.* 423, 428-9.

[36] G. P. Fletcher, 'Prolonging Life: Some Legal Considerations', op. cit., 77 (his emphasis). See also P. D. G. Skegg, op. cit., 429 n. 34.

'artificial' was unsatisfactory,[37] but his distinction between causing and permitting death could stand independently of that distinction.

Fletcher chose an easy example for himself when he wrote that if the patient was beyond recovery and on the verge of death 'one balks at saying that the activity causes death.' He used this example as the starting-point of his argument which led to the conclusion that 'Because we are prompted to refer to the activity of turning off the respirator as activity permitting death to occur, rather than causing death, we may classify the case as an omission rather than as an act.' It is possible to provide other instances where the termination of artificial ventilation would normally be described as causing death to occur, rather than simply permitting death. Such a description would be natural if someone turned off a ventilator which had maintained a fully conscious and reasonably healthy poliomyelitis patient for several years, and could have continued to do so for years to come.

Fletcher recognized that attitudes, and hence classification, could change. However, he did not take account of the fact that the termination of artificial ventilation might be classified differently according to the medical condition of the person being ventilated. This is not the only complication that he overlooked. Usage may vary according to who it is that turns off the ventilator. Even where it is accepted that it would be natural to describe the conduct of a doctor who terminated artificial ventilation as 'permitting death', it does not follow that such language would be used if the patient's ventilator was switched off by a relative who stood to gain financially if the patient died sooner rather than later. But, as will become apparent later in this chapter, the fact that a relative's conduct might be classified as an act, when a doctor's conduct would be classified as an omission, could prove to be an advantage of this approach.

There is not simply the complication that the same conduct

---

[37] The provision of artificial ventilation 'interferes artificially in the pattern of events' whether the patient is conscious or unconscious, and whether the dependence upon artificial ventilation is temporary or permanent. The administration of insulin to a diabetic can also be regarded as interfering artificially in the pattern of events.

can be described differently depending upon the condition of
the patient being ventilated, or who it is that turns off the
ventilator. There is the further complication that sometimes
the same conduct can be described perfectly naturally in
terms of either permitting or causing death. Even where a
doctor turned off a ventilator which was maintaining a patient
who was 'beyond recovery and on the verge of death', many
people might consider it perfectly natural to say that the
doctor's conduct caused death to occur at the time when it
did. However it would be possible to retain Fletcher's emphasis
on linguistic usage, while recognizing the existence of cases
which can be described as permitting or causing death. For
although many cases of permitting death can also be described
as in some sense causing death, there are many cases of causing death which would not be described as permitting death.
There is a comparatively restricted category of cases where a
person may be said to have permitted death to occur. Many
of these would undoubtedly be considered omissions. The
others are very closely analogous, and could be treated as
omissions by adopting the rule that, where it is natural to say
that a person has permitted something to occur, his conduct
in so doing should be considered an omission, for the purpose
of the law of homicide. It would be irrelevant that the conduct could also be described as causing death.

Nowadays it is more usual to distinguish between killing
and letting die than between causing and permitting death.[38]
The test can easily be re-expressed in these terms. As re-
formulated, the test would be that, where it is natural to say
that a person has let someone die, his conduct should be
regarded as an omission for the purpose of the law of
homicide. Where the doctor was under a duty to continue
with artificial ventilation, his omission would therefore be a
cause of death. But where he was not under a duty to continue to provide artificial ventilation, the law of homicide
would not take account of his conduct. Whatever his state of
mind, the doctor could not be held to have committed
murder, or manslaughter.

Even if judges were persuaded that this test would at

[38] Cf. G. P. Fletcher, *Rethinking Criminal Law*, 610.

present work satisfactorily, they might be reluctant to adopt a test the future application of which could be affected by fortuitous changes in linguistic usage. It can, of course, be argued that if the distinction became of legal significance there would be more discussion about it, and this discussion might affect the way in which the terms were used in the future.[39] If there was no better way of avoiding the conclusion that a doctor would be guilty of murder if he terminated artificial ventilation, in circumstances where there was widespread agreement that he should be free to do so, the uncertainty about future usage should not dissuade a court from adopting this approach. But it is as well to consider other ways of dealing with the problem.

Another approach

It is not only by invoking a distinction between causing and permitting death, or between killing and letting die, that the withdrawal of artificial ventilation could sometimes be classified as an omission, rather than as an act.[40] As Professor Glanville Williams has written:[41]

Giving up trying to keep a patient alive may involve something other than literal inaction. It may involve telling the sister in charge to discontinue certain treatment. It may involve moving the patient from one ward to another, or from hospital to home. It may involve disconnecting

---

[39] In *Rethinking Criminal Law*, 610, Fletcher recognizes that 'some people might object to relying upon our intuitions or on our sense for English usage in working out important legal distinctions'. But he goes on to say 'it is not clear that we have any choice', and expresses the hope that 'in a community of theorists thinking and discussing these problems, we could minimize the personal idiosyncrasies in a consensus about the distinction that are critical in our system of criminal law'. But it would be a mistake to underrate the difficulty of this task at a time when the distinction is under attack from various quarters. See e.g. Jonathan Glover, *Causing Death and Saving Lives* (1977), ch. 7; John Harris, *Violence and Responsibility* (1980) (but see [A. J. L. Gormally], 'Is there a morally significant difference between killing and letting die?', *Linacre Papers* (No. 2, 1978), esp. 15–16; John Finnis, *Natural Law and Natural Rights* (1980), 195).

[40] '[T]he act/omission distinction does not rest upon what is done, or upon a concept of willed muscular contraction, but upon the impact of what is done on the victim': Roger Leng, Note, 'Death and the Criminal Law' (1982) 45 *M.L.R.* 206, 208–9. For a very tentative (and extraordinary) proposal, see Helen Benyon, 'Doctors as Murderers' [1982] *Crim. L.R.* 17, 23.

[41] Glanville Williams, 'Euthanasia' (1973) 41 *Med.-Leg. J.* 14, 20–1. See also Williams, *Textbook*, 236–7.

the mechanical respirator that is keeping the patient alive. If an 'act' is defined as a willed movement (including a movement of the vocal organs), all these are acts; but they need not be regarded as acts for the purpose of the moral and legal rule, because in substance they merely put into effect a decision to take no further steps. The moral and legal rule, which distinguishes between acts and omissions, must be interpreted in accordance with the substance of the matter.

In the case of artificial ventilation, the difference between the doctor responsible for the patient choosing not to replace a cylinder of gas on a gas-powered ventilator, or turning off the supply of electricity on a standard ventilator is, at most, minimal.[42] In both cases, the ethically important question is whether artificial ventilation should be continued. If the courts treated the doctor's conduct in turning off the ventilator as an omission, they could focus on the ethically important question of whether there was a duty to provide artificial ventilation. By treating the withdrawal of artificial ventilation in the same way as the withholding of further artificial ventilation, they could avoid putting asunder what common sense would place together.

This approach has much to commend it. But it has one drawback, which might make judges cautious about accepting it. For, although it would work satisfactorily where there was an appropriate duty-relationship between the patient and person who turns off the ventilator, it could lead to difficulties where there was no duty-relationship, recognized by the law of homicide. Take the example of someone who had a business competitor who was temporarily dependent on artificial ventilation. If the termination of artificial ventilation is to be regarded as an omission he would not commit murder if he switched off his rival's ventilator, with the intention that the rival should die. He would clearly have a murderous intent, but if his conduct were regarded as an omission it would not count in law as a cause of death, for he was not under a duty to provide artificial ventilation.[43]

Professor Glanville Williams has responded to criticism along these lines with the comment that:[44]

[42] Cf. ibid. 21 and 237, respectively.
[43] Cf. *R.* v. *Miller* [1983] 2 W.L.R. 539, [1983] 1 All E.R. 978 (H.L.) ('act', followed by omission to prevent or minimize resultant damage to property).
[44] Williams, *Textbook*, Suppl. (1979), p. [9]. The criticism had appeared in

from the practical point of view this is not a serious objection. Nurses would be under the same kind of duty as the doctor. The intervention of an unauthorised intruder is most improbable. If it be the case that the patient is beyond hope, there is no great social need to regard the intervention as murder anyway.

The intervention of an unauthorized intruder is certainly 'most improbable', and it would still be far from probable if it were known that outsiders would not incur criminal liability if they disconnected a ventilator.[45] Nevertheless, a judge might be reluctant to accede to a submission that a doctor's conduct should be regarded as an omission if the consequence of that view would be that intruders, however unlikely, would not incur criminal liability if they disconnected any of the ventilators which are, at any one time, maintaining hundreds of ventilator-dependent patients in this country.[46] Furthermore, even if it were conceded that 'If it be the case that the patient is beyond hope, there is no great social need to regard the intervention as murder anyway', a judge might not overlook the fact that a substantial proportion of those on artificial ventilation are only temporarily dependent upon it, and will in due course recover.[47]

It is possible to modify this approach to meet the objection about the intervention of an intruder. The withdrawal of artificial ventilation could be regarded as an omission where there was a duty-relationship between the parties, recognized by the law of homicide, but as an act where there was no duty-relationship.[48] Where artificial ventilation was withdrawn

P. D. G. Skegg, 'The Termination of Life-Support Measures and the Law of Murder' (1978) 41 *M.L.R.* 423, 432.

[45] Or if they turned off the supply of oxygen, while letting the ventilator continue.

[46] Intensive therapy units are closely monitored. However, some ventilators can now be used at home, where patients might be more vulnerable to unauthorized intruders.

[47] See e.g. J. F. Nunn, J. S. Milledge, and J. Singaraya, 'Survival of Patients Ventilated in an Intensive Therapy Unit' [1979] 1 *Br. Med. J.* 1525-7 (study of 100 consecutive patients who were artificially ventilated for more than four hours in the intensive therapy unit of a district general hospital: 67 survived treatment in the unit, 47 were discharged from hospital, and 30 survived for four years).

[48] I mentioned this as a possibility in an earlier article, but simply commented 'This would be open to the objection that it is undesirable that the same physical movements should be classified either as an act or as an omission, depending on who it was that switched off the ventilator.' (P. D. G. Skegg, op. cit., 432.) Professor

by a person who was under a duty of care in relation to the patient's treatment, or by someone acting at the direction of such a person, it could be regarded as an omission. Hence it would count as a cause of death if there was a duty to provide further artificial ventilation, but not if there was in the circumstances no such duty. However, where artificial ventilation was withdrawn by an outsider that person would deprive the patient of the aid he was receiving, and his intervention could be regarded as an act causing death.[49]

To classify the same physical conduct as an act or as an omission, depending upon whose conduct was involved, would not on the face of it be at all satisfactory. But any judicial reluctance to accept this approach, in this context, might be overcome by a consideration of other circumstances where the courts would probably classify a doctor's conduct as an omission, but an intruder's conduct as an act. Where a doctor responsible for the patient's care decides that, if the patient has another cardiac arrest, no steps should be taken to resuscitate him, the doctor may make the appropriate entry on the patient's chart.[50] When the patient does have another cardiac arrest and the nurses, following the doctor's instruction, omit to resuscitate him, it is sensible to analyse the entire course of conduct as an omission to resuscitate the patient. It would be undesirable to distinguish, in this context, between an act on the doctor's part and an omission on the nurse's part. The doctor's conduct should not be seen as

Glanville Williams did not mention the possibility in the original edition of his *Textbook*. But in the Supplement he noted the suggestion that a medical practice considered proper in the circumstances should not be regarded as a cause of death in contemplation of law, and wrote that 'if we are allowed to play with language in this way, it could equally well be said that the intruder who switches off the machine commits an act, while the doctor who does so merely omits to continue to treat.' (Williams, *Textbook*, Suppl. p. [9].) But see also Glanville Williams, Letter, 'Switching Off Life Support Machines' [1977] *Crim. L.R.* 635, where he does not rest his suggestion on this condition.

[49] Cf. I. M. Kennedy, 'Switching Off Life Support Machines: The Legal Implications' [1977] *Crim. L.R.* 443, 448 n. 19; G. P. Fletcher, *Rethinking Criminal Law*, 609–10; Williams, *Textbook*, Suppl. p. [9].

[50] Current practice in one hospital known to the author is to write 'No 222', 222 being the number dialled to call the emergency resuscitation team which would otherwise be summoned to attempt to resuscitate the patient. See generally Editorial, 'Cardiac Resuscitation in Hospital: More Restraint Needed?' [1982] 1 *Lancet* 27–8.

an act causing death, but as part of the overall omission to resuscitate the patient. Assuming the patient would have lived longer if resuscitation had been provided, the doctor's conduct should only be regarded as a cause of death, for the purpose of the law of homicide, if there was a duty to resuscitate the patient in these circumstances. But if an intruder gained access to the patient's chart and made the appropriate entry, in consequence of which the nurses omitted to resuscitate the patient, his conduct should be regarded as an act for the purpose of the law of homicide. If the patient would have lived longer had the intruder not made that entry, his act would undoubtedly count as a cause of death. Were it regarded as an omission, the law could not take cognizance of it unless the intruder was under a relevant 'homicide duty'—which would rarely be the case.

Similarly, it may be argued that it would be desirable for the courts to regard the withdrawal of artificial ventilation as an omission when done by someone who was a member of the medical team caring for the patient, but as an act when done by an intruder. This would enable a member of the medical team to terminate artificial ventilation, if in the circumstances there would not have been any duty to continue to provide it had the ventilator stopped of its own accord.

III A DEFENCE?

It is extremely unlikely that a doctor would be prosecuted for murder for turning off a ventilator, in circumstances in which it could be regarded as good medical practice to do so. If there were such a prosecution, a judge would be more likely to encourage a jury to take the view that the doctor's conduct was not in law a cause of death, than openly to provide a justification for an intentional killing.[51] Openly to provide a defence for an intentional killing of a patient would raise the broader issue of active euthanasia, a matter which most judges would be anxious to leave to Parliament.[52]

[51] The courts have often been very reluctant openly to admit a defence of necessity: see ch. 6, n. 66.
[52] See generally Lord Devlin, *The Judge* (1979), 10.

However, if a patient objected to further artificial ventilation, and its continuation would necessitate touchings which would then constitute a criminal offence,[53] a judge might accept that there was a legal justification for turning off the ventilator, even though the doctor knew that the patient would then die.[54] But in such a case it could be said that the termination of artificial ventilation was a proper medical practice, and also that there was no duty to continue to provide artificial ventilation. So if either of the approaches discussed above were adopted, the question of a justification would not arise. The doctor's conduct would not be regarded in law as a cause of death, so there would be nothing that required justification.

IV CONCLUSION

There are several ways by which the courts could avoid the conclusion that a doctor would always be guilty of murder if he terminated the artificial ventilation of a patient whom he knew to be dependent upon it. None of the ways discussed in this chapter is entirely satisfactory.[55] But a judge would be likely to adopt some such approach, rather than direct a jury that a doctor was guilty of murder if he terminated artificial ventilation when it was good medical practice to do so.

The matter discussed in this chapter provides a dilemma for lawyers, rather than for doctors. Doctors can be reassured by the fact that in recent years both the Lord Chancellor and the Lord Chief Justice have dealt with cases in which doctors terminated the artificial ventilation of ventilator-dependent patients, who their Lordships assumed were still alive when

[53] For an account of circumstances in which a doctor is free to proceed without consent, see ch. 5.

[54] Cf. Criminal Law Act 1967, s. 3(1) ('A person may use such force as is reasonable in the circumstances in the prevention of crime.'). A more extensive defence was proposed by I. M. Kennedy, op. cit., 449–51. (*Quaere*, the adequacy of the reasons adduced in support of it.) For another possible defence, which would apply only in very exceptional circumstances, see P. D. G. Skegg, op. cit., 435.

[55] One possible solution would be a statute providing that a doctor is justified in terminating his patient's treatment whenever he would be justified in withholding such treatment. See Note, 'Scarce Medical Resources' (1969) 69 *Columbia Law Review* 620, 627.

ventilation was terminated. Although the cases did not necessitate any consideration of the doctors' legal position, it is significant that the judgments did not contain the least hint of criticism of the practice of turning off ventilators which were maintaining very severely brain-damaged patients.[56]

In the overwhelmingly unlikely event of a doctor being prosecuted for terminating the artificial ventilation of such a patient, judges would be likely to develop, modify, refine, or even fudge, legal concepts, rather than direct the jury that the doctor was guilty of murder. In the almost unthinkable event of a judge directing the jury that the doctor was guilty of murder in such circumstances, the likelihood of a jury convicting the doctor would still be slight. The problem could then be overcome for the future by equipping ventilators with a device that would automatically switch off a ventilator after twelve hours if it were not reset for another twelve. Further artificial ventilation could then be withheld, and there would be no need for a doctor to do anything to terminate artificial ventilation.

[56] The termination of artificial ventilation was mentioned only in passing in the speech of Lord Hailsham L.C. in *R.* v. *Cunningham* [1982] A.C. 566, 573, but it was a central issue in the judgment that Lord Lane C.J. delivered in *R.* v. *Malcherek* [1981] 1 W.L.R. 690.

9

DEATH

Death, I suppose, may be a process rather than an
instantaneous event . . .

Viscount Simon L.C., 1945[1]

In the past the cessation of spontaneous respiration and
circulation rapidly resulted in the cessation of all brain function. Similarly the cessation of all brain function rapidly
led to the cessation of respiration and circulation. This being
so, it was entirely reasonable to use the absence of heartbeat and breathing as the criteria for determining that a
patient was dead.

In recent decades, however, advances in medical technology have made it possible to sustain brain function despite
the absence of spontaneous respiration and circulation.
Furthermore, it is now possible to maintain respiration and
circulation for a time even though the patient's brain is not
able to function again. Where only the higher regions of the
brain have ceased to function, spontaneous respiration and
circulation may continue for months or even years.

These developments have been followed by a reassessment
of the traditional criteria for distinguishing between human
life and death. One view that has found widespread support is
that an individual is dead if all the functions of his brain have
irreversibly ceased, even though his heart continues to beat
because artificial ventilation has been provided. Patients in
this state are often described as 'brain dead'.

Another view is also finding support. Adherents of this
view argue that, if the individual's brain is damaged to an
extent that precludes his ever returning to consciousness, he
is dead even though his body continues to breathe normally.
Patients in this irreversible non-cognitive state are sometimes

[1] *Hickman* v. *Peacey* [1945] A.C. 304, 317.

said to be in a persistent vegetative state, or to have sustained 'cognitive death'.

Much of this chapter will be taken up with a discussion of whether patients whose hearts continue to beat but who have sustained brain death, or even only cognitive death, are now dead for the purpose of English law. This will be followed by a discussion of whether patients should ever be regarded as dead if their heartbeat has ceased, but there has not yet been an irreversible cessation of brain function.

I GENERAL ISSUES

It has been said that a patient dies at the 'time which the doctors in the particular case *say* was the time of his death',[2] and that 'the question of what is death . . . is a technical, professional medical matter'.[3] These statements, and many like them,[4] suggest a misunderstanding of the issues involved.

It is convenient to consider first the oft-repeated view that for legal purposes a patient is dead when a doctor says he is dead. In recent decades doctors have sometimes disagreed about whether a patient can ever be said to be dead if heartbeat continues, even though brain death has been established.[5] The disagreement has not been about the medical facts, but

[2] R. K. Fullagar, Q.C., 'The Lore and Law of Tissue Homotransplantation' (1966) 10 *Proceedings of the Medico-Legal Society of Victoria* 161, 162. He also said that in the eyes of the law a man was dead at 'that point of time at which the preponderance of credible medical testimony holds that he was dead'. The discussion concerning Lord Kilbrandon's statement (cited in the next note) will also apply to this statement.

[3] Lord Kilbrandon, in *Ethics in Medical Progress* (1966, edd. G. E. W. Wolstenholme and M. O'Connor), 213. See also ibid. 158.

[4] See e.g. *Report of Law Reform Committee [of General Council of the Bar] on the Law relating to Organ Transplantation* (adopted by the Council on 20 July 1971), p. 14 (abridged version printed in (1971) 72 *Law Guardian* 23, 29); *Report of the Committee on Death Certification and Coroners* (Cmnd. 4810; 1971), para. 17. 20. See also Edmund Davies, 'Transplants', 636; Ormrod, 'Ethics', 23; Lord Scarman, 'Legal Liability and Medicine' (1981) 74 *J. Roy. Soc. Med.* 11, 14–15.

[5] For an example of doctors rejecting the view that a patient who is brain dead is no longer a living human being, see D. W. Evans and L. C. Lum, Letter, 'Brain Death' [1980] 2 *Lancet* 1022 (Report of Conference of Medical Royal Colleges on *Diagnosis of Brain Death* said to define a very grave prognosis, but 'must not be confused with a diagonosis of death'). See also J. B. Briggs and D. N. H. Hamilton, 'Kidney Transplantation' (1976) 34 *Health Bulletin* 191, 195; D. W. Evans, Letter to the Editor, *The Times*, 13 September 1982.

about broader ethical and social issues. It would be unsatisfactory if for legal purposes a patient in London was dead,
while a patient in an identical medical condition in Oxford
was alive, simply because the doctors involved held different
opinions as to whether patients in that condition were alive
or dead. The inadequacy of the view that a patient is dead
when doctors say that he is dead becomes even more apparent on those rare occasions when a patient is certified as
dead but subsequently 'wakes up' in the mortuary. Such a
patient is clearly alive for legal purposes, even though doctors
have declared that he is dead.

The view that 'the question of what is death . . . is a technical professional medical matter' often raises no difficulties.
But it results from an over-simplification which, in some
borderline cases, is seriously misleading. It fails to distinguish
between the medical 'facts' about a patient's condition and
the separate issue of whether, given these facts, the patient
should be considered alive or dead.[6]

One reason why the distinction between the two issues has
not been more generally recognized is that in most cases it is
agreed on all sides that if certain medical facts are established
the patient is, or is not, alive.[7] Everyone accepts that a member of the species *Homo sapiens* whose respiratory, circu-
tory, and neurological activities are continuing normally is
alive. Similarly, everyone accepts that when all respiratory,
circulatory, and neurological activity has irreversibly ceased,
the patient is dead.

So fundamental does the distinction between human life
and death seem that it is hardly surprising that lawyers and
others have assumed that there is some moment of 'true
death' which can be ascertained by scientific inquiry. If this
were so, the law could indeed leave it to the medical profession to decide whether a patient whose heart continued to

---

[6] The distinction is recognized in Brian Hogan, 'A Note on Death' [1972] *Crim.
L.R.* 80-4 and Williams, *Textbook*, 235. See also P. D. G. Skegg, 'Irreversibly
Comatose Individuals: "Alive" or "Dead"?' [1974] *C.L.J.* 130-44.

[7] Another reason may have ben the difficulty of finding a satisfactory terminology to express the different issues. But see now A. M. Capron and L. R. Kass, 'A
Statutory Definition of the Standards for Determining Human Death: An Appraisal and a Proposal' (1972) 121 *University of Pennsylvania Law Review* 87,
102-4; R. M. Veatch, *Death, Dying, and the Biological Revolution* (1976), 21-54.

beat, but who had sustained brain death or cognitive death, was alive or dead. But unfortunately this is not the case. As has been said with reference to the beginning of life, our conceptual unities have sharp edges which do not exist in nature.[8]

The stage in the process of dying at which the patient is to be regarded as 'dead' involves an element of choice. This should be particularly apparent now that various jurisdictions have enacted differing statutory definitions of death, so that some patients will be regarded as dead in one jurisdiction when they would be regarded as still alive in another.[9] In the United Kingdom some patients are now regarded as dead by doctors who used to regard patients in the same condition as alive.[10] It is not simply new medical knowledge that has brought about this reclassification.

Doctors have often stressed that dying is a process.[11] The Conference of Medical Royal Colleges, in its report, *Diagnosis of Death*, said that:[12]

Exceptionally, as a result of massive trauma, death occurs instantaneously or near-instantaneously. Far more commonly, death is not an event, it is a process, the various organs and systems supporting the continuation of life failing and eventually ceasing altogether to function, successively and at different times.

Nevertheless, for legal purposes it is necessary to make a

[8] Glanville Williams, 'Euthanasia and Abortion' (1966) 38 *University of Colorado Law Review* 178, 201.

[9] For the text of various statutory provisions, see President's Commission, App. C and App. E.

[10] Compare the views expressed by Professor R. Y. Calne in 1966 and in 1975. See R. Y. Calne in *Ethics in Medical Progress*, op. cit., n. 3, 73 ('I feel that if a patient has a heartbeat he cannot be regarded as a cadaver'); R. Y. Calne *et al.*, Letter to the Editor, *The Times*, 6 February 1975 ('the mechanical ventilation of a corpse'; 'if authorization has been obtained, organs can be removed for transplantation either before or after the heart has stopped beating').

[11] In fact, they have sometimes said that death is a process. But strictly speaking it is dying, not death, that is a process. Death is neither a process nor an event, but a state. See generally W. C. Charron, 'Death: A Philosophical Perspective on the Legal Definitions' [1975] *Washington University Law Quarterly* 979, esp. 990; J. L. Bernat, C. M. Culver, and B. Gert, 'On the Definition and Criterion of Death' (1981) 94 *Annals of Internal Medicine* 389.

[12] [1979] 1 *Br. Med. J.* 332, para. 2; [1979] 1 *Lancet* 261-2, para. 2. (The punctuation in the passage quoted follows that which appeared in the *Lancet*. In the *British Medical Journal* the word 'event', in the second sentence, was followed by a colon rather than a comma.)

sharp distinction between the living and the dead, as the application of various rules of law depends upon the individual being alive or dead. As yet, the law does not recognize any intermediate stage.[13]

Whether someone has sustained brain death, or cognitive death, is a technical medical issue. It is, of course, possible to make some distinction between the basic data (for example, electrocerebral silence for a specified period), and the inferences which may be drawn from those data (for example, that the patient will never recover consciousness). But this is not of importance here. What is important is that once it is established that the patient has sustained brain death, or cognitive death, there still remains the question whether he should, for that reason alone, be regarded as dead. This is not simply a technical medical issue.

The courts should approach the question of whether a body is that of a living human being, for the purpose of a particular rule of law, in the same way as they approach any other question of whether a particular object comes within a category mentioned in a rule of law. Where a special meaning has been assigned to a term the courts must seek to give effect to it. But in the absence of a special legal meaning, and in the absence of any indication that the term is a technical one, or is being used in some special sense, the courts must normally seek to give it its ordinary meaning where it has a clearly settled one. If the object comes clearly within the accepted meaning of the term, then only the most overwhelming considerations could justify the courts taking the view that the object was outside the scope of the law in question. However, the less certain the conventional usage, the more the courts must take account of other considerations, before deciding whether to hold that the object falls within, or without, the rule in question.

In practice the courts will be very reluctant to take a different view from that adopted by prominent members of the

[13] It is highly unlikely that, in the absence of statutory reform, any English court would accept the view that there is an intermediate stage between life and death, to which the rules relating to living human beings, or human corpses, do not apply. It would be possible to introduce such a status by legislation, and to provide an appropriate legal regimen. But this is not a likely consequence of the current debate about brain death.

medical profession. But unless doctors can carry the wider public with them, if they wish to treat as corpses bodies which have hitherto been regarded as alive, the courts should not act as if the courts had no role to play in the resolution of the issue. It is not simply a technical medical matter.

II BRAIN DEATH

A patient who is brain dead has not simply lost the capacity for consciousness. All the functions of his brain have permanently and irreversibly ceased. In consequence, he will not be able to breathe spontaneously again. Even if artificial ventilation is provided heartbeat will normally cease within a few days.

There is usually a close connection between brain death and the cessation of spontaneous respiration and circulation.[14] Brain death normally follows on the permanent cessation of respiration or circulation. Where brain death occurs first (as, for example, from a head injury) spontaneous respiration, and hence circulation, will cease. But if the patient is already on a ventilator, or if artificial ventilation is provided promptly, it is often possible to sustain bodily functions for a time after the occurrence of brain death.[15] The heart, the liver, and the kidneys will continue to function. Spinal cord function may persist, so reflex movements of the limbs will sometimes occur in response to stimuli.[16] Indeed, spontaneous movements sometimes occur without apparent stimuli.[17] These bodies can even develop pneumonia or septicaemia.

Where brain death occurs after the irreversible cessation of

[14] The concept of 'death of the brain', and its relevance to the death of other organs, was discussed in M. F. X. Bichat, *Recherches physiologiques sur la vie et la mort* (1800).

[15] See e.g. B. Jennett, 'Death, Determination of' in *Dict. Med. Ethics* 128 ('commonly for only 48 to 72 hours'); B. Jennett and C. Hessett, 'Brain Death in Britain as reflected in Renal Donors' (1981) 283 *Br. Med. J.* 359 ('the heart always stops within 14 days (usually much sooner) even though ventilation is maintained'); F. Plum and J. B. Posner, *The Diagnosis of Stupor and Coma* (3rd edn., 1980), 313 ('within a few days or, rarely, after several weeks').

[16] E. O. Jørgensen, 'Spinal Man after Brain Death' (1973) 28 *Acta Neurochirurgica* 259-73.

[17] B. Jennett, J. Gleave, and P. Wilson, 'Brain Death in Three Neurosurgical Units' (1981) 282 *Br. Med. J.* 533, 537. See generally L. P. Ivan, 'Spinal Reflexes in Cerebral Death' (1973) 23 *Neurology* 650-2.

respiration and circulation it has long been accepted that the patient is dead. But this discussion will focus on those cases where brain death occurs before the irreversible cessation of respiration and circulation, and, until the final part of this chapter,[18] the term 'brain death' will be employed in relation to these patients alone.

Once there has been an irreversible cessation of brain-stem function the brain as a whole can no longer function—even though biological activity may continue for a short time in isolated parts of the brain.[19] Brain-stem death can therefore be viewed as synonymous with brain death. However a distinction is sometimes drawn between 'brain-stem death' and 'total brain death'.[20] This distinction can be misleading,[21] as it is widely recognized that once brain-stem death occurs there is not merely no possibility of a return to spontaneous respiration, but there is also no possibility of a return to consciousness.[22] When brain-stem death occurs it can be said that there is an irreversible cessation of brain function, as:[23]

In measuring *functions*, physicians are not concerned with mere *activity* in cells or groups of cells if such activity (metabolic, electrical, etc.) is not manifested in some way that has significance for the organism as a whole. The same is true of the cells of the heart and lungs; they too may continue to have metabolic and electrical activity after death has been diagnosed by cardiopulmonary standards.

The brain cells which may remain alive for a time after brain-stem death has occurred are not able to contribute anything

[18] i.e. pt. IV, 'Death before Brain Death?' (pp. 223-7).

[19] For an account of the function of the brain-stem, and the mechanism of brain-stem death, see C. Pallis, 'From Brain Death to Brain Stem Death' (1982) 285 *Br. Med. J.* 1487, 1489-90. For an account of the loss of various brain functions, see President's Commission, 16-18, 27-8.

[20] See e.g. N. J. Legg and P. F. Prior, Letter, 'Brain Death' [1980] 2 *Lancet* 1378; R. Paul, Letter, 'The Brain Death Debate' [1981] 1 *Lancet* 502. See also J. Korein, 'Terminology, Definitions, and Usage' (1978) 315 *Annals N.Y. Acad. Sci.* 6, 7-8; G. F. Molinari, 'Brain Death, Irreversible Coma, and words doctors use' (1982) 32 *Neurology* 400-2, esp. 401.

[21] But it does have the advantage that it avoids the need for discussion of what counts as a 'function' of the brain. The term 'brain-stem death' is likely to be used much more widely in future, in place of the term 'brain death'.

[22] See C. Pallis and B. MacGillivray, Letter, 'Brain Death and the EEG' [1980] 2 *Lancet* 1085 ('The utter dependence of a *viable* and *conscious* human being on a functioning brainstem is not difficult to grasp.').

[23] President's Commission, 28-9. See also ibid. 75.

to ongoing bodily activities.[24] Hence a statement issued on behalf of the Conference of Medical Royal Colleges accepts that 'permanent functional death of the brain stem constitutes brain death'.[25]

The Conference of Medical Royal Colleges has accepted that brain death occurs when 'all functions of the brain have permanently and irreversibly ceased'.[26] This terminology will be adopted for the purpose of this discussion. Patients will be regarded as brain-dead once it is established that there has been an irreversible cessation of all brain function, whether or not there is continuing activity in isolated parts of the brain.[27]

Background and current status

The debate about brain death resulted from the availability of artificial ventilators. Contemporary descriptions of patients who had sustained brain death began with a paper by Mollaret and Goulon in 1959.[28] They described the clinical and electroencephalographic findings in twenty-three cases of what they termed *coma dépassé*, a state beyond coma. They did not assert that such patients were dead, but their paper, and others that soon followed, led to a consideration of the question.[29] Developments in organ transplantation soon made

[24] Cf. Linacre Report, 14.

[25] 'Diagnosis of Brain Death' [1976] 2 *Br. Med. J.* 1187, [1976] 2 *Lancet* 1069. See also Code of Practice, para. 27; C. Pallis, 'Reappraising Death' (1982) 285 *Br. Med. J.* 1409 ('the necessary and sufficient component of brain death is death of the brain stem'); C. Pallis, 'From Brain Death to Brain Stem Death' (1982) 285 *Br. Med. J.* 1487, 1489 ('The irreversible cessation of brain stem function implies death of *the brain as a whole*.').

[26] *Diagnosis of Death* [1979] 1 *Br. Med. J.* 332, para. 7; [1979] 1 *Lancet* 261, 262, para. 7.

[27] The Law Reform Commission of Canada, in its report on *Criteria for the Determination of Death* (Report 15, 1981), recommended the enactment of a provision which stated, in part, that 'a person is dead when an irreversible cessation of all that person's brain functions has occurred'. The Commission preferred the term 'functions' to 'activities' because it 'did not wish to prevent diagnosis of death, only because there could still exist some . . . measurable "*activities*" that are not symptoms of real "*function*" ' (ibid. 17). See, similarly, the statute and comments quoted in President's Commission, 67, 117, 119.

[28] P. Mollaret and M. Goulon, 'Le Coma Dépassé (Mémoire Préliminaire)' (1959) 101 *Revue Neurologique* 3-15.

[29] For information about developments in the decade following the French studies, see D. Silverman *et al.*, 'Cerebral Death and the Electroencephalogram' (1969) 209 *J.A.M.A.* 1505, 1507; J. Katz and A. M. Capron, *Catastrophic Diseases:*

the issue an important one far beyond professional neurological circles.

An event of major importance was the publication in 1968
of the 'Report of the Ad Hoc Committee of the Harvard
Medical School to Examine the Definition of Brain Death'.[30]
Although the report was entitled *A Definition of Irreversible
Coma*, the Committee was concerned with brain death rather
than cognitive death.[31] The Committee did not restrict itself
to defining that state, and listing the criteria for identifying it
in practice. The first sentence of the report stated that the
Committee's primary purpose was to define irreversible coma
'as a new criterion for death'. The Committee did not suggest
that patients who had a permanently non-functioning brain,
but who were maintained on ventilators, had hitherto been
regarded as dead. However the Committee suggested that
responsible medical opinion was ready to adopt new criteria
for pronouncing death to have occurred in those cases. Subsequent events in the United States confirmed this view.

In some parts of the world there was ready acceptance of
the notion that once brain death was established the patient
was dead, even though cardiac arrest had not occurred. There
were many who held this view in the United Kingdom,[32] but
it had still not found general acceptance by 1975. It was for
this reason that a Committee set up by the British Transplantation Society recommended that there was a 'need to
accept' that a person was dead when it was established that

Who Decides What? (1975), 207 n. 128. See also A. Milhaud, (1978) 315 *Ann.
N.Y. Acad. Sci.* 434. For evidence of earlier questioning about the status of some
bodies that were maintained on artificial ventilators, see the replies of Pope Pius
XII on 24 November 1957 to some questions concerning resuscitation: (1957) 49
Acta Apostolicae Sedis 1027–33.

[30] H. K. Beecher *et al.*, 'A Definition of Irreversible Coma' (1968) 205 *J.A.M.A.*
337–40. The important Minnesota criteria were published three years later: see
A. Mohandas and S. N. Chou, 'Brain Death: A Clinical and Pathological Study'
(1971) 35 *Journal of Neurosurgery* 211–18.

[31] In the second paragraph of the report that Committee stated that it was
concerned 'with those comatose individuals who have no discernible central
nervous system activity'. This statement, and the subsequent discussion of 'un-
responsitivity', supports the view that, far from drawing the line short of brain
death, the Committee went beyond it by requiring an absence of spinal cord
function.

[32] See e.g. J. B. Brierley *et al.*, 'Neocortical Death After Cardiac Arrest' [1971]
2 *Lancet* 560, 565.

he had 'suffered from an irreversible cessation of brain function and was incapable of spontaneous respiration'.[33] An
editorial in the *Medico-Legal Journal* in 1975 observed that
the concept of brain death 'is still regarded warily in the
United Kingdom',[34] and one leading exponent of the new
view wrote that its implications 'are difficult for the public
(and even for many doctors) to grasp'.[35] Another leading
exponent of the new approach claimed no more than that
brain death was a concept 'which is now increasingly recognized by doctors dealing with the critically ill'.[36]

An important development occurred in 1976, when the
Conference of Medical Royal Colleges approved of diagnostic
criteria for the determination of brain death,[37] and presented
them in a report entitled *Diagnosis of Brain Death*.[38] The
report stated that it was 'agreed that permanent functional
death of the brain stem constitutes brain death and that once
this has occurred further artificial support is fruitless and
should be withdrawn'. But the report did not express any
view on whether such patients could be regarded as dead
before artificial ventilation was withdrawn, and cardiac arrest
occurred.[39] However the *Lancet* published the report with an

[33] R. Y. Calne *et al.*, 'The Shortage of Organs for Clinical Transplantation'
[1975] 1 *Br. Med. J.* 251, 254. For hostile reaction to this recommendation, see
e.g. *The Times*, 3 February 1975, p. 3; 20 February 1975, p. 14. See also Editorial,
The Times, 31 January 1975.

[34] Editorial, 'The Beating-Heart Cadaver' (1975) 43 *Med.-Leg. J.* 37. See also
A. Jones and W. F. Bodmer, *Our Future Inheritance: Choice or Chance?* (1974), 92.

[35] C. Pallis, Letter to the Editor, *The Times*, 3 December 1975.

[36] B. Jennett, 'The Donor Doctor's Dilemma: Observations on the Recognition and Management of Brain Death' (1975) 1 *Journal of Medical Ethics* 63.

[37] By 1978 there were more than 30 published sets of criteria for brain death:
see P. McL. Black, 'Brain Death' (1978) 299 *New England Journal of Medicine*
338-44, 393-401, esp. 395-6. See also, now, 'Guidelines for the Determination
of Death' (1981) 246 *J.A.M.A.* 2184-6 (Report of the Medical Consultants on the
Diagnosis of Death to the President's Commission for the Study of Ethical Problems in Medicine and Biomedical and Behavioral Research).

[38] [1976] 2 *Br. Med. J.* 1187-8; [1976] 2 *Lancet* 1069-70. After the British
Transplantation Society Working Party, in its 'Discussion Document' cited n. 33
above, had proposed criteria for determining brain death, the Transplant Advisory
Panel set up a working party to consider criteria for brain death. These criteria
were subsequently considered by two separate subcommittees of the Royal
College of Physicians of London and of the Faculty of Anaesthetists. The report
was prepared for the Conference of Medical Royal Colleges and their Faculties in
the United Kingdom by the Secretary of the Conference, Professor Gordon Robson: see D. Pond, Letter, 'Brain Death' [1980] 2 *Lancet* 1306.

[39] A doctor who played an important role in the proceedings of the Confer-

introductory statement which asserted that the document which followed 'describes in general terms the diagnosis of death and sets out detailed diagnostic criteria for establishing when death has occurred in cases where vital functions are being maintained mechanically'.[40] This was by no means an isolated example of misinterpretation of the report.[41] The confusion resulted from a failure to recognize that it is one thing to agree upon diagnostic criteria to determine brain death, but quite another to make an ethical and social judgment that once this has been established the patient is dead, even though the heart continues to pump blood around the body.

Transplant surgeons were among the many doctors and others who mistakenly thought that the statement indicated that the Conference of Medical Royal Colleges had agreed that once brain death was established the patient was dead. In consequence, some changed their practice and commenced removing organs for transplantation before artificial ventilation was finally discontinued.[42]

By the later 1970s there appeared to be much greater acceptance of the view that a patient was dead once brain death had occurred.[43] But there was some inconsistency. For example, transplant surgeons who were strongly committed to the new approach sometimes spoke of the need to remove kidneys 'within one hour of death'. What they meant was

ence has informed me that the reason for this omission was that it would not then have been possible to obtain agreement on this matter.

[40] [1976] 2 *Lancet* 1069.

[41] Although there was no equivalent passage in the version of the report published in the *British Medical Journal*, an editorial in that journal demonstrated the same misunderstanding of the report: 'Brain Death' [1976] 2 *Br. Med. J.* 1157–8 ('It sets out clear guidelines for the diagnosis of death . . .').

[42] As evidence of the change of practice after the mid 1970s, see e.g. Professor R. Y. Calne's comments, under the heading 'Tissue Transplant', in successive editions of the *Dictionary of Medical Ethics*. In the first edition, which was published in 1977, he stated that in the United Kingdom 'it is usual to wait until circulation ceases before organ removal begins' (p. 325). In the revised edition, published in 1981, he stated 'All heart and liver grafts and most kidney transplants are now taken from . . . "heart-beating cadavers".' (p. 438.) Cf. n. 10, above.

[43] It is likely that the misapprehension that the matter was simply a technical medical one, and also the misunderstanding about what had been agreed upon by the Conference of Medical Royal Colleges in 1976, aided the acceptance of this view.

within one hour of the cessation of effective respiration and circulation which, on their view, could occur many hours after the patient was dead.[44] When brain death was established, but artificial ventilation was continued for a time, it was not uncommon for doctors to record that death occurred at or after the time when artificial ventilation was finally terminated.[45]

In 1979 there were two developments which made it seem particularly likely that English courts would in future accept the view that once brain death was established a person was dead, even though heartbeat continued. One was the publication by the Conference of Medical Royal Colleges of a report entitled *Diagnosis of Death*.[46] This did what many had wrongly assumed that the earlier report had done. It accepted the view that, 'Whatever the mode of its production, brain death represents the stage at which a patient becomes truly dead, because by then all functions of the brain have permanently and irreversibly ceased.'[47] The final paragraph stated it was the conclusion of the Conference 'that the identification of brain death means that the patient is dead, whether or not the function of some organs, such as a heart beat, is still maintained by artificial means'.[48]

Later in 1979 the Department of Health and Social Security published a Code of Practice to regulate the removal of cadaveric organs for transplantation.[49] The Code was prepared by a Working Party set up by the United Kingdom Health Departments, which included the Chairman of the Association of Community Health Councils, a coroner, and an academic lawyer, as well as a wide range of medical personnel. The Code of Practice embodied the view of the Working Party that death could be diagnosed 'by the irreversible

---

[44] For a later, and striking, example of similar usage, see Editorial, 'Brain Death' [1981] 1 *Lancet* 363-5 (on no less than eleven occasions, in the course of this editorial, 'died' was used as a synonym for terminal cardiac arrest—despite the fact that in all cases brain death had already been established).

[45] One of the objects of paragraph 29 of the Code of Practice, which was published in October 1979 (see n. 49, this page), was to avoid this practice in future.

[46] [1979] 1 *Br. Med. J.* 332; [1979] 1 *Lancet* 261-2.

[47] Para. 7.

[48] Para. 9.

[49] *The Removal of Cadaveric Organs for Transplantation: A Code of Practice* (H.M.S.O., 1979).

cessation of brain-stem function—''brain death'' '.[50] It approved of the practice of maintaining artificial ventilation and heartbeat until the completion of the removal of organs for transplantation.[51]

The publication of the report entitled *Diagnosis of Death*, and of the Code of Practice which accepted the approach adopted in that report, caused very little controversy. It became apparent that there was widespread acceptance of the view that brain death can be equated with the death of a human being. The fact that this view had found widespread acceptance was further demonstrated in 1980, when a much-publicized programme on BBC television[52] resulted in prolonged public and professional debate concerning the criteria for determining brain death. A striking characteristic of the programme, and of the discussion in the months that followed, was the acceptance of the view that once there has been an adequate determination of brain death the patient is rightly regarded as dead. The controversy had the incidental effect of disseminating yet more widely the view that a person can be dead even though his heart continues to beat.[53]

In March 1981 the English Court of Appeal (Criminal Division) dealt with two cases which appeared to provide an excellent opportunity for authoritative judicial acceptance of the view that a person may be regarded as dead for legal purposes once brain death is established. The cases—*R.* v.

[50] Ibid. para. 27. The Working Party had agreed to adopt this view before steps were taken to bring the matter before the Conference of Medical Royal Colleges. The Chairman of the Working Party was Lord Smith, a former Chairman of the Conference.

[51] Para. 33.

[52] 'Transplants: are the donors really dead?' ('Panorama', 13 October 1980). For an account of the programme, see C. Pallis, 'Medicine and the Media' (1980) 281 *Br. Med. J.* 1064; B. Silcock, 'Facts behind the transplant row', *Sunday Times*, 9 November 1980, p. 14. The debate continued for many months in the correspondence columns of the *British Medical Journal* and the *Lancet*.

[53] The debate resulted in the re-examination, but eventual vindication, of the diagnostic criteria for brain death which the Conference of Medical Royal Colleges had agreed upon in 1976. It led to the publication of evidence which supported those criteria (see, especially, B. Jennett, J. Gleave, and P. Wilson, 'Brain Death in Three Neurosurgical Units' (1981) 282 *Br. Med. J.* 533-9), and also to the Conference of Medical Royal Colleges agreeing to recommend certain procedural safeguards to be followed in determining brain death (see J. G. Robson, Letter, 'Brain Death' (1981) 283 *Br. Med. J.* 505).

Malcherek and *R.* v. *Steel*[54]—were both ones of murder. The assailants had both inflicted injuries which resulted in their victims being connected to ventilators. The victims were maintained on ventilators until doctors were of the opinion that brain death had occurred. Artificial ventilation was then terminated. The assailants both contended that the respective trial judges should not have withdrawn the issue of causation from the jury, as there was evidence that the cause of death was the termination of artificial ventilation.

The judge at Malcherek's original trial was reported to have said, 'To have kept her on the respirator would have been, in effect, to ventilate a corpse.'[55] This statement, and his ruling that there was no evidence to show that the victim was still alive when the doctors switched off the machine,[56] indicated the trial judge's acceptance of the view that once brain death is established a person is dead for the purpose of the law of homicide, even though the heart continues to beat. However the Court of Appeal took the view that 'This is not the occasion for any decision as to what constitutes death.'[57]

In delivering the judgment of the Court of Appeal, Lord Lane C.J. said that modern techniques have undoubtedly resulted in the blurring of many of the conventional and traditional concepts of death. He said:[58]

There is, it seems, a body of opinion in the medical profession that there is only one true test of death and that is the irreversible death of the brain stem, which controls the basic functions of the body such as breathing. When that occurs it is said the body has died, even though by mechanical means the lungs are being caused to operate and some circulation of blood is taking place.

---

[54] [1981] 1 W.L.R. 690. The court comprised Lord Lane C.J., Ormrod L.J., and Smith J. Lord Lane C.J. stated, in the opening sentence of the judgment of the court, 'These two appeals, one an appeal and the other an application, raise similar points and it was accordingly thought convenient that they should be dealt with together, and that is what has happened.' For details of the hearing, see 'Point of death: no judicial definition' (1981) 282 *Br. Med. J.* 1083–4.

[55] *Guardian*, 13 November 1979, p. 2 (news report), per Willis J. This information is not contained in the reports of the case before the Court of Appeal. (The briefer news reports in *The Times*, 13 November 1979, p. 2, and the *Daily Telegraph*, 13 November 1979, p. 19, were much less informative than the one in the *Guardian*.)

[56] *Guardian*, 13 November 1979, p. 2 (news report).

[57] [1981] 1 W.L.R. 694E.

[58] Ibid. 694F–G.

But he did not adopt this view as a way of resolving the issue
before him.

Lord Lane C.J. said that in each of the two cases there was
no doubt that, whatever test was applied,[59]

the victim died; that is to say, applying the traditional test, all body
functions, breathing and heart beat and brain function came to an end,
at the latest, soon after the ventilator was disconnected.

He said:[60]

There is no evidence in the present case that at the time of conventional
death, after the life support machinery was disconnected, the original
wound or injury was other than a continuing, operating and indeed substantial cause of the death of the victim . . .

Although Lord Lane C.J. did speak of a medical practitioner
coming to the conclusion 'that the patient is for practical
purposes dead',[61] he did not make use of the opportunity to
state that once brain death is established a patient is dead for
the purpose of English law.

There is a remarkable similarity between the approach the
Court of Appeal adopted in *R.* v. *Malcherek* and that adopted
almost three years earlier by the Scottish High Court of Justi-
ciary in *Finlayson* v. *H.M. Advocate*.[62] There, too, the court
was concerned with a question of causation which could have
been avoided entirely if it had been accepted that once brain
death was established the patient was dead. However, the
case was dealt with on the assumption that the victim did not
die until after artificial ventilation was terminated, even
though brain death had already occurred. Soon after the decision in *R.* v. *Malcherek* the House of Lords heard an appeal in
which Lord Hailsham L.C. said that the victim 'died . . .
when, in view of the fact that he was virtually already dead,
the breathing machine on which he had been placed . . . was
finally switched off'.[63] There was no consideration of whether
a patient could be regarded as dead before the heart stopped
beating.

---

[59] Ibid. 694H.   [60] Ibid. 696G.   [61] Ibid. 697D.
[62] [1978] S.L.T. (Notes) 60. *Finlayson* v. *H.M. Advocate* was not cited to the
Court of Appeal in *R.* v. *Malcherek*.
[63] *R.* v. *Cunningham* [1982] A.C. 566, 573.

Despite the judicial references to patients being 'for all practical purposes dead', or 'virtually dead', the English and Scottish appellate courts have not yet accepted the view that once brain death is established the patient is rightly regarded as dead, even though bodily functions are maintained by artificial ventilation. Far from seeking an opportunity to accept this view, the courts have side-stepped the issue when the opportunity has arisen. Nevertheless, if faced with a case where there was no way of avoiding the issue,[64] it is now highly likely that the courts would accept that once brain death is established an individual is to be regarded as dead for legal purposes.[65]

In an article written almost a decade ago, I claimed that 'although the conventional view may be changing' individuals who had sustained brain death were still ordinarily regarded as living human beings.[66] I went on to assert that the conventional view was still so clearly established that it would probably not be open to the courts to regard them as other than living human beings, and that certainly 'nothing less than the most overwhelming considerations—such as do not exist here—would justify the courts going against current usage'.[67] The situation now seems very different. The view that brain-dead individuals are no longer living human beings has received such wide acceptance that a court would need strong reasons for insisting that they are still to be regarded as alive for legal purposes. And, although the arguments in support of the equation of brain death with human death are not all equally strong, and although its acceptance is not without any dangers, there is no sufficient reason for the courts to reject the new view. This assertion requires explanation.

Practical advantages

Brain-dead patients whose hearts continue to beat might well have to come to be regarded as dead, even if there had not been any doubts about the propriety of terminating artificial

[64] For examples of such cases, see P. D. G. Skegg, 'Irreversibly Comatose Individuals: "Alive" or "Dead"?' [1974] *C.L.J.* 130, 131–2.

[65] See Ormrod, 'Ethics', 23, and also Lord Scarman, 'Legal Liability and Medicine' (1981) 74 *J. Roy. Soc. Med.* 11, 15.

[66] P. D. G. Skegg, op. cit., 136.

[67] Ibid. 137.

ventilation if they were still 'alive', or any question of using their organs for transplantation.[68] But there can be little doubt that these considerations have been very influential, and that without them the change would not have come about as quickly as it has done.[69] The seminal Harvard Report mentioned these factors alone as the 'reasons' for the 'new criterion of death' which it proposed. They merit closer scrutiny than they were given there, or than they have received in much of the discussion which has followed.

If some ventilator-dependent patients are regarded as dead this does avoid the need to consider the legality of withdrawing artificial ventilation from them. Furthermore, to regard some ventilator-dependent patients as dead also prevents the person who caused the injuries, which made the patient ventilator-dependent, from claiming that it was the withdrawal of artificial ventilation rather than the injuries which caused the death. These are real advantages, although their importance has sometimes been exaggerated.

Before the widespread acceptance of the view that once brain death is established the patient is dead, there had been many hundreds of cases in the United Kingdom in which doctors had withdrawn artificial ventilation from severely brain-damaged patients, with the consequence that respiration and circulation had ceased. This practice does not appear to have given rise to any legal proceedings against a doctor, much less to a doctor being convicted or held liable to pay damages. Had the matter come before the courts there would have been several ways in which they could have avoided finding the doctor liable.[70]

Regarding some ventilator-dependent patients as already

[68] See ibid. 138–9 for some additional considerations. But see also ibid. 142.
[69] In the United Kingdom it was a Committee set up by the British Transplantation Society which first recommended that a person should be regarded as dead once brain death was established (see n. 33, above), and discussions in groups specifically concerned with transplantation led eventually to the statements of the Conference of Medical Royal Colleges in 1976 and in 1979. See n. 38 and n. 50, above. See also A. E. Walker, 'The Death of a Brain' (1969) 124 *Johns Hopkins Medical Journal* 190 ('The paradox of a dead brain in a living body has been known to neurologists and neurosurgeons for some years. It occasioned little interest, however, until organ transplantation developed when it was realized that such states provided ideal donors of heart and other organs.').
[70] See ch. 8.

dead could simplify the trial of the person responsible for the condition which made the patient ventilator-dependent.[71] However, in the United Kingdom there has long been reason to believe that, even if brain-dead patients were regarded as alive at the time when artificial ventilation was finally terminated, the withdrawal would not of itself break the chain of causation.[72] Recent decisions of appellate courts have put the matter beyond doubt.[73]

If doctors had not in the past felt free to terminate artificial ventilation once brain death was established, this would not have resulted in large numbers of bodies being 'kept alive' indefinitely. Heartbeat can rarely be maintained for more than a few days. But it would have had serious consequences for transplantation. This is because doctors have frequently removed organs from brain-dead bodies once artificial ventilation has been terminated and heartbeat has ceased. If the artificial ventilation of such bodies had continued until heartbeat ceased, the organs would not have been suitable for transplantation. However in the United Kingdom many doctors were terminating the artificial ventilation of severely brain-damaged patients long before it came to be accepted that at least many of these patients were already dead.[74]

It is not only the desirability of terminating artificial ventilation which has been offered as a reason for regarding brain-dead individuals as dead. It has also been said that, unless organs can be removed from bodies which are being maintained on

[71] It also simplifies inquests into the death.

[72] The leading English case was *R.* v. *Smith* [1959] 2 Q.B. 35, 42–3. See also *R.* v. *Hennigan* [1971] 3 All E.R. 133, 135; *R.* v. *Blaue* [1975] 1 W.L.R. 1411, 1415; *R.* v. *Cato* [1976] 1 W.L.R. 110, 117. The issue did not arise in the trial of the assailant of Potter, for he was not charged with murder or manslaughter, but with assault: see Brian Hogan, 'A Note on Death' [1972] *Crim. L.R.* 80, 81. For a report of the inquest, see *The Times*, 26 July 1963, p. 9, [1963] 2 *Br. Med. J.* 394.

[73] *Finlayson* v. *H.M. Advocate* [1978] S.L.T. (Notes) 60; *R.* v. *Malcherek, R.* v. *Steel* [1981] 1 W.L.R. 690. (For contemporary news reports of the original trials of Malcherek and of Steel, see the *Guardian*, 13 November 1979, p. 2, and *The Times*, 14 December 1979, p. 4, respectively.) See also *R.* v. *Kitching and Adams* [1976] 6 W.W.R. 697, 715 (Man. C.A.); *R.* v. *Page* (Manitoba, 1970) unreported, but an account given in *Report on a Statutory Definition of Death* (Manitoba Law Reform Commission, Report No. 16, 1974), 17–18.)

[74] See ch. 8, n. 4.

ventilators, the chances of successful organ transplantation are significantly reduced. However the Code of Practice prepared by a Committee which included several experienced transplant surgeons, did not suggest that it was essential that kidneys be removed from bodies in which the heart was still beating.[75] It said that kidneys 'must be removed within 60 minutes of cessation of circulation and it is desirable that this time is kept as short as practicable—less than 30 minutes if possible'.[76] The liver and heart must be removed more promptly if they are to be used for transplantation: a leading transplant surgeon has said they must be removed within fifteen minutes of the cessation of circulation, if they are not to be irreversibly damaged.[77] The organs will certainly be in a better state if they are not deprived of oxygenated blood for any time before they are removed. Nevertheless, the benefit of removing them while the body is still being ventilated, and the heart is still beating, is not as significant as has sometimes been claimed. Of course, even a very substantial benefit would not of itself be a sufficient reason for regarding as dead patients who had hitherto been regarded as alive.

There are other advantages if brain-dead patients are regarded as having died. One relates to transplantation, although not to the desirability of removing organs from bodies in which the heart is still beating. This is that prior to the removal of organs for transplantation it is often desirable to administer drugs to maintain the condition of the organs, and also to carry out various tests. The potential donor will rarely have consented to these, and only some of them can be regarded as being in any sense for his benefit. Where they are not, they will be illegal, unless the potential donor is already dead.

[75] There are a great number of factors which affect the 'success rate' of different transplant units, and it is difficult to isolate any one factor (see generally P. J. Morris, 'Results of Renal Transplantation' in *Kidney Transplantation* (1979, ed. P. J. Morris), 377–88, esp. 381–3). In the United Kingdom in the mid- to late 1970s some of the very best results were from units which did not remove kidneys from bodies in which the heart was still beating. Figures sometimes cited include cases where the operation to remove kidneys commenced an appreciable time after the cessation of circulation.

[76] Code of Practice, para. 33.

[77] R. Y. Calne, 'Tissue Transplant', in *Dict. Med. Ethics* 435, 437. Cf. Code of Practice, para. 33.

Another advantage of regarding brain-dead individuals as dead is demonstrated by one instance in which a still-functioning body, of an individual who had sustained brain death, was used to provide cross-circulation therapy for a patient who had developed acute hepatic failure and encephalopathy.[78] Such bodies could sometimes be maintained for a day or two to enable medical students occasionally to practise anatomy on a still-functioning body, rather than on the long-dead ones to which they are normally restricted.[79] The bodies could also be used for doctors to try some surgical techniques, or to study the effects of certain drugs.[80] But again, it must be insisted that these advantages[81] are not of themselves a sufficient reason for regarding such bodies as corpses, rather than as living human beings.

The basic arguments

Many of those who believe that brain-dead individuals should be regarded as dead appear to assume that there is no need for any argument in support of that view.[82] Of those who do provide reasons, some mention only the practical advantages of the new approach. Others concentrate on the fact that once brain death has occurred the patient's condition is hopeless, and that heartbeat will cease within a short time in any event.[83] But some do consider more fundamental issues. They discuss the role of the brain in relation to the life of a human being, and conclude that when the brain can no

[78] R. W. Summers *et al.*, 'Acute Hepatic Coma Treated by Cross Circulation With Irreversibly Comatose Donor' (1970) 214 *J.A.M.A.* 2297-301.

[79] The Anatomy Acts have long demonstrated acceptance of the view that, subject to certain conditions, dead bodies may be retained for a time unburied, to aid medical education.

[80] D. N. Walton, *Brain Death* (1980), 48, and see also ibid. 37 for some other possibilities.

[81] These advantages might be much more significant if it becomes possible to maintain brain-dead patients on ventilators for longer periods.

[82] M. B. Green and D. Wikler, 'Brain Death and Personal Identity' (1980) 9 *Philosophy & Public Affairs* 105, n. 2. ('Though the literature on brain death is large, it has been remarkably free of argument. The medical literature, especially, gives the reader the impression that no argument is needed.')

[83] The fact that a patient's condition is hopeless, and that conventional death will occur within a short time in any event, is not a sufficient reason for regarding the patient as already dead—although much of the debate in the United Kingdom, following the controversial 'Panorama' programme on BBC television, appeared to proceed on the assumption that it was.

longer fulfil that role the person is dead. Such arguments
divide into two categories: those which emphasize 'higher'
(or cognitive) functions, and those which emphasize 'lower'
(or vegetative) functions. Taken on their own, both arguments could have consequences which are more radical than
those who employ them appear to realize.

The Australian Law Reform Commission has stressed that
when brain death occurs 'The patient can never again have
consciousness, memory, knowledge, thought, feeling, sight,
hearing, touch, speech, or any other sense of any kind',[84]
and appeared to regard this as of crucial significance. Similarly, the Law Reform Commission of Canada has said that
death is considered to be 'the permanent and irreversible
cessation of conscious and relational life'.[85] Both those statements appeared in publications which supported the view
that a patient should be regarded as dead once brain death
occurs. They are by no means untypical. But, if accepted,
such arguments lead to the conclusion that a patient is dead
once cognitive death occurs, rather than only when brain
death occurs.[86] They stress the irreversible loss of cognitive
function, and do not rely on the absence of regulative functions. Whether patients should be regarded as dead once
cognitive death occurs is an issue which will be considered
later in this chapter; at this stage it is enough to stress that,
taken alone, such arguments do not provide a good reason
for drawing the line between life and death at the time when
brain death occurs.

Other advocates of brain-dead individuals being regarded as
dead have focused on the role of the brain in maintaining the
integrated functioning of the body as a whole. For example,
the report on *Diagnosis of Death*[87] issued by the Conference
of Medical Royal Colleges, emphasized the relationship
between brain function and other bodily functions. 'Higher'

[84] *Human Tissue Transplants* (Law Reform Commission, Report No. 7, 1977),
54. See, similarly, President's Commission 83; although see generally ch. 3 of that
report.

[85] *Criteria for the Determination of Death* (Law Reform Commission of
Canada, Working Paper 23, 1979), 57.

[86] This was recognized in the Law Reform Commission of Canada's Report
No. 15, *Criteria for the Determination of Death* (1981), 15–16.

[87] See p. 194, above.

brain functions were not expressly mentioned. Those who stress that once brain death has occurred there is a 'breakdown in integrated operation of the crucial trisystemic (heart–lungs–brain) functioning'[88] do provide a reason for distinguishing between patients who have sustained brain death and patients who have simply sustained cognitive death. But if the fact that 'the body is preserved from organic and cellular destruction only by means of an artificially intruded pumping system'[89] is, on its own, a sufficient reason for regarding a patient as dead, then polio victims who are permanently dependent on artificial ventilation are also dead.[90]

One writer who considers that patients who have sustained brain death should be regarded as dead, whereas those who have simply sustained cognitive death should be regarded as alive, stresses that human life is bodily life.[91] He says that it is appropriate 'that our empirical criterion of death should be one that speaks unambiguously and indubitably of "the disintegration of the body" ', and he equates brain death with the 'irreversible cessation of integrated organic functioning'.[92] But, when artificial ventilation is provided, brain death does not lead immediately to the disintegration of the body. It is true that once brain death occurs the total disintegration of the body can rarely be postponed for more than a few days (or, in the case of children, a few weeks).[93] But with other

[88] A. M. Capron, 'Legal Definition of Death' (1978) 315 *Ann. N.Y. Acad. Sci.* 349, 353.

[89] G. R. Dunstan, 'Definitions of Death: Ethical Considerations', in *Gradwohl's Legal Medicine* (3rd edn., 1976, ed. F. E. Camps, completed by A. E. Robinson and B. G. B. Lucas), 53, 55.

[90] See B. Jennett, 'Irrecoverable Brain Damage After Resuscitation: Brain Death and Other Syndromes' (1976) 5 *Resuscitation* 49, 51 ('Respiratory paralysis and inability to move may result from polyneuritis, poliomyelitis and myasthenia gravis, and such patients may survive for long periods if artificial ventilation is maintained.').

[91] 'Determining the Fact of Death', in 'Ordinary and Extraordinary Means of Prolonging Life', *Linacre Papers* (No. 3, 1979), 28, 30–1. The author uses the term 'neocortical death' rather than 'cognitive death'.

[92] Ibid. 31. See also G. Grisez and J. M. Boyle, *Life and Death with Liberty and Justice* (1979), 76–8.

[93] See p. 188, n. 15, and see also J. Korein, 'Brain Death', in *Anesthesia and Neurosurgery* (edd. J. E. Cottrell and H. Turndorf, 1980), 282, 316 ('children and infants . . . may persist in a state of brain death with full resuscitative support for . . . as long as 30 days or more'). As yet there has been only limited success in overcoming the effects of the absence of brain-stem function in regulating blood pressure and temperature.

patients the fact that the disintegration of the body is imminent and inevitable, is not regarded as a reason for placing them in the same category as those in which the disintegration has already occurred.

Taken singly, neither the absence of cognitive function, nor the inability to maintain integrated bodily functions without artificial assistance, provides a basis for distinguishing between patients who are brain dead and some other patients whom advocates of the new approach wish to regard as alive. But where these factors result from the irreversible cessation of brain function they can, taken together, provide a basis for making a distinction between patients who are brain dead and patients who have only sustained cognitive death, or who are permanently dependent on artificial ventilation.

One of the first of the comparatively few reports or articles which rely explicitly on factors involving the absence of both 'higher' and 'lower' brain function was a 'Status Report' on brain death which was published in 1977.[94] Having pointed out that the fact that someone would be useful to others if pronounced dead should not alone be a sufficient reason for considering that person dead, the report went on to say that the principal reason for deciding that a person is dead should be based on a fundamental understanding of the nature of man.[95] The report recognized that all members of society will not be able to agree precisely on an acceptable formulation of man's nature, but said:[96]

Almost all segments of society will agree that some capacity to think, to perceive, to respond, and to regulate and integrate bodily functions is essential to human nature. Thus, if none of these brain functions are present and will ever return, it is no longer appropriate to consider a person as a whole as being alive.

But before a conclusion is reached concerning the desirability of equating brain death with the death of a human being, it is as well to take account of the possible disadvantages of this approach, and to consider the alternatives.

---

[94] F. J. Veitch *et al.*, 'Brain Death. 1. A Status Report of Medical and Ethical Considerations' (1977) 238 *J.A.M.A.* 1651-5. See also, now, President's Commission, 36.

[95] But see J. L. Bernart, C. M. Culver, and B. Gert, 'On the Definition and Criterion of Death' (1981) 94 *Annals of Internal Medicine* 389, 390, for a critical assessment of this approach.   [96] F. J. Veitch *et al.*, op. cit., 1653.

Disadvantages

It has long been recognized that some bodily functions continue long after the patient is regarded by all as dead. For example, it is widely known that nails and hair continue to grow. But in the past it would have been thought contradictory to say that the patient was dead, but that his body was 'kept alive', or 'survived', for several days. However, this is said of bodies which have sustained brain death, but which are maintained on artificial ventilators. Of course, heartbeat will not persist for long if artificial ventilation is withdrawn, but this is also the case with other patients who are entirely dependent on artificial ventilation.

When a patient is brain dead, but is maintained on an artificial ventilator, the cardio-vascular, gastro-intestinal, and urinary systems continue to function. The body is warm, consumes oxygen, and may react to painful stimuli. It would be difficult to describe this as a 'dead body'. Yet until very recently, if a person had died, not merely he but also his body was regarded as dead. The bodily functions which continued for a time after 'death' were of a very different order from those which continue when the body of a brain-dead patient is maintained on an artificial ventilator.

Those who believe that patients who have sustained cognitive death should be regarded as dead will welcome the development of a distinction between personal life and bodily life. But many people do not wish to see the boundary between human life and death brought forward to the stage when cognitive death occurs. For some of them, this divorce between personal and bodily life is less attractive, and may be accounted a disadvantage of the new approach.

It can, however, be argued that a divorce between personal and bodily life would have taken place even if it had not been suggested that patients who have sustained brain death may be regarded as dead. For if someone was beheaded it would now be possible to maintain the rest of his body on a ventilator, for a short time. The cardio-vascular, gastro-intestinal, and urinary systems could be continued. The body would be warm, would consume oxygen, and might react to painful stimuli. Yet the head could have been cremated. Surely, it could be argued, no one would regard such a body as a living human being. No one would dispute that the person had died, even though it could be said that the body was 'kept alive' or 'survived'.

This is true, and goes a little way towards meeting the objection that to accept that brain-dead patients are dead is to introduce a distinction between personal and bodily life which could otherwise have been avoided.[97] But in practice the likelihood of persons being beheaded, and their bodies maintained on ventilators, is extremely slight. The theoretical possibility would probably not have eroded the traditional identification of personal and bodily life. Furthermore, a headless body does not look like a living human being,[98] whereas a patient who is brain dead, and is maintained on a ventilator, will not normally look different from some other unconscious ventilator-dependent patients.

The introduction of a distinction between personal and bodily life could be seen as a disadvantage of the new approach. But even if this is accepted, it may be argued that it is more than counterbalanced by other considerations.

[97] It may be argued that such a distinction is already made prior to live birth. But this issue is notoriously controversial, and many would not wish to see it used as a precedent for what is done to human beings who have been born alive. If the presence or absence of brain function were thought to be of crucial significance at the beginning as well as at the end of life, this could have radical consequences in relation to attitudes towards abortion. Furthermore, it could be argued that even a newly fertilized zygote has a capacity for exercising brain function in the future, whereas this capacity has (by definition) been irreversibly lost when brain death occurs.

[98] But this would not be a sufficient reason to exclude, from the category of living human beings, the isolated head of a human being in which brain death, or at any rate cognitive death, had not yet occurred. The isolated head of a monkey, if perfused with oxygenated blood under a sufficient pressure, can look, bite, and make noises (R. J. White et al., 'Primate Cephalic Transplantation: Neurogenic Separation, Vascular Association' (1971) 3 Transplantation Proceedings 602-4). If a dog's head is experimentally severed from the body, and kept alive by an appropriate life-support system, the head will eat, salivate, blink, sleep and respond to stimuli, such as its name being called (J. Korein, 'The Problem of Brain Death: Development and History' (1978) 315 Ann. N.Y. Acad. Sci. 19, 27-8). Similar experiments have apparently been conducted on human heads of 12-17 weeks gestation, which consumed nutriments (H. A. H. van Till, 'Legal Aspects of the Definition and Diagnosis of Death', in Handbook of Clinical Neurology (edd. P. J. Vinken and G. W. Bruyn), vol. xxiv (1976), 787, 818). If the head of a human being who had been born alive was maintained in this state, and still had cognitive function, the human being should certainly not be regarded as dead for legal purposes.

Alternatives[99]

The irreversible cessation of all brain function is undoubtedly a more appropriate test of death than any of those which are concerned exclusively with respiratory and circulatory activities.[1] But it would be wrong to assume that a choice must be made between those approaches, for it would be possible to combine elements of both.[2]

One possibility would be to take the view that a person should not be regarded as dead until there has been an irreversible cessation, not simply of brain function, but also of respiration and circulation.[3] 'Beating-heart cadavers' would then be a contradiction in terms. But as it is possible to recommence artificial respiration and circulation in some bodies in which respiration and circulation have ceased, and brain death has occurred, this would bring back into the category of the living some bodies which have long been regarded as dead. Quite apart from the introduction of a greater degree of uncertainty about when the cessation was irreversible,[4] such an approach would handicap doctors in obtaining organs for transplantation. It is one thing to be cautious about bringing forward the time of death simply to serve the interests of transplant surgeons and their patients; it is quite another to put that time back, in a way which would unnecessarily hinder the practice of transplantation.

[99] It is assumed that there is not at present any prospect of the law recognizing an intermediate stage between life and death (see n. 13, above). This discussion therefore proceeds on the assumption that patients who have sustained brain death must be classified as either alive or dead, for the purpose of English law.

[1] For a discussion, see P. D. G. Skegg, 'Irreversibly Comatose Individuals: "Alive" or "Dead"?' [1974] C.L.J. 130, 138-9.

[2] It could be argued that brain death—as opposed to cognitive death—is not concerned exclusively with brain function. Once brain death occurs there is an irreversible cessation of spontaneous respiration.

[3] To avoid lengthening this discussion unnecessarily, the alternatives discussed will all involve the cessation of both respiration and circulation. It would (for example) be possible to focus on the cessation of respiration, whether spontaneous or artificial, but to disregard circulation. For the sake of simplicity, it will be assumed that the cessation of heartbeat is synonymous with the cessation of circulation. This is not always the case in practice.

[4] Some uncertainty is unavoidable. But this is usually restricted to uncertainty about whether the cessation of respiration and circulation was irreversible, or else about whether the cessation of brain function was irreversible. This approach combines all three considerations.

A less stringent alternative would be the irreversible cessation of all brain function, together with the permanent cessation of respiration and circulation. But even if a doctor waits until the heart stops beating before removing organs for transplantation, the making of an incision prior to the removal of the organs for transplantation sometimes has the effect of causing heartbeat to recommence. On this approach, the doctor would in such cases have made an incision in a body which, as it turned out, was still that of a living human being. Had he done nothing the body would already have been a corpse, for the cessation would have been permanent.

Of course, it would be possible to jettison the requirement that the cessation of respiration and circulation be permanent. A patient could be regarded as dead once there was an irreversible cessation of all brain function, together with a cessation —be it temporary or permanent—of respiration and circulation. Once death had occurred the body could then be maintained on a ventilator until it was convenient to remove organs for transplantation. But this approach would not avoid the apparent contradiction of corpses being 'kept alive'. And as there would not be any obvious difference in the medical condition of bodies before circulation ceased and after it had been recommenced, this approach would achieve very little. This would also be so with a test of the irreversible cessation of brain function together with the cessation of spontaneous respiration and circulation. If brain death has occurred, spontaneous respiration will already have ceased —and it may be argued that circulation which would not be continuing unless artificial ventilation was provided is not itself spontaneous. If it is regarded as spontaneous, it may be asked whether there is any point in requiring a doctor to wait until heartbeat ceases before the patient is regarded as dead, especially as he would then be free to recommence artificial ventilation. Again, there would be a 'beating-heart cadaver'.

The alternative which merits closest consideration is that death occurs when the patient has sustained cognitive death, even though brain-stem function continues. If this view is accepted it would follow that patients who had sustained brain death were also dead, so a consideration of this alternative can be postponed until the next part of this chapter.

Conclusion

On the basis of this review of the arguments for and against regarding a patient as dead once brain death has occurred, there do not appear to be sufficient grounds for a judge to reject what is now the commonly accepted view. Indeed, even if the judge had complete freedom in the matter, it would be desirable that he adopt the view that a patient is dead once there has been an irreversible cessation of all brain function.

III COGNITIVE DEATH

Brain functions can be divided into two categories: those related to vegetative functions and those relating to cognition. Vegetative functions do not require awareness, but the brain-stem plays a crucial role in relation to some of them. Spontaneous breathing may occur if the brain-stem continues to function, even though other parts of the brain can never function again. Cognition includes elements of alert awareness, perception, reasoning, problem-solving, memory, and decision making. Cognition is not possible unless the upper levels of the brain, as well as the brain-stem, can still function.[5]

If the supply of oxygenated blood ceases, the higher regions of the brain are the first to be irreversibly damaged. The brain-stem is more resistant to the deprivation of oxygen. When doctors seek to resuscitate a patient, following a cardiac arrest, they will rarely know to what extent, if any, the brain is damaged. However, after breathing has been restored it may become apparent that the patient's brain is damaged to such an extent that he is in an irreversibly non-cognitive condition, even though brain-stem functions continue. Systemic death may not occur for months, or even years.[6]

---

[5] See generally J. Korein, 'The Problem of Brain Death: Development and History' (1978) 315 *Ann. N.Y. Acad. Sci.* 19, 21.

[6] For a case concerning a patient in this state, see *In the Matter of Karen Quinlan* (1976) 355 A. 2d 647, esp. 654–5 (N.J.).

Terminology

Patients who are in this irreversible non-cognitive condition[7] are sometimes said to have sustained cognitive death.[8] Other terms which have been used include cerebral death,[9] irreversible coma,[10] persistent vegetative state,[11] and neocortical death.[12] None of these terms is ideal for the purpose of this discussion.[13]

Cerebral death has often been used as a synonym for brain death,[14] so its use in this different sense can lead to confusion.[15] Irreversible coma has also been used interchangeably with brain death.[16] It also has the disadvantage that many

[7] Leading neurologists have used expressions similar to this, e.g. 'vegetative or noncognitive components of the nervous system' (F. Plum); 'the irreversible, non-cognitive state' (J. Korein): (1978) 315 *Ann. N.Y. Acad. Sci.* 225, 319n, respectively.

[8] H. R. Beresford, 'Cognitive Death: Differential Problems and Legal Overtones' (1978) 315 *Ann. N.Y. Acad. Sci.* 339-45, but see ibid. 348. The term has also been used in discussion by F. Plum and by A. M. Capron. See (1978) 315 *Ann. N.Y. Acad. Sci.* 292, 359, respectively.

[9] J. Korein, 'Terminology, Definitions, and Usage' (1978) 315 *Ann. N.Y. Acad. Sci.* 6, 7.

[10] See F. Plum and J. B. Posner, *The Diagnosis of Stupor and Coma* (3rd edn., 1980), 313.

[11] B. Jennett and F. Plum, 'Persistent Vegetative State After Brain Damage' [1972] 1 *Lancet* 734-7.

[12] J. B. Brierley *et al.*, 'Neocortical Death After Cardiac Arrest' [1971] 2 *Lancet* 560-5.

[13] For a discussion of other terms, including akinetic mutism and the appallic syndrome, see B. Jennett and F. Plum, op. cit., 735-6; S. A. Schneck, 'Brain Death and Prolonged States of Impaired Responsiveness' (1981) 58 *Denver Law Journal* 608, 618-20; and see also F. Plum and J. B. Posner, op. cit., 7-8. Akinetic mutism and the appallic syndrome (or state) are both used to refer to some patients in an irreversible non-cognitive condition. But there are other patients in this condition to whom these terms do not refer, and the terms have also been used to refer to some patients who are not in an irreversible non-cognitive state.

[14] See e.g. 'An Appraisal of the Criteria of Cerebral Death' (1977) 237 *J.A.M.A.* 982-6. See also M. J. G. Harrison, 'The Diagnosis of Brain Death' (1976) 16 *British Journal of Hospital Medicine* 320, 323.

[15] See also D. L. Stickel, 'The Brain Death Criterion of Human Death. An Analysis and Reflection on the *1977 New York Conference on Brain Death*' (1979) 6 *Ethics in Science and Medicine* 171, 181 ('There was some ambiguity . . . in the use of "cerebral death". This term literally means death of the cerebrum (right and left hemispheres), but it was more often used to mean death of the entire brain.').

[16] See e.g. 'A Definition of Irreversible Coma' (Report of the Ad Hoc Committee of the Harvard Medical School to Examine the Definition of Brain Death) (1968) 205 *J.A.M.A.* 337-40; D. Silverman *et al.*, 'Irreversible Coma Associated with Electrocerebral Silence' (1970) 20 *Neurology* 525-33.

patients in an irreversibly non-cognitive condition are not comatose in the usual sense[17] of the term. They are not all in a state of sleep-like unresponsiveness. Some of them are in a state of wakefulness, although without awareness.[18] Patients in this latter category are sometimes said to be in a persistent vegetative state.[19] This term has become so established in relation to those non-cognitive patients who are not in the usual sense comatose that it would now be confusing to use it to refer also to those who do not open their eyes and have cycles of sleeping and waking.[20]

What is needed here is a broader term which embraces all patients in an irreversibly non-cognitive condition, whether or not they are in a state of sleep-like insensibility. The term neocortical death would have some advantages for the purpose of this discussion, provided that the term was understood to refer to any irreversible loss of cognitive function, and not solely to the destruction of the neocortex. But this was not the sense in which the term was originally used. Furthermore, for the purpose of this discussion there are advantages in using a term which does not imply that any one part of the brain determines the presence or absence of cognitive activity. The broader issues remain the same whatever view is taken on this matter.

It has been suggested that it is misleading to make use of the word 'death' in a context in which it is not generally

[17] B. Jennett and G. Teasdale, 'Aspects of Coma after Severe Head Injury' [1977] 1 *Lancet* 878-81.

[18] F. Plum and J. B. Posner, op. cit., 3 (continuous sleep-like coma almost never lasts more than 2 to 4 weeks). See also ibid. 314.

[19] B. Jennett and F. Plum, op. cit., 734-7. See also F. Plum and J. B. Posner, op. cit., 6-7.

[20] When Jennett and Plum first suggested the use of the term persistent vegetative state they explained that they were concerned to identify an irrecoverable state, but that until the criteria needed to establish that prediction reliably had been confirmed 'persistent' was a safer term than 'irreversible'. Plum has since described the use of 'persistent' as 'unfortunate' ((1978) 315 *Ann. N.Y. Acad. Sci.* 224), and the term has been used by others in relation to patients who subsequently recovered from the vegetative state: see e.g. K. Higashi *et al.*, 'Epidemiological Studies on Patients with a Persistent Vegetative State' (1977) 40 *Journal of Neurology, Neurosurgery, and Psychiatry* 876-85. Jennett has stated that recovery from the persistent vegetative state, as he defines it, does not occur: B. Jennett, 'Prognosis after Head Injury', *Handbook of Clinical Neurology* (edd. P. J. Vinken and G. W. Bruyn), vol. xxiv (1976), 669, 673. See also F. Plum and J. B. Posner, op. cit., 6-7.

agreed that the patient is dead.[21] But if there is an assumption that to talk of cognitive death (or brain death, or neocortical death) necessarily implies that the patient is dead, it is as well to contradict that assumption. The 'death' of a particular organ or function should not, without argument, be equated with the death of a human being. Had the term *coma dépassé* been used instead of 'brain death', it would certainly be undesirable to use the word 'death' in describing patients in an irreversible non-cognitive condition. But it is now too late to avoid employing the term 'brain death', and the use of the word 'death' in relation to the irreversible loss of other functions helps to refute the notion that because the brain, or any part or function thereof, can be described as 'dead', it necessarily follows that the patient is to be regarded as dead.

In the discussion that follows, the term 'cognitive death' will sometimes be used to refer to those patients who are in an irreversibly non-cognitive condition, but who have not lost brain-stem function. If these patients are dead for legal purposes, it would necessarily follow that patients who are brain dead are also dead for legal purposes. For the purpose of this discussion it will be assumed that it can be established that some patients are in an irreversibly non-cognitive condition, even though they are not brain dead.

Current legal status

Many of the arguments for regarding as dead those patients whose hearts continue to beat, but who are brain dead, apply also to those who are in an irreversible non-cognitive condition. But the fundamental argument is that, once cognitive death has occurred, the person may be said to have ceased to exist, even if the body continues to breathe spontaneously. Doctors, as well as philosophers and theologians, have supported this approach. For example, one doctor (who uses 'cerebral death' to refer to what is here described as 'cognitive death') has written:[22]

The personal, identifiable life of an individual human can be equated with the living function of that part of the brain called the cerebrum.

[21] Cf. R. Nesbakken, (1978) 315 *Ann. N.Y. Acad. Sci.* 348.
[22] S. D. Olinger, 'Medical Death' (1975) 27 *Baylor Law Review* 22, 22–4.

Cerebral function is manifested in consciousness, awareness, memory, anticipation, recognition and emotions. . . . There is no human life in the [irreversible] absence of these. . . .

I would emphasize . . . that 'cerebral death' and 'brain death' are different things, and that the term 'cerebral death' expresses the medical concept which is equated with the death of the individual person.

If a doctor acted upon this view in practice, and removed a heart from a patient who had sustained cognitive death, but whose brain-stem was still functioning, the courts might be forced to consider the issue. It could come before the courts in other ways also. For example, the defendant in a personal injury claim could argue that as the plaintiff had sustained cognitive death he was no longer a living person, and hence not entitled to damages on the basis that he was still alive.[23]

Were such a case to come before the courts, it would be particularly important that the courts make a clear distinction between the medical facts about the patient's condition and the separate issue of whether, given those facts, the patient was to be regarded as alive or dead.[24] Whether the patient is in an irreversible non-cognitive condition is undoubtedly a medical question. But whether a patient in this condition is alive or dead, for the purpose of English law, is not a matter on which the courts should feel obliged to follow the views of the doctors who gave evidence, or even the views of the medical profession generally. A good statutory definition of death would put the issue beyond doubt. But in the absence of any statutory definition, the courts should here give effect to current usage.

It is now well over a decade since a Member of Parliament said, in the course of a debate in the House of Commons,[25]

[23] The *Report of the Royal Commission on Civil Liability and Compensation for Personal Injury* (Cmnd. 7054-I; 1978), paras. 393–8, proceeded on the assumption that a plaintiff who had been rendered permanently unconscious by his injuries was not yet dead for legal purposes.

[24] This distinction may have been overlooked by Lord Edmund-Davies when he said that 'many doctors now regard as dead a patient who is in a state of deep and irremedial unconsciousness, even though his heart still beats and he still draws breath. One day the doctors will have to make up their minds about the matter, otherwise the Courts will have to decide the dispute for them.' Lord Edmund-Davies, 'On Dying and Dying Well: Legal Aspects' (1977) 70 *Proc. Roy. Soc. Med.* 73. See also Lord Scarman, 'Legal Liability and Medicine' (1981) 74 *J. Roy. Soc. Med.* 11, 15.

[25] (1969) 785 Parl. Deb. H.C. 898 (Mr Eric Ogden, MP).

I cannot accept that dead people breathe. As long as a body is breathing, I cannot accept that it is dead. . . . It might be a remnant of emotion; it might be 100,000 years of history, but to my simple view, and in that of most people outside the House, dead people do not breathe and as long as a person is breathing he cannot be said to be dead.

Since that time the conventional view concerning brain death has changed, and many writers—medical, philosophical, and theological—have also argued that patients who have sustained cognitive death are also dead. But the view that 'as long as a person is breathing he cannot be said to be dead' is still so generally held that the courts should not at present take a different view, even if that view were supported by medical experts.[26]

The arguments

For the foreseeable future, conventional usage will be so clear that patients in an irreversible non-cognitive state must be regarded as alive for the purpose of English law. But the currently accepted view is likely to come under increasing attack, and it is possible that opinion will become so divided that the courts will have to take account of other considerations. It is therefore as well to consider some of the arguments and considerations which might, in that event, influence the courts.

Many of the reasons which have been put forward for regarding as dead those patients who have sustained brain death apply also to those patients who have sustained cognitive death. For example, the first of the two reasons offered in the Harvard Report,[27] in support of the 'new criterion for death', was that:[28]

Improvements in resuscitative and supportive measures have led to increased efforts to save those who are desperately injured. Sometimes

[26] In practice, doctors invariably regard such patients as alive. The report entitled *Diagnosis of Death*, issued by the Conference of Medical Royal Colleges in 1979, says that 'brain death represents the stage at which a patient becomes truly dead' ([1979] 1 *Br. Med. J.* 332, para. 7; [1979] 1 *Lancet* 261, 262, para. 7). However, editorials in the *Lancet* and the *British Medical Journal* have mentioned the possibility of the more radical approach, and not expressed opposition to it. See 'Death of a Human Being' [1971] 2 *Lancet* 590–1; 'Brain Death' [1975] 1 *Br. Med. J.* 356. Cf. *Thurlow* v. *Thurlow* [1976] Fam. 32, 45G–H.

[27] H. K. Beecher *et al.*, 'A Definition of Irreversible Coma' (1968) 205 *J.A.M.A.* 337–40.

[28] Ibid. 337. The other 'reason' was that 'Obsolete criteria for the definition

these efforts have only partial success so that the result is an individual whose heart continues to beat but whose brain is irreversibly damaged. The burden is great on patients who suffer permanent loss of intellect, on their families, on the hospitals, and on those in need of hospital beds already occupied by these comatose patients.

Although this consideration can hardly stand on its own as a sufficient reason for regarding anyone as dead,[29] it has much greater application to those who have sustained cognitive death than to those who have sustained brain death. Even if doctors were not free to withdraw artificial ventilation when brain death was established, those bodies can rarely be kept functioning for more than a few days. By contrast, patients who have sustained cognitive death may continue in that state for months, and sometimes even years.

The other reason often given for regarding brain-dead patients as dead is the desirability of doctors being free to remove organs from such bodies for transplantation. Patients who have sustained cognitive death would be a particularly suitable source of organs for transplantation, as their hearts, livers, and kidneys will often be in excellent condition. But such patients would provide a very small proportion of the organs required for transplantation, so the possible benefit to transplantation if those patients were regarded as dead would not be comparable with the benefit which would accrue in the saving of medical resources.[30]

of death can lead to controversy in obtaining organs for transplantation.' Of course, criteria should not be regarded as obsolete simply because they conflict with the interests of transplant surgeons and their patients—although see W. J. Dempster, 'The Donor Crisis in Organ Transplantation' in *Matters of Life and Death* (1970, ed. E. Shotter), 49-53, esp. 51.

[29] The fact that resuscitation sometimes has only 'partial success', with the consequence that the patient's brain is 'irreversibly damaged', is not generally considered as a good reason for regarding a patient as dead. Children who do not breathe at birth are often resuscitated, but by this time they have sometimes suffered irreversible brain damage, as a result of which they are permanently handicapped. They are not regarded as dead. It is hard to see what great 'burden' is borne by a patient who has sustained brain death (or cognitive death). Whatever it is, it is one of which he will never be aware. It is true that the burden is sometimes great on the families and on hospitals, and that resources have been used on these patients which could otherwise have been used to benefit other patients. But this is also the case with other patients who are nevertheless regarded as alive.

[30] Some of the other incidental advantages of regarding brain-dead patients as dead would be present in increased measure if patients who had sustained cognitive death were regarded as dead. There would then be the possibility of using

The debate about cognitive death has been unlike much of that about brain death, for most of those who favour patients in an irreversibly non-cognitive condition being regarded as dead have not relied on the incidental advantages of such an approach.[31] They have focused on more fundamental issues.[32] Death being the cessation of life, many of them have sought to determine what is distinctive about the life of a human person, as opposed to other members of the animal kingdom. They argue that if a person's brain is damaged to such an extent that he can never return to consciousness, can never perform any cognitive function, then that person has died. The Co-ordinator of the Protection of Life Project of the Law Reform Commission of Canada, E. W. Keyserlingk, has taken this view. In a study written for the Commission, he stated:[33]

In my view, if the medical tests have in fact determined that there is no potential for spontaneous cerebral brain function, even if spontaneous respiration continues, then the human person is dead. Obviously this view is based on the conviction that man is essentially more than a biological 'respiratory' being, and is essentially a rational, experiencing, communicating being. It is based as well on the strong medical evidence that the specific loci in the brain in which these latter functions reside are cerebral or higher brain centres.

At least in the short term[34] the problem is: if a patient

these bodies to provide cross-circulation therapy, for the practice of anatomy, experimental surgery, and studies of the effects of drugs.

[31] See, however, J. B. Brierley et al., 'Neocortical Death after Cardiac Arrest' [1971] 2 Lancet 560, 565. Having raised the question whether, once neocortical death is established, the patient is still alive, the authors state 'Perhaps the most important consideration is the suffering imposed upon the relatives by a person with whom they can no longer communicate but who breathes without the aid of a machine.'

[32] In addition to the writers cited in nn. 38, 42, 44, and 46, below, see also e.g. Jonathan Glover, Causing Death and Saving Lives (1977), 43-5; Norman Anderson, Issues of Life and Death (1978 edn.), 109. See also Bernard Häring, Medical Ethics (1972), 133-4; W. C. Charron, 'Death: A Philosophical Perspective on the Legal Definitions' [1975] Washington University Law Quarterly 979, 1001-4; 'Life and Death with Liberty and Justice' (Book Review) [1979] 2 Lancet 1220.

[33] E. W. Keyserlingk, Sanctity of Life or Quality of Life (Law Reform Commission of Canada, Protection of Life Series, Study Paper), (1979), 62. But see ibid. 62-3, 130; cf. ibid. 64, 187.

[34] That is, in the absence of any statute creating an intermediate legal status so that a body could be regarded as no longer that of a living human being, but not yet a corpse.

who has sustained cognitive death is not to be regarded as a
living human person, what is he? The problem arises no less
acutely with those who are born without the higher regions
of the brain—so-called anencephalic 'monsters'—whom
Keyserlingk suggests could be 'deemed "personally" dead at
birth'.[35] Many patients in both categories will not 'survive'
for long. But some will 'live' for years. If they are not to
count as living persons (so that, for example, offences against
the person cannot be committed against them), what is their
legal status? Are these bodies, in which breathing and heartbeat is still continuing spontaneously, to be regarded as
corpses? If that is not acceptable, may they be regarded as
animals—so that, for example, restrictions concerning
experimentation on animals apply to them? Or are they the
subject neither of the law relating to living persons, nor to
human corpses, nor animals? The answer given in relation to
anencephalics need not be the same as for those who have
simply sustained cognitive death. For even if anencephalics
were not regarded as persons for legal purposes,[36] this would
not be conclusive as to whether someone who was once a
living human person, but is now in an irreversible non-cognitive
condition, has therefore ceased to be a person in law.[37]

If the courts were to hold that someone who was once a
living person, but who had sustained cognitive death, was
dead for legal purposes, it is difficult to see that there could
be any legal objection to these spontaneously breathing
bodies being cremated or buried.[38]

[35] E. W. Keyserlingk, op. cit., 62.

[36] Coke and Blackstone stated that 'monsters' 'brought forth' in marriage, but
which 'hath not the shape of mankind' could not inherit land, but that if it 'hath
human shape', it could (Co. Litt. f. 7b; 2 Bl. Comm. 246-7); see also Braçt. f. 438
a-b; cf. ff. 5a, 70a. This was apparently because of the belief that the former were
fathered by an animal (cf. 3 Co. Inst. 59 'a great lady had committed buggery
with a baboon, and conceived by it'). In British hospitals anencephalic neonates
are regarded—as they would have been by Coke and Blackstone—as human
beings, although doctors and nurses do not strive to keep them alive. On 'monsters'
generally, see *Doodeward* v. *Spence* (1908) 6 C.L.R. 406, 419-20; S. B. Atkinson,
'Life, Birth, and Live-Birth' (1904) 20 *L.Q.R.* 134, 139; Williams, *Sanctity*, 31-3;
Glanville Williams, Letter, 'Legal Protection of Life of the Unborn and Newly Born'
[1964] 1 *Br. Med. J.* 500; C. Howard, *Criminal Law* (4th edn., 1982), 25; and see
also *Euthanasia, Aiding Suicide and Cessation of Treatment* (Law Reform Commission of Canada, Working Paper 28, 1982), pp. 33-4.

[37] But see n. 47, below.

[38] Of course, a statutory prohibition could be enacted. But see R. Puccetti,

Even if a judge did have freedom of decision in this matter he might consider that, although there are very significant differences between patients who have sustained cognitive death and patients who have not lost their cognitive faculties, there are also significant differences between patients who have sustained cognitive death but continue to breathe spontaneously and almost all corpses. He would be likely to recognize that a move to regard as dead all patients who have sustained cognitive death would be very controversial, and that a trial was a particularly unsuitable occasion to determine such an issue.[39] Even if a judge was personally in favour of a statute providing that a person is dead once cognitive death occurs, considerations such as these could be expected to lead him to persist with the view that—in the absence of statutory intervention—a patient who is breathing spontaneously is not to be regarded as dead. He would not consider that it was for him to introduce a fundamental distinction between personal and bodily life.

Of course, it could be argued that acceptance of the view that a patient who has sustained brain death is dead, even though his heart continues to beat, has already involved acceptance of a distinction between human personal life, and human biological life, in relation to some bodies which would not in the past have been regarded as corpses. A patient who has sustained brain death may be maintained on a ventilator for some days before systemic death occurs. But the fact that there has been a relatively small departure from the traditional approach, whereby a person was not regarded as dead before his heart stopped pumping blood around his body, is not necessarily an argument for a much more striking departure.[40] The argument may lead to doubt as to the wisdom of having

'The Conquest of Death' (1976) 59 *The Monist* 249, 252 ('When reasonably assured of a loved one's neocortical death, it would not have the slightest interest for me that this person was still breathing when prepared for burial, however grisly it might seem to those who have to do that. . . . And if the notion of burying a breathing corpse is repulsive, then I suggest we simply stop it from breathing.').

[39] Cf. *R.* v. *Kitching and Adams* [1976] 6 W.W.R. 697, 714 (Man. C.A.). See also Lord Devlin, *The Judge* (1979), 10.

[40] The contrast would be less striking if it became possible to maintain dead bodies on ventilators for long periods.

taken the first step, rather than encourage the taking of the second or third.[41]

As dying is invariably a process, it is not surprising that wherever the line between life and death is drawn there will be cases on either side of it which do not appear all that different. The problem would be shifted, rather than avoided, if patients in an irreversibly non-cognitive condition were regarded as dead. It would then be possible to point to those patients whose brains were damaged to such an extent that they could never have more than a minimal degree of cognition. Why, it could be asked, should the possibility of such an extremely limited function be considered so significant as to warrant making such a fundamental distinction between this patient and one in whom this very limited capacity was absent?

The 'slippery slope' argument may be seen as a reason for drawing the line short of cognitive death. One writer who supports the view that patients in an irreversible non-cognitive state are no longer living persons has proposed a list of 'possible human criteria'. One of these is minimal intelligence, and concerning this he writes that 'An individual of the species *Homo sapiens* who falls below the IQ grade of 40-mark in a standard Stanford–Binet test, amplified if you like by other tests, is questionably a person; below the 20-mark, not a person.'[42] Others who favour the view that patients who have sustained cognitive death should be regarded as dead also use arguments which, if logically applied, would deny the status of a living human person to others who are not in an irreversible non-cognitive condition.[43] Indeed, the

[41] Were it not for the interests of those who may benefit from transplantation, there would have been advantages in accepting that a doctor was justified in terminating life-support measures once brain death was established, but persisting with the view that such patients should not be regarded as dead until respiration and circulation ceased. Death would then still be seen to involve actual, rather than sometimes simply the imminent, cessation of bodily functioning.

[42] Joseph Fletcher, 'Medicine and the Nature of Man' (1973) 1 *Science, Medicine and Man* 93, 97; and see also his *Humanhood: Essays in Biomedical Ethics* (1979), 12. Fletcher had earlier written that 'True guilt arises only from an offence against a person, and a Down's is not a person': Joseph Fletcher, 'The Right to Die', *Atlantic Monthly*, April 1968, p. 64.

[43] See e.g. R. M. Veatch, *Death, Dying, and the Biological Revolution* (1976), 42 ('While consciousness is certainly important, man's social nature and embodiment seem to me to be the truly essential characteristics. I therefore believe that death is most appropriately thought of as the irreversible loss of the embodied

approach of most of those who believe that patients who
have sustained cognitive death should be regarded as dead,
could lead to the conclusion that some patients who have not
reached this stage are also dead. They identify certain functions, capacities, or qualities as essential to 'personal' or truly
'human' life, and go on to say that where these have been
irreversibly lost, 'personal' or 'human' life has ceased, so the
individual is by definition dead.[44] There is unlikely to be
agreement as to what are these 'indicators of humanhood'[45]
or personhood.[46] The irreversible loss of cognitive functions
is at present the lowest common denominator, but there is
no reason why this approach should be restricted to these
cases alone.[47]

capacity for social interaction'), but see D. N. Walton, *Brain Death* (1980),
86 n. 17.

[44] See e.g. R. M. Veatch, 'The Definition of Death: Ethical, Philosophical, and
Policy Confusion' (1978) 315 *Ann. N.Y. Acad. Sci.* 307, 308 ('The philosophical,
conceptual question is, "What is it that is so essential to our concept of human
life such that when it is lost we should treat the individual as dead?" '). See also
R. M. Veatch, 'The Whole-Brain-Oriented Concept of Death: An Outmoded Philosophical Formulation' (1975) 3 *Journal of Thanatology* 13–30.

[45] The phrase is that of Joseph Fletcher: see his 'Four Indicators of Humanhood
—The Enquiry Matures' (1974) 4 *Hastings Center Report* (6), 4–7.

[46] The concept of 'personhood' plays an important role in the thinking of
E. W. Keyserlingk. He says that 'in the *strict sense*' person is a concept 'applicable
to normal adult humans as moral agents' although there is a second, 'social' concept of person 'in the *less than strict sense*'. His example of this less-than-strict
sense is that of the child in the parent–child relationship, 'in which the child is
treated as person though it is not one strictly': E. W. Keyserlingk, *Sanctity of Life
or Quality of Life*, op. cit. p. 217, n. 33, 101. *Quaere*, whether a child who is not
treated as a person is a person in either of these senses. (Keyserlingk later writes of
the need to give determinative place to 'minimal potential capacity to *experience
and relate*' (ibid. 103)—although elsewhere he states that 'If one argues that a fœtus
has the *potentiality* to become a person, one has conceded that it isn't now one.'
(Ibid. 205, n. 135.).) Other writers have a concept of 'person' which excludes
some born and still-living members of the species *Homo sapiens*, but includes
some members of other species: see Peter Singer, *Practical Ethics* (1979), 79,
93–9, 122–5; Michael Tooley, 'Decisions to Terminate Life and the Concept of
Person' in *Ethical Issues Relating to Life and Death* (1979, ed. J. Ladd), 62, 66–8,
80–1, 85–6, 91–2, esp. 92 n. 2. But see Linacre Report, 28.

[47] But see M. B. Green and D. Wikler, 'Brain Death and Personal Identity'
(1980) 9 *Philosophy & Public Affairs* 105–33, esp. 127–8. Following other
personal identity theorists, they take the view that a given person ceases to exist
'with the destruction of whatever processes there are which normally underlie
that person's psychological continuity and connectedness'. They go on to say, 'We
know these processes are essentially neurological, so that irreversible cessation of
upper-brain functioning constitutes the death of that person.' They stress that it
does not follow from their argument that all humans lacking the substrate of

Thus far, this discussion of cognitive death has proceeded on the assumption that it is possible to determine with certainty that some patients who are not brain dead are nevertheless in an irreversible non-cognitive condition. Many doctors believe that this is so,[48] but there is less agreement about the identification of this state than there now is about the identification of brain death. Hence it could be argued that it is, at the very least, premature to accept that a person whom doctors believe to be in an irreversibly non-cognitive condition is dead for legal purposes.[49]

Even once it is generally accepted that in some cases it can be established with certainty that a patient is in an irreversibly non-cognitive condition, there are likely to be many other cases in which it is not clear whether or not patients have sustained cognitive death. Doctors would doubtless treat them as alive until death was conclusively established, as they do patients who may be brain dead. But the problem would occur over a longer time-scale than it does with brain death, and it would be unsatisfactory if a great number of long-term patients were suspected of being dead, but were being treated as alive simply because death had not been established conclusively. There could also be undesirable consequences if the law failed to provide a presumption that such patients were alive until it was clearly established that they were dead.

---

consciousness are dead, for they point out that 'the identity criteria for the anencephalic, never-to-be conscious infant do not involve causal substrates for higher level psychological continuity'. But a different personal identity theory could lead to different conclusions as to when 'a given person ceases to exist'.

[48] See e.g. J. Pearson, J. Korein, and P. Braunstein, 'Morphology of Defectively Perfused Brains in Patients with Persistent Extracranial Circulation' (1978) 315 *Ann. N.Y. Acad. Sci.* 265–71.

[49] One of the leading Continental legal writers on death defines person as 'a psychical-physical (or psychosomatic) human entity; a human being with awareness', but takes the view that 'In the present state of science we should adhere to the thesis that only the death of the whole brain (neither more nor less) means the death of a person': H. A. H. van Till, 'Legal Aspects of the Definition and Diagnosis of Death' in *Handbook of Clinical Neurology* (edd. P. J. Vinken and G. W. Bruyn), vol. xxiv (1976), 787, 790, 819; and see also 821. See, similarly, D. N. Walton, 'Epistemology of Brain Death Determination' (1981) 2 *Metamedicine* 259, 268–73. See also J. Korein, 'The Problem of Brain Death: Development and History' (1978) 315 *Ann. N.Y. Acad. Sci.* 19, 27.

Conclusion

The conclusion, then, is that while patients who have sustained brain death can now be regarded as dead for the purpose of English law, those who have merely sustained cognitive death will not now, or in the near future, be regarded as dead for the purpose of English law. Even if conventional usage becomes much less clear, and doctors come to favour reclassification, judges should be wary of giving effect to the new view in advance of its very widespread acceptance, or its adoption by statute.

IV DEATH BEFORE BRAIN DEATH?

In recent years debate has centred on the circumstances in which a patient with a beating heart may be regarded as dead for legal purposes. There has been much less discussion of when a patient whose heart has stopped beating may be regarded as alive.

There are undoubtedly some circumstances in which a patient must be regarded as alive, even though his heart has stopped beating for a time. Quite apart from elective cardiac arrest in the course of open-heart surgery, spontaneous cardiac arrest is often followed by successful resuscitation.[50] Although such patients are sometimes said to have 'died', but to have been 'brought back to life',[51] for legal purposes death must be a once-and-for-all occurrence. If respiration and circulation are restored in a patient who is not brain dead, he is obviously alive. He must also be regarded as having been alive during the time his heart ceased beating.

But what of the patient whose respiration and circulation cease, and who is not successfully resuscitated? Is the patient to be considered dead from the time respiration and circulation ceased, or from some later time? Professor Glanville Williams has twice discussed an imaginary situation in which a potential legatee plunges a dagger into a patient after his heart has stopped beating, thereby ensuring that the patient

---

[50] Conference of Medical Royal Colleges, *Diagnosis of Death*, [1979] 1 *Br. Med. J.* 332, para. 4; [1979] 1 *Lancet* 261, 262, para. 4.

[51] See e.g. *Lim* v. *Camden and Islington Area Health Authority* [1979] Q.B. 196, 214; *Croke* v. *Wiseman* [1982] 1 W.L.R. 71, 74.

is not resuscitated. Would this be an offence against the person, or would he be merely interfering with a corpse? A quarter of a century ago Professor Williams suggested that:[52]

perhaps death is only when the heart stops beating beyond the known limit of medical recall. On this view, we cannot tell whether a man is dead or merely in a state of suspended animation, until such time has elapsed as puts revivification out of the question. But such a definition would introduce some indeterminacy into the time of death.

More recently he wrote that it seems 'that the legal moment of death is not to be postponed by reference to a possible resuscitation that does not take place, because the contrary view would create formidable difficulties'.[53] On this approach the potential legatee would simply have interfered with a corpse, even if but for that interference the patient would have been resuscitated.

Professor Williams's approach would not avoid all uncertainty. Immediately after respiration and circulation ceased it would sometimes be impossible to determine whether the body was that of a living human being or whether it was a corpse. It would all depend upon whether the patient was subsequently resuscitated. Nevertheless, in many circumstances Professor Williams's approach would make it easier to specify a precise 'moment of death' than would an approach involving a test of irreversibility. But this advantage has not been sufficient to lead legislatures or law reform bodies to prefer a test of permanency to one of irreversibility in this context. If adopted, Professor Williams's approach would have remarkable consequences. If a patient's respiration and circulation ceased, in circumstances where he could easily be resuscitated, a doctor would always be free to 'let the patient die'. The patient would then be accounted dead from the time of the cessation, and the doctor could hardly be said to be under a duty to resuscitate what was, in retrospect, already a corpse.[54]

[52] Williams, *Sanctity*, 18. At the time Professor Glanville Williams was writing it had not been suggested that brain death was a suitable criterion of death.

[53] Williams, *Textbook*, 236 n. 5.

[54] It is unlikely that the doctor would be under a contractual or other duty to take steps to resuscitate what, in the absence of resuscitation, would already be a corpse. Even if the doctor was in breach of a duty to resuscitate the body, it would be difficult to regard his omission to do so as a cause of death—given that,

And, as Professor Williams recognizes,[55] a surgeon would not commit any offence against the person if he removed that patient's heart for transplantation, even if the patient could still have been resuscitated.

Until there has been an irreversible cessation of the function or functions which are accepted as being of crucial significance, a patient should not be regarded as dead. But it would now be wrong to assume that, in cases where respiration and circulation have ceased, the only alternatives to tests focusing on the 'permanent' cessation of respiration and circulation are ones focusing on their 'irreversible' cessation.[56] For, now that it is accepted that a patient will not be regarded as alive if he is brain dead, even though his heart continues to beat, the question arises whether a patient should ever be regarded as dead before there is an irreversible cessation of brain function. In other words, should brain death be the sole, or simply an alternative, test of death? Leading Commonwealth law reform bodies have expressed different views on this matter.

In Australia the Law Reform Commission has recommended enactment of a provision stating:[57]

A person has died when there has occurred:
(a) irreversible cessation of all function of the brain of the person; or
(b) irreversible cessation of circulation of blood in the body of the person.

On this approach, if the irreversible cessation of the circulation

on this analysis, the patient would be regarded as having died before the doctor was in breach of his duty.

[55] Williams, *Textbook*, 236 n. 5.

[56] It would be possible to focus on respiration alone, circulation alone, or both together. To simplify the discussion, only the latter possibility is considered here.

[57] *Human Tissue Transplants* (Law Reform Commission, Report No. 7, 1977), 63. For legislation resulting from this proposal, see e.g. Transplantation and Anatomy Ordinance 1978 (A.C.T.), s. 45; and (less satisfactorily) the Transplantation and Anatomy Act 1979 (Queensland), s. 45. In the United States, the President's Commission for the Study of Ethical Problems in Medicine and Biomedical and Behavioral Research has made a similar recommendation: see the Commission's Report, *Defining Death* (1981), esp. pp. 2, 53, 73, 74 (critically reviewed by J. L. Bernat, C. M. Culver, and B. Gert, 'Defining Death in Theory and Practice' (1982) 12 *Hastings Center Report* (1) 5-9).

of blood occurs before brain death, the patient is already dead for legal purposes.

By contrast, the Law Reform Commission of Canada has recommended the enactment of a provision stating that for all purposes within the jurisdiction of the Parliament of Canada:[58]

(1) a person is dead when an irreversible cessation of all that person's brain functions has occurred.

(2) the irreversible cessation of brain functions can be determined by the prolonged absence of spontaneous circulatory and respiratory functions.

(3) when the determination of the prolonged absence of spontaneous circulatory and respiratory functions is made impossible by the use of artificial means of support, the irreversible cessation of brain functions can be determined by any means recognized by the ordinary standards of current medical practice.

On this approach, brain death is the crucial factor in all cases, even though it will often be determined by the prolonged absence of the conventional signs of life, rather than by the more complicated tests which are necessary when the body is being maintained on a ventilator.

The Canadian proposal avoids giving the impression that there are two definitions of death, and shows how the traditional tests can be linked to the new approach.[59] In the United Kingdom the Conference of Medical Royal Colleges' report on *Diagnosis of Death* lends support to an approach in which the occurrence of brain death is always the event of crucial importance. Having stated that to most people the one aspect of death that is beyond doubt is its irreversibility, the report explained that although brain death sometimes occurs before the failure of heartbeat and respiration, in the majority of cases 'successive organic failures eventually reach

[58] *Criteria for the Determination of Death* (Law Reform Commission of Canada, Report 15, 1981), esp. p. 25. See, similarly, the Law Reform Commission of Saskatchewan's *Proposal for a Definition of Death Act* (1980), 15. For an account of similar Norwegian regulations, see R. Nesbakken, (1978) 315 *Ann. N.Y. Acad. Sci.* 319.

[59] Cf. P. D. G. Skegg, 'The Case for a Statutory "Definition of Death" ' (1976) 2 *Journal of Medical Ethics* 190, 191.

a point at which brain death occurs and this is the point of no return'.[60] It went on to state that whatever the mode of its production 'brain death represents the stage at which a patient becomes truly dead, because by then all functions of the brain have permanently and irreversibly ceased'.[61] This statement may well encourage the English courts to adopt the view that, just as a patient is not to be regarded as alive after brain death has occurred, nor is a patient to be regarded as dead before brain death occurs.[62]

[60] [1979] 1 *Br. Med. J.* 332, para. 5; [1979] 1 *Lancet* 261, 262, para. 5.

[61] Ibid., para. 7. See also C. Pallis, 'Reappraising Death' (1982) 285 *Br. Med. J.* 1409, 1410 ('A person is . . . not dead unless his brain is dead. Arrest of the heart and circulation indicate death only when they persist long enough for the brain to die.'). See, similarly, W. H. Sweet, Editorial, 'Brain Death' (1978) 299 *New England Journal of Medicine* 410.

[62] The issue is of greater theoretical (see D. N. Walton, *Brain Death* (1980), 53–5) than practical importance. On the close connection between the irreversible cessation of respiration and circulation, and brain death, see B. Jennett, 'Death, Determination of' in *Dict. Med. Ethics* 128; J. Korein, 'Brain Death' in *Anesthesia and Neurosurgery* (edd. J. E. Cottrell and H. Turndorf, 1980), 282, 285.

PART IV
AFTER LIFE

10

THE USE OF CORPSES FOR
THERAPEUTIC PURPOSES

> [I]n modern times the requirements of science are
> larger than formerly, and when they are so extensive
> it seems to me that we ought not to entertain any
> prejudice against the obtaining of dead bodies for the
> laudable purposes of dissection, but we ought rather
> to look at the matter with a view to utility . . .
>
> Willes J., 1858[1]

Until 1952 there was no statute which provided for the use,
for therapeutic purposes, of any part of a human corpse. In
that year the Corneal Grafting Act was enacted. It made
provision for the authorization of the removal of eyes from
corpses, so they could be used for therapeutic purposes.[2] The
Corneal Grafting Act was replaced in 1961 by the broader
provisions of section 1 of the Human Tissue Act.[3] This is
now the one statute which deals with the use of corpses for
therapeutic purposes.

In this chapter it is proposed to consider the application of
the Human Tissue Act to the removal of parts of corpses for
therapeutic purposes. The maintenance and use for therapeutic
purposes of whole corpses will then be discussed.[4]

I THE REMOVAL AND USE OF PARTS OF CORPSES

Section 1 of the Human Tissue Act 1961 provides that,
where certain conditions are met, the person lawfully in possession of the body of a deceased person may authorize the

---

[1] *R.* v. *Feist* (1858) Dears. & Bell 590, 598.

[2] See Corneal Grafting Act 1952, s. 1.

[3] The Corneal Grafting Act was repealed by s. 4(2) of the Human Tissue Act
1961.

[4] For an explanation of some of the terms used in this chapter, see n. 10
('coronial inquiry'), n. 33 ('hospital authority'), and n. 63 ('any relevant objection').

removal of parts of it for therapeutic purposes, or for the purposes of medical education or research.[5] The section goes on to provide that, when certain further conditions are fulfilled, the removal and use of those parts is lawful.[6]

A PERSON LAWFULLY IN POSSESSION OF THE BODY

The 'person' lawfully in possession of the body is a crucial figure in the provisions of the Human Tissue Act, for that person alone may give authority under the act.[7] An important question is whether a health authority is normally lawfully in possession of corpses which lie in its hospitals. If it is, then persons designated by it[8] will frequently be able to authorize the removal and use of parts of corpses. But if it is not in lawful possession of such bodies, it would often be more difficult to obtain valid authorization.

The right to possession

The English courts have taken the view that a human corpse is not the subject of property.[9] Despite this, they have accepted that certain persons sometimes have a right to possession of a corpse. They have recognized a right to possession for the purpose of a coronial inquiry,[10] and for the purpose of disposing of the body.[11]

[5] For the purpose of s. 1, blood and skin are just as much a 'part' of the body as organs such as kidneys. It is a Human Tissue, not simply a Human Organs, Act.

[6] Human Tissue Act 1961, s. 1(3).

[7] By virtue of s. 19 of the Interpretation Act 1889, 'person' here includes 'any body of persons corporate or unincorporate'. (See also Interpretation Act 1978, s. 5, Sch. 1.)

[8] See Human Tissue Act 1961, s. 1(7).

[9] The cases are discussed in P. D. G. Skegg, 'Human Corpses, Medical Specimens and the Law of Property' (1975) 4 *Anglo-American Law Review* 412-25. See also Williams, *Textbook*, 678-80.

[10] *R.* v. *Bristol Coroner, ex p. Kerr* [1974] Q.B. 652, 658-9. See also Coroners Amendment Act 1926, s. 24(1), and n. 14, below. In this chapter 'coronial inquiry' will be used to refer to coroners' inquests, and also to those cases (see n. 13) where coroners have power to order post-mortem examinations if they believe that as a result of such examinations an inquest may prove to be unnecessary.

[11] *R.* v. *Fox* (1841) 2 Q.B. 246; *Williams* v. *Williams* (1882) 20 Ch. D. 659, 664-5. See also *Doodeward* v. *Spence* (1908) 6 C.L.R. 406, 411; *Hunter* v. *Hunter* (1930) 65 O.L.R. 586, 596; *Edmonds* v. *Armstrong Funeral Home Ltd.* [1931] 1 D.L.R. 676, 679-80. There are various restrictions on this right, e.g. Public Health Act 1936, ss. 162-163. 'Dispose' is used in this chapter to embrace burial (the concern of most of the cases), cremation, and any other means of disposing of a

A coroner is required to inquire into virtually[12] all cases in which he is informed that there is a dead body lying in his jurisdiction, and there is reasonable cause to suspect that the person died a sudden death of which the cause is unknown, or a violent or unnatural death.[13] In these cases the coroner has the prior right to possession of the body.[14]

If the death is not one into which a coroner is required to inquire, or if the coroner has completed his inquiries,[15] there will normally be someone else who has the right to possession of the body.[16] If the executor has taken office, or an administrator has been appointed, then that person will have the right to possession of the corpse for the purpose of

body. For examples of judicial use of this term, see *R.* v. *Price* (1884) 12 Q.B.D. 247, 250 per Stephen J.; *Scottish Burial Reform and Cremation Society Ltd.* v. *Glasgow Corporation* [1968] A.C. 138, 150 per Lord Upjohn. See also National Assistance Act 1948, s. 50(1).

[12] The reason for this qualification is the Visiting Forces Act 1952, s. 7(1). See also Coroners Act 1980, ss. 2, 3(2).

[13] Coroners Act 1887, s. 3(1). (See also *R.* v. *West Yorkshire Coroner, ex p. Smith* [1983] Q.B. 335.) He is also required to inquire into deaths in prison (Coroners Act 1887, s. 3(1); see also Capital Punishment Amendment Act 1868, s. 5) or in the detention barracks of the armed forces (Army Act 1955, s. 128; Air Force Act 1955, s. 128; Naval Detention Quarters Rules 1973 (S.1.1973/270), r. 93. See also Coroners Act 1980, ss. 2-3). The coroner is required to hold an inquest in all of the cases mentioned in this note, and in the text above (see Coroners Act 1887, s. 3(1); Coroners (Amendment) Act 1926, s. 21(3)), except for those of sudden death from an unknown cause. With these cases he has the power to order a post-mortem examination if he is of the opinion that such an examination may prove an inquest to be unnecessary (see Coroners (Amendment) Act 1926, s. 21(1), amended by Coroners Act 1980, s. 1; Sch. 1, para. 6).

[14] *R.* v. *Bristol Coroner, ex p. Kerr* [1974] Q.B. 652, 658-9. The case was concerned with the coroner's right to possession for the purpose of an inquest, but there can be no doubt that the same principle would apply where (see n. 13) the coroner had the power to order a post-mortem examination, without necessarily holding an inquest. See also Coroners (Amendment) Act 1926, s. 24.

[15] The coroner has the power to permit the earlier release of the body: see Coroners (Amendment) Act 1926, s. 14(2).

[16] The right to possession is sometimes said to be based on a duty to do something in connection with the body. But the 'duty' is not always enforceable: *Rogers* v. *Price* (1829) 3 Y. & J. 28, 36. Cf. *Mutasa* v. *A.-G.* [1980] Q.B. 114, 118-20; *Albert* v. *Lavin* [1982] A.C. 546, 565C. Many of the cases cited nn. 17-23 focus on the duty to dispose of the body, rather than on the concomitant right to possession of it for that purpose. This 'duty to dispose of the body' is distinct from an incumbent's duty to perform the burial service in certain circumstances (see *Halsbury*, vol. x, paras. 1135, 1139) and from the contractual or other duty an undertaker or other person may take upon himself. It would be more realistic to speak of a duty to arrange for the disposal of the body.

disposal.[17] But in most cases an executor will not have taken office, much less an administrator been appointed, by the time it is desired to remove parts for therapeutic purposes. There are three categories of persons who may then have a right to possession of the body for the purpose of disposal.[18] They are certain close relatives of the deceased (in particular, the husband of a deceased wife[19] and the father of a deceased infant[20]),[21] the occupier of the premises in which the deceased died,[22] and the occupier of the premises in which his body now lies.[23] Where these three categories do not coincide in the one person, it is not at present possible to be certain who has the right to possession of the body for the purpose of

[17] See *Tugwell* v. *Heyman* (1812) 3 Camp. 298, 299; *Rogers* v. *Price* (1829) 3 Y. & J. 28, 36, 38; *R.* v. *Fox* (1841) 2 Q.B. 246; *Williams* v. *Williams* (1882) 20 Ch. D. 659, 664; *Hunter* v. *Hunter* (1930) 65 O.L.R. 586, 596; *Schara Tzedeck* v. *Royal Trust Co.* [1952] 4 D.L.R. 529, 535. See also *Ambrose* v. *Kerrison* (1851) 10 C.B. 776, 779; *Sharp* v. *Lush* (1879) 10 Ch. D. 468, 472; *Rees* v. *Hughes* [1946] K.B. 517, 524.

[18] Where it appears to the local authority that no suitable arrangements for the disposal of the body have been or are being made, the authority is itself under a statutory duty to dispose of the body (National Assistance Act 1948, s. 50 as amended; see also Public Health Act 1936, s. 162; Child Care Act 1980, s. 25), and will have the right to possession for that purpose. But only in the most exceptional circumstances would this duty have fallen on the local authority while there was still any question of using parts of the body for therapeutic purposes.

[19] *Jenkins* v. *Tucker* (1778) 1 Bl. H. 90, 93; *Ambrose* v. *Kerrison* (1851) 10 C.B. 776, 779; *Bradshaw* v. *Beard* (1862) 12 C.B. (N.S.) 344, 348; *Clark* v. *London General Omnibus Co. Ltd.* [1906] 2 K.B. 648, 663–4; *Edmonds* v. *Armstrong Funeral Home Ltd.* [1931] 1 D.L.R. 676, 679. *Rees* v. *Hughes* [1946] K.B. 517, which is often cited in this context, concerned the duty to bear the cost of disposal of the body of a deceased wife. Even where a wife leaves an estate the husband will sometimes be under a duty to arrange for the disposal of the body.

[20] *R.* v. *Vann* (1851) 2 Den. 325, 327, 330; *R.* v. *Price* (1884) 12 Q.B.D. 247, 254; *Clark* v. *London General Omnibus Co. Ltd.* [1906] 1 K.B. 648, 659 (though cf. 663). See also Children Act 1948, s. 18(1).

[21] Sometimes a wife and a mother are probably under a similar obligation: see *Re Montgomery, Lumbers* v. *Montgomery* (1911) 17 W.L.R. 77, 81 (Man.). It is uncertain whether other relatives are ever under such an obligation. The principle which Willes J. laid down in *Bradshaw* v. *Beard* (1862) 12 C.B. (N.S.) 344, 348 might be susceptible of wider application. S. G. Hume, 'Dead Bodies' (1956) 2 *Sydney Law Review* 109, 112–13 discusses some of the possibilities. However, he does not always distinguish between the duty to arrange for the disposal of the corpse and the duty to bear the cost of disposal.

[22] *R.* v. *Stewart* (1840) 12 Ad. & E. 773, 778–9. See also *R.* v. *Feist* (1858) Dears. & Bell 590; National Assistance Act 1948, s. 50(3); Children Act 1948, s. 18(1).

[23] *Bradshaw* v. *Beard* (1862) 12 C.B. (N.S.) 344, 348.

disposal.[24] But in the case of a person who died in hospital, or whose body now lies there, a court may be expected to adopt the view that it is the close relatives, rather than the health authority, who have the right to possession of the body for the purpose of disposal.

Lawful possession

Where the person with custody of the body also has the right to immediate possession of it, he is clearly in lawful possession of the body.[25] At the other extreme, where the person with custody of the body has, after a reasonable time, refused to comply with the request of the person entitled to immediate possession that the body be made available to him, he is clearly not in lawful possession of it.[26] The uncertainty arises with the intermediate category, where the person with possession of the body has no right to possession for the purpose of a coronial inquiry or disposal, but has not failed to comply with a request to make the body available to the person entitled to immediate possession. Health authorities are frequently in this position in relation to bodies which lie in their institutions.

Although the Anatomy Act 1832 and the Corneal Grafting Act 1952 both referred to the party lawfully in possession of the body,[27] the phrase does not appear to have given rise to controversy until after the enactment of the Human Tissue Act.[28] When the Human Tissue Bill was before Parliament, Government spokesmen stated that a hospital authority was lawfully in possession of a body which lay in the hospital, at least until it was claimed for disposal.[29] The same view was

[24] In theory, there is always someone who is under the legal duty to dispose of the body: *R.* v. *Stewart* (1840) 12 Ad. & E. 773, 778. In practice, it is not always clear who that person is.

[25] *R.* v. *Price* (1884) 12 Q.B.D. 247, 254.

[26] *R.* v. *Scott* (1842) 2 Q.B. 248. The report of this case, like that of *R.* v. *Fox* (1841) 2 Q.B. 246, speaks of failing to 'deliver up', rather than failing to 'make available'. However the latter expression seems more appropriate where there is no contract or bailment.

[27] Anatomy Act 1832, ss. 7, 8, and 10; Corneal Grafting Act 1952, s. 1(1), (2).

[28] One reason for this may be that the marginal note to s. 7 of the Anatomy Act 1832 stated that 'Persons having lawful Custody of Bodies may permit them to undergo Anatomical Examination in certain Cases.'

[29] (1960) 632 Parl. Deb. H.C. 1232 (Miss Edith Pitt, MP, Parliamentary Secretary to the Ministry of Health), 1254, 1257 (Mr J. Enoch Powell, MP, Minister

expressed in a memorandum on the Act issued by the Ministry
of Health.[30] The challenge to this view came in the late 1960s,
when the Medical Defence Union announced that it had been
advised by leading counsel that, save in the exceptional case,
the hospital where a person died was not lawfully in possession of the body for the purpose of the Act.[31] Counsel
advised that it was the executors or close family who were
lawfully in possession of the body. The subsequent statements
and actions of one Secretary of State for Social Services were
interpreted in some quarters as indicating that he shared the
view accepted by the Medical Defence Union.[32]

Subsequently, the Department of Health and Social Security reasserted the view that a hospital authority is normally
the person lawfully in possession of a dead body which
lies in a hospital.[33] This view is in accordance with extrajudicial statements of Lord Kilbrandon[34] and Lord Edmund-

of Health); (1961) 643 Parl. Deb. H.C. 832, 836 (Miss Edith Pitt, MP); (1961)
233 Parl. Deb. H.L. 57 (Lord Newton).

[30] H.M. (61) 98, para. 6.

[31] P. H. Addison (Secretary, Medical Defence Union), Letter to the Editor,
'Human Tissue Act' [1968] 1 *Br. Med. J.* 516. This opinion was given by two
leading counsel on two separate occasions: see P. H. Addison, Letter to the
Editor, 'Kidney Donation and the Law' [1973] 3 *Br. Med. J.* 409.

[32] This was the interpretation of the legal correspondents of *The Times* and
the *British Medical Journal*. See Marcel Berlins, 'Why Doctors Refuse to Operate',
The Times, 16 December 1974, p. 14; 'Kidney Transplants and the Law' [1975] 3
Br. Med. J. 107. In fact, Sir Keith Joseph was careful not to express any opinion
on the legal position. (See e.g. (1973) 851 Parl. Deb. H.C. *189*; (1973) 855 Parl.
Deb. H.C. *182*; (1973) 858 Parl. Deb. H.C. 355.) His statement that the donor
cards issued by his Department were not intended to authorize a surgeon to proceed without further enquiry ((1973) 860 Parl. Deb. H.C. *353*) is explicable in
terms of his view—expressed on the earlier occasions, cited in this note—that
whatever the legal position, the next of kin should be consulted.

[33] See H.S.C. (I.S.) 156 (June 1975). Paragraph 6 of this Guidance Circular
states: 'If a person dies in hospital, the person lawfully in possession of the body,
at least until the executors or relatives ask for the body to be handed to them, is
the Area Health Authority or the Board of Governors responsible for the hospital.
In the case of a private institution or a Services hospital, the person lawfully in
possession would be the managers and the Commanding Officer respectively.' In
paragraph 7 it is said that: 'If a person is brought into hospital dead the Health
Authority will be lawfully in possession of the body as in paragraph 6, although in
such cases the Coroner will normally be involved.' In the remainder of this chapter, the term 'hospital authority' will be used to refer to the health authority,
board of governors, managers, commanding officer, or whoever else has the
control and management of the hospital in question.

[34] Lord Kilbrandon, in *Ethics in Medical Progress* (1966, edd. G. E. W. Wolstenholme and M. O'Connor), 51. Lord Kilbrandon apparently repeated this

Davies,[35] and with the views expressed by the great majority of legal writers who have considered the matter.[36] But are there good reasons for this view? Almost all of those who have offered reasons have relied on *R. v. Feist*,[37] or section 1(7) of the Human Tissue Act, or both. Unfortunately it is not certain that either *R. v. Feist* or section 1(7) establish that a person has lawful possession of a corpse when he has no recognized right to possession.

In *R. v. Feist* it was accepted that the master of a workhouse was the party lawfully in possession of the bodies of paupers who died there, even though the deceased had relatives who attended the funerals.[38] There was no indication that lawful possession was dependent on any established right to possession, and one judge used 'lawful custody' as a synonym for lawful possession.[39] However, it is possible that the master was under a duty to dispose of the body, and hence had the right to possession for that purpose.[40] This being so, the case does not establish conclusively that a person having control or management of an institution is normally in lawful possession of bodies which lie on the premises.

Section 1(7) states that:

> In the case of a body lying in a hospital, nursing home or other institution, any authority under this section may be given on behalf of the person having the control and management thereof by any officer or person designated for that purpose by the first-mentioned person.

This implies that a hospital authority will sometimes be in

view in an unpublished lecture: see D. W. Meyers, *The Human Body and the Law* (1970), 107.

[35] Edmund Davies, 'Transplants', 637.

[36] See e.g. Gerald Dworkin, 'The Law Relating to Organ Transplantation in England' (1970) 33 *M.L.R.* 353, 366–7; David Lanham, 'Transplants and the Human Tissue Act 1961' (1971) 11 *Med. Sci. Law* 16, 19; Speller, *Hospitals*, 328.

[37] (1858) Dears. & Bell 590.

[38] *Quaere*, whether in law it was not the poor law authority, rather than their servant, the master of the workhouse, which was in possession of the body. See generally *Richard v. Nowlan* (1959) 19 D.L.R. (2d) 229, 231–2.

[39] Dears. & Bell 597, per Wightman J.

[40] See *R. v. Stewart* (1840) 12 Ad. & E. 773, 778–9; *Bradshaw v. Beard* (1862) 12 C.B. (N.S.) 344, 348.

lawful possession of bodies that lie in the hospital.[41] However, it is scarcely arguable that this provision indicates that
the hospital authority would be in lawful possession of a
body which it had repeatedly refused to make available to
the person entitled to immediate possession of it.[42] And once
it is accepted that this provision does not establish that a
hospital authority is always lawfully in possession of bodies
which lie in the hospital, it must also be accepted that it does
not establish that a hospital authority is in lawful possession
whenever its possession is not unlawful, rather than simply
when it also has the right to immediate possession.[43]

The strongest indication that lawful possession is not
dependent on the right to possession is provided, not by
section 1(7), but by section 1(5). This states that:

> Where a person has reason to believe that an inquest may
> be required to be held on any body or that a post-mortem
> examination of any body may be required by the coroner,
> he shall not, except with the consent of the coroner,—
> (a) give an authority under this section in respect of the
>   body; or
> (b) act on such an authority given by any other person.

On being informed that there is a dead body lying within his
jurisdiction, and that there is reasonable cause to suspect that
the person has died a sudden death of which the cause is
unknown or a violent or unnatural death, the coroner is

---

[41] It also implies that it will not be within an employee's implied power to
give authority on behalf of the institution. The Department of Health and Social
Security has advised health authorities and boards of governors that it would be
appropriate to designate senior administrators, doctors, or nurses to exercise this
function. As its Guidance Circular states, the designation may be by name or by
post, and may cover more than one person or post (H.S.C. (I.S.) 156, para. 8).
As to who has control and management of various institutions, see Speller,
Hospitals, 328-9.

[42] Cf. *R.* v. *Fox* (1841) 2 Q.B. 246; *R.* v. *Scott* (1842) 2 Q.B. 248.

[43] It could be argued that as well as enabling designated persons to act on
behalf of the person having control and management of an institution, s. 1(7)
enables the person having control and management, or his designate, to give
authority where there is a body lying in the institution, whether or not on general
principles he would be the person lawfully in possession of it. But a court would
probably read the phrase 'any authority under this section' in the light of s. 1(1)
and s. 1(2), which provide for authorization to be given by the person lawfully in
possession of the body.

almost always under a duty to act,[44] and has the right to immediate possession of the body. However, paragraph (a) implies that even after the coroner has been informed, and therefore has the right to immediate possession,[45] someone else may nevertheless be the person lawfully in possession of the body and hence able to give authority under the Act. Section 1(6) of the Human Tissue Act also lends support to the view that lawful possession is not dependent on the right to immediate possession. It provides that:

> No authority shall be given under this section in respect of any body by a person entrusted with the body for the purpose only of its interment or cremation.

This implies that an undertaker—who, in his professional capacity, will not be the person with the right to possession of the body—will sometimes be the person lawfully in possession of it.[46]

All things considered, it seems that possession should here be distinguished from the right to possession, and the possession which is not unlawful should be regarded as lawful.[47]

If the person with the right to immediate possession claims the body, and the hospital fails after a reasonable time to make the body available, its possession would become unlawful. But

---

[44] For the relevant statutes, see n. 13 above.

[45] The right to possession has been based on the duty to act, and a coroner is not under a duty to act before he is informed of the relevant circumstances. But if the death is one into which the coroner will be under a duty to inquire, he should be regarded as having the right to immediate possession of the corpse from the time of death. In such circumstances, a hospital authority should not be regarded as acting unlawfully in declining to permit the relatives, or their agents, to remove the body before the coroner is informed.

[46] Cf. (1960) 632 Parl. Deb. H.C. 1238 (Mr Kenneth Robinson, MP) ('I understand that it was recently held in connection with a rather unpleasant case which came to the attention of the House that a mortuary keeper was also a "person lawfully in possession of the body".').

[47] Other considerations which support this conclusion include the fact that it will sometimes be uncertain who has the right to immediate possession; that this person may not be available; and that even if he were available he would often be less well placed to make any necessary enquiries than would the person with custody of the body. In the report of *R.* v. *Scott* (1842) 2 Q.B. 248 'possession' was used as a synonym for 'custody', in relation to the detention of a corpse. And in *R.* v. *Bristol Coroner, ex p. Kerr* [1974] Q.B. 652, 658, Lord Widgery C.J. used 'possession of the body' as a synonym for physical control of the body. See also *Doodeward* v. *Spence* (1908) 6 C.L.R. 404, 414.

until there has been a failure to comply with a request that
the body be released or delivered to the person with the right
to immediate possession of it, the hospital authority will
remain the person lawfully in possession of the body. Persons
designated by it can therefore act on its behalf in authorizing
the removal, for use for therapeutic purposes, of parts of the
body.[48]

B CONDITIONS OF AUTHORIZATION

Section 1 of the Human Tissue Act specifies the circumstances
in which the person lawfully in possession of the body may
authorize the removal of parts from it. The conditions of
authorization vary according to whether or not the person
lawfully in possession of the body is relying on a request of
the deceased that his body be so used. But there are two
restrictions which apply in all cases. One is that no authority
may be given by a person entrusted with the body for the
purpose only of its interment or cremation.[49] The other is
that if the person lawfully in possession of the body has
reason to believe that an inquest may be required to be held
on the body, or that a post-mortem examination of the body

---

[48] It is possible to anticipate two objections to the view favoured here. It
could be argued that it is a contradiction in terms to say that a person has lawful
possession of a body if he has no legally protected right to possession. However,
to give effect to this objection would be to give an unnecessarily exaggerated
effect to the technicality of the 'no property' rule (see n. 9 above). Were it not for
this rule, the appropriation of the body from a person who had physical control
of the body, without any right to immediate possession of it, would sometimes be
theft (see Theft Act 1968, ss. 1, 4, 5(1)). Furthermore, the law sanctions his dealing with the body, in that if he takes it upon himself to arrange for its disposal,
he can sometimes recover the reasonable expenses thereof—even from the person
who had the right to possession of the body for that purpose. (See e.g. *Tugwell*
v. *Heyman* (1812) 3 Camp. 298; *Rogers* v. *Price* (1829) 3 Y. & J. 28; *Ambrose*
v. *Kerrison* (1851) 10 C.B. 776; *Bradshaw* v. *Beard* (1862) 12 C.B. (N.S.) 344;
Sharp v. *Lush* (1879) 10 Ch. D. 468, 472; *Schara Tzedeck* v. *Royal Trust Co.*
[1952] 4 D.L.R. 529, 535.) This supports the view that his possession is lawful.
Another possible objection to the view favoured here is that s. 7 of the Anatomy Act
1832 speaks of 'any executor or other party having lawful possession of the body
of any deceased person', which could be interpreted as implying that an executor
is in lawful possession of a body whether or not he has physical control of it.
However, the fact that the phrase quoted is followed by the words 'and not being
an undertaker or other party intrusted with the body for the purpose only of its
interment' counts against this interpretation, for it implies that such a person may
be the person lawfully in possession of the body.

[49] S. 1(6), quoted above.

may be required by the coroner, he may not give his authority without the consent of the coroner.[50]

The Act does not place any restrictions on the manner, or the circumstances, in which a coroner may consent. However, it does not follow that a coroner has an unfettered discretion to give or withhold consent. Any person exercising a statutory discretion is required to take account of relevant considerations, and to exclude extraneous considerations.[51] One relevant consideration is undoubtedly the likely effect of the removal on the coroner's inquiries. However, this consideration does not stand on its own, and the coroner is free to take account of other relevant considerations, such as the benefits which may accrue from the use of the part in question.[52] As well as taking account of all relevant considerations, the coroner must exclude all extraneous considerations. A coroner's dislike of a particular transplant surgeon, or belief that the law should require the written consent of a relative, would clearly be extraneous considerations. A coroner would be acting unlawfully if he permitted such matters to influence his decision.

Pursuant to a request of the deceased: the 'opting in' provision

In discussions of possible schemes for permitting the use of parts of corpses for medical purposes, a distinction is often drawn between an 'opting in' approach and an 'opting out' approach. Under an 'opting in' scheme it would not be possible to remove parts of a body unless the deceased had indicated that he wished his body to be used in this way.

---

[50] S. 1(5), quoted above. Cf. Corneal Grafting Act 1952, s. 1(4). See generally Home Office Circular, No. 65/1977; 'Coroners and Transplants' [1977] 1 *Br. Med. J.* 1418; and David Lanham, op. cit., 21-2. S. 1(9) of the Human Tissue Act 1961 provides that: 'In the application of this section to Scotland, for subsection (5) there shall be substituted the following subsection:— "(5) Nothing in this section shall authorise the removal of any part from a body in any case where the procurator fiscal has objected to such removal." '

[51] See e.g. *Associated Provincial Picture Houses, Ltd.* v. *Wednesbury Corporation* [1948] 1 K.B. 223, 229; *Padfield* v. *Minister of Agriculture, Fisheries and Food* [1968] A.C. 997; *Anisminic Ltd.* v. *Foreign Compensation Commission* [1969] 2 A.C. 147, 171. See generally *Halsbury*, vol. i, para. 61.

[52] Had it been intended that a coroner should never give his consent where the removal might affect his inquiries into the death, this could easily have been spelt out in the Act.

Under an 'opting out' scheme, parts of a body could be removed unless the deceased had indicated that he did not wish this to be done. Section 1 of the Human Tissue Act is not based simply on the 'opting in' principle, but section 1(1) can be characterized as an 'opting in' provision. It states that:

> If any person, either in writing at any time or orally in the presence of two or more witnesses during his last illness, has expressed a request that his body or any specified part of his body be used after his death for therapeutic purposes or for purposes of medical education or research, the person lawfully in possession of his body after his death may, unless he has reason to believe that the request was subsequently withdrawn, authorise the removal from the body of any part or, as the case may be, the specified part, for use in accordance with the request.

Under section 1(1), authorization may be given where the person 'has expressed a request'. On the face of it, it is the expression of a request which is important, and the question whether the person was able to understand what he was doing does not arise. However, it could be argued that a request, like consent, requires some understanding and that unless a person has some understanding he cannot have a request to express, even if he uses appropriate words.[53] There is no reason to believe that the word 'request' must be used —the expression of a wish or desire would probably be sufficient. It is less certain that mere consent would, in theory, suffice. Just as consent is more than mere submission,[54] so a request is more than mere consent.

The request may be made in writing at any time, in which case it need not be in any particular form, or be witnessed. A printed 'donor card', appropriately worded, and signed by the deceased in his lifetime, would undoubtedly be considered adequate.[55] If the deceased had written out his

[53] Cf. Beattie J., 'Medico-Legal Aspects of Organ Transplantation in New Zealand' [1972] *New Zealand Law Journal* 36, 37 ('No age limit is prescribed but it would appear that if a child is old enough to understand and make the request it is valid for a formal request.').

[54] *R.* v. *Day* (1841) 9 C. & P. 722, 724.

[55] See Interpretation Act 1889, s. 20 ('expressions referring to writing shall, unless the contrary intention appears, be construed as including references to

request by hand, it probably need not be signed. It is also possible for authorization to be given on the basis of a request made orally in the presence of two or more witnesses during the 'last illness' of the deceased.[56] A person may make a request in respect of 'his body or any specified part of his body', and the request may be limited to one or two of the three specified purposes.[57]

Where the conditions specified in section 1(1) have been fulfilled, the person lawfully in possession of the body (or, in cases to which section 1(7) applies, any person designated by him) may[58] authorize the removal of any part of the body, for use in accordance with the request. The views of the deceased's spouse, relatives, or friends are, as a matter of law, irrelevant.[59] But although their views can be disregarded, the person lawfully in possession of the body is free to take account of them when deciding whether to give effect to the request of the deceased.

Apart from a request of the deceased: the 'opting out' provision

It is not only where the deceased has requested that his body be used for therapeutic or other purposes, after his death, that authorization can be given for the removal of parts. The person lawfully in possession of the body (or, where section 1(7) applies, any person designated by him) can sometimes authorize the removal and use of parts of the body even though there is no reason to believe that the deceased would

---

printing . . . and other modes of representing or reproducing words in a visible form'). This provision continues to apply to the interpretation of the Human Tissue Act—although see now Interpretation Act 1978, Sch. 1 (where the definition of 'writing' would have the same effect in relation to 'donor cards').

[56] Cf. Anatomy Act 1832, s. 7 ('the illness whereof he died').

[57] The request may be withdrawn in any way, at any time. But although the person lawfully in possession of the body may not give his authorization if he has reason to believe that the request was subsequently withdrawn, he is not obliged to enquire whether it was withdrawn.

[58] Cf. Anatomy Act 1832, s. 8 ('shall').

[59] If a person who has the right to immediate possession of the body disapproves of the proposed course of conduct, he could sometimes prevent anyone authorizing the removal by requesting that the body be handed over to him or his agent.

have wished his body to be used in this way. Section 1(2) provides that:

> Without prejudice to the foregoing subsection, the person lawfully in possession of the body of a deceased person may authorise the removal of any part from the body for use for the said purposes if, having made such reasonable enquiry as may be practicable, he has no reason to believe—
> (a) that the deceased had expressed an objection to his body being so dealt with after his death, and had not withdrawn it; or
> (b) that the surviving spouse or any surviving relative of the deceased objects to the body being so dealt with.

In the absence of paragraph (b), section 1(2) would be a straightforward 'opting out' provision. As it is, it must be regarded as a modified form of 'opting out' provision.[60] However, it differs from the 'opting out' schemes which have sometimes been proposed[61] in that there is no provision for a register in which objections could be recorded, and which would have to be consulted before authorization is given.

The person lawfully in possession of the body may not authorize the removal of parts of it if he has reason to believe that the deceased had expressed an objection to this being done, and had not withdrawn this objection. Nor may he do so if he has reason to believe that the surviving spouse, or any surviving relative of the deceased, objects to the body being used in this way.[62] But if having made 'such reasonable

---

[60] See also Anatomy Act 1832, s. 7; Corneal Grafting Act 1952, s. 1(2) (repealed by Human Tissue Act 1961, s. 4(2)).

[61] See e.g. Organ Transplants Bill 1969; Transplant of Human Organs Bill 1973.

[62] It has been said that 'You cannot consent to a thing unless you have knowledge of it' (*Re Caughey, ex p. Ford* (1876) 1 Ch. D. 521, 528 per Jessel M.R.). Similarly, it could be said that a person cannot object to something being done unless he is aware of the proposal to do it. But it may also be argued that a person can have a sufficiently clear and consistent attitude to certain conduct for it to be said that he 'objects' to it, even though he is ignorant of a particular proposal to act. Even on this broader interpretation of 'objects', there would still be many people who could not be said to object, even though on being informed of a particular proposal they might well object. The problem in practice is that the person lawfully in possession of the body could not know into which category of actual or potential objector a spouse or relative came. At present, it would be wise to act as if section 1(2)(b) read 'objects or would object', rather than simply 'objects'. However, it may be noted that in the one reported case on the analogous

enquiry as may be practicable' he has no reason to believe that there is any relevant objection,[63] he may authorize the removal and use of parts of the body.

The Act does not provide any definition of 'relative', but the separate reference to 'any surviving spouse' lends support to the view that in this context 'relative' does not include persons to whom the deceased was related only by marriage.[64] The courts have given a restrictive interpretation to 'relative' or 'relation' when used by a testator in his will.[65] However this is because 'else it would be uncertain; for the relation may be infinite',[66] and it would be unwise to assume that 'relative' would be interpreted in a limited sense in this context. The original memorandum on the Act advised hospital authorities of the Minister's opinion that the word 'should be interpreted in the widest sense, to include those who claim a quite distant relationship to the deceased'.[67] The current guidance circular is more equivocal. It simply advises that there are 'some circumstances' in which 'relative' should be interpreted 'in the widest sense, e.g. to include those who although claiming only a distant relationship are nevertheless closely concerned with the deceased'.[68] In fact, there is no warrant for interpreting the word differently according to the circumstances. The circular appears to confuse the issue of who is a relative with the issue of whether it is reasonable and practicable to enquire of a particular relative.

Section 1(2) could easily have been drafted so that the person lawfully in possession of the body could never authorize

---

section in the Anatomy Act 1832 (*R.* v. *Feist* (1858) Dears. & Bell 590), the court did not give the word 'requires' such an extended interpretation. This was despite the fact that the jury found that the four sets of relatives would have required the bodies to be interred without undergoing anatomical examination, if the person lawfully in possession of the bodies had not fraudulently misled them into believing that the bodies were being buried.

[63] The expression 'any relevant objection' will be used in this discussion to refer to any former or current objection which would, if known to the person lawfully in possession of the body, preclude his authorizing the removal of a part of the body. See paras. (a) and (b) of s. 1(2).

[64] Cf. *Re Griffiths, Griffiths* v. *Griffiths* [1926] V.L.R. 212, 217.

[65] See e.g. *Anon.* (1716) 1 P. Wms. 327; *Re Bridgen, Chaytor* v. *Edwin* [1938] Ch. 205, 208–10.

[66] *Anon.* (1716) 1 P. Wms. 327.

[67] H.M. (61) 98, para. 8.

[68] H.S.C. (I.S.) 156, para. 11.

the removal of parts of it, unless the surviving spouse and any relatives of the deceased had agreed to this being done. But it imposes no such requirement. Nor does it require the person lawfully in possession of the body to make all possible enquiries whether there is a relevant objection. It requires only 'such reasonable enquiry as may be practicable'.

If the requirement of 'reasonable enquiry' stood on its own, there could clearly be considerable discussion of the extent to which the impracticability of an enquiry should be given weight in determining whether that enquiry was 'reasonable'. But section 1(2) does not require the making of all reasonable enquiries, but only 'such reasonable enquiry as may be practicable'. Putting aside the issue of practicability, what enquiries are reasonable?

As no court has considered the interpretation of section 1(2), it is not possible to obtain any direct assistance from decided cases. In these circumstances, it would seem sensible to look first at the extent to which the law generally gives effect to the objections of the deceased, the surviving spouse, and any relatives, in relation to what is done with the body. If the law generally gave great weight to their views, this would indicate that an enquiry would not be reasonable unless it was fairly extensive. However, an examination of the position in English law reveals that the views of these persons are very often irrelevant. An executor is free to arrange for the cremation of a body even though he is aware that the deceased expressed an objection to his body being cremated after his death.[69] Alternatively, the executor is free to bury the body, even though he knows that the deceased left written instructions that his body was to be cremated,[70] and that the surviving spouse and relatives also favour that course. Under the Anatomy Act 1832 'any executor or other party having lawful possession of the body of any deceased person, and not being an undertaker or other party intrusted with the body for the purpose only of

[69] Reg. 4 of the Cremation Regulations 1930 (S.R. & O. 1930/1016) stated 'It shall not be lawful to cremate the remains of any person who is known to have left a written direction to the contrary', but this revoked by Cremation Regulations 1965 (S.I. 1965/1146), reg. 7(a). See, however, National Assistance Act 1948, s. 50(6); Child Care Act 1980, s. 25(1).

[70] See *Williams* v. *Williams* (1882) 20 Ch. D. 659.

interment'[71] may permit the body to undergo anatomical examination, unless to his knowledge the deceased 'expressed his desire, either in writing at any time . . . or verbally in the presence of two or more witnesses during the illness whereof he died' that his body 'might not undergo such examination', or unless 'the surviving husband or wife, or any known relative of the deceased person, shall require the body to be interred without such examination'.[72] He is under no obligation to consult the surviving spouse or relatives, or to enquire whether the deceased had indicated that he did not wish his body to be used in this way.[73] There is no clear trend in the law in favour of giving effect to the views of the deceased or the surviving spouse or relatives. It was four years after the enactment of the Human Tissue Act 1961 that the Cremation Regulations were altered so as to permit the cremation of someone who was known to have left written instructions to the contrary.[74]

If a court had to determine what amounts to a reasonable enquiry in this context, it might wish to take account, not merely of the general legal position, but also of current social attitudes. The problem here is that current attitudes are very diverse. It may well be, however, that a substantial portion of British society considers the wishes of the deceased, the surviving spouse, and at least some relatives, to be of greater importance than the law normally allows.[75] It may also be the case that many people regard the removal and use of some parts of the body to be much more controversial than the removal and use of other parts, or the performance of a post-mortem examination.[76] A court might take account of these considerations, both to assist in the determination of

[71] Cf. Human Tissue Act 1961, s. 1(6) ('interment or cremation').

[72] Anatomy Act 1832, s. 7.

[73] Nor did the equivalent section of the Corneal Grafting Act impose any obligation to make any enquiries. See Corneal Grafting Act 1952, s. 1(2).

[74] See n. 69.

[75] See generally *Public Attitudes to Kidney Donation* (Report of a survey prepared by Marplan Ltd. for the Central Office of Information on behalf of the Department of Health and Social Security, August 1979), pp. ix, 72.

[76] The issue of what constitutes 'such reasonable enquiry as may be practicable' also arises in relation to post-mortem examinations which are not directed or requested by the coroner or any other competent lawful authority: see Human Tissue Act 1961, s. 2(2).

what is a reasonable enquiry in particular circumstances, and also to counterbalance what might otherwise be the implications of the general legal position. But for the most part neither general legal principles nor current social attitudes are of much assistance in determining what is a reasonable enquiry, for the purpose of section 1(2).

In determining whether the person lawfully in possession of the body has made reasonable enquiries, some weight must clearly be given to the resources—both in terms of finance and manpower—available to him, and to the other claims on those resources. Where a hospital authority is the person lawfully in possession of a body, it is clearly not reasonable for all other administrative activities to cease for a day, while staff assist in an enquiry as to whether any one of the dozens of traceable relatives of the deceased have any objection to the removal of a pituitary gland.[77] It would not be reasonable for even one employee to put the hospital authority to the considerable expense of telephoning dozens of relatives in distant parts of the world, many of whom may have had no contact with the deceased during his lifetime. Even if such relatives were available locally, it would not be necessary to contact all of them before the person lawfully in possession of the body could be said to have made reasonable enquiries. When the person lawfully in possession of the body is a private individual, the limitation on resources may have to be given still greater weight.

In deciding whether it was reasonable to enquire of a particular person, it would sometimes be necessary to take account of that person's age and his physical and emotional condition, as well as his relationship to the deceased. For example, it would generally be unreasonable to enquire of young children, or of someone who was critically ill as a result of the accident in which the potential donor died.[78]

[77] Pituitaries are required for the preparation of growth hormone, to treat some types of growth retardation in children. See generally Editorial, 'Post-mortem Tissue Problems' [1978] 2 *Br. Med. J.* 382.

[78] There are, of course, other relevant factors, in addition to those mentioned in the text above. One is the likely utility of such an enquiry. It could be said that reasonable enquiries had been made even though every available colleague or friend of the deceased had not been asked whether the deceased ever expressed an objection to the use of his body for the envisaged purpose. Although it is possible that any one of them might recall some relevant statement of the deceased, the

In determining what amounts to a reasonable enquiry, a court would be influenced by widely held views concerning what is a reasonable enquiry.[79] It has long been accepted that a reasonable enquiry normally requires no more than enquiring of the spouse, or a close relative, whether he or she objects; and whether he or she has reason to believe that the deceased expressed an objection, or that some other person, whose objection is relevant, objects. Even where a more extensive enquiry is practicable, this enquiry is generally regarded as reasonable. Given this consensus, it is unlikely that a court would take a different view.

Section 1(2), it has already been stressed, does not require the making of all reasonable enquiries. It requires only 'such reasonable enquiry as may be practicable'. An important issue is whether, in determining the practicability of an enquiry, it is permissible to take account of the time within which the part must be removed if it is to be of use for the desired purpose. It has been said that the practicability of the enquiry must relate to the steps taken to trace the relatives, not to the practicability of using the body, since the basis of the provision is to allow a relative to object if he so wishes.[80] However, the Long Title of the Act indicates that the overall purpose of section 1 was 'to make provision with respect to the use of parts of bodies of deceased persons for therapeutic purposes and purposes of medical education and research'. The purpose of section 1(2) is not simply to allow any relative to object if he so wishes. If it was, it would require the person lawfully in possession of the body to contact every relative and enquire whether he or she objects. As it stands, section 1(2) attempts a compromise between the interests of the parties specified and the interests of those who may benefit from the use of parts of the body. For this reason, it requires only 'such reasonable enquiry as may be practicable'. In determining the practicability of an enquiry, there is no warrant for excluding from consideration the time within

likelihood of the enquiry producing relevant information would normally be too slight for it to be unreasonable to omit to make it.

[79] See generally H.M. (61) 98, para. 8; H.S.C. (I.S.) 156, para. 11; Code of Practice, para. 14. See also (1968) 764 Parl. Deb. H.C. 38 (Mr Kenneth Robinson, MP, Minister of Health).

[80] Gerald Dworkin, 'The Law Relating to Organ Transplantation in England'

which a part must be removed, if it is to be of use for the intended and approved purpose. Indeed, this factor will sometimes be crucial. When it is desired to remove a kidney for transplantation, it will often not be practicable to make as extensive enquiries as it would be if it was desired to remove a bone for the purpose of medical education.[81]

Section 1(2) does not require the making of enquiries which are unreasonable or impracticable. But the question arises whether authorization can ever be given without any enquiry being made, on the ground that no enquiry was both reasonable and practicable. On one view, section 1(2) requires that at least some enquiry always be made before the person lawfully in possession of the body authorizes the removal.[82] On another view, an enquiry need only be made if it is both reasonable and practicable to make one.[83] On this interpretation, if no enquiry was both reasonable and practicable the person lawfully in possession of the body could still authorize the removal and use of any part of the body if he had no reason to believe that there was a relevant objection. In such circumstances, section 1(2) would operate like its predecessor in the Corneal Grafting Act 1952, where there was no obligation to make an enquiry in any circumstances.[84] If a choice must be made between these two approaches, the second

(1970) 33 *M.L.R.* 353, 367. *Quaere*, whether the distinction is as clear as might at first appear. The available time would often be a crucial factor in either case. Many relatives who could not be traced in an hour could be traced in a day, a week, or a month. *Quaere*, also, what factors would, on this view, affect the practicability of steps to trace relatives. Finance might appear to be one possibility. But this and other factors might also have to be excluded if it is accepted that 'the basis of the provision is to allow the relative to object if he so wishes'.

[81] A person does not become lawfully in possession of the body until death occurs, and the Act does not require enquiries to commence in anticipation of death. Nevertheless, it will sometimes be desirable to lay at least the foundations for an enquiry, before death has occurred, or been established. This may involve checking hospital records to find the name and telephone number of the next of kin, and the religion of the patient.

[82] Edmund Davies, 'Transplants', 637 ('[T]he surviving spouse and relatives . . . may be all entirely unknown. Even if known, they may be far distant and quick communication impossible. Nevertheless, the Statute . . . does not enable the hospital to say that, if the emergency is so great that time does not permit of *any* enquiry, none is "practicable" and therefore none need be attempted.').

[83] S. R. Speller, *Law of Doctor and Patient* (1973), 174, n. 19 ('If no inquiries are reasonably practicable, then authority may be given without any inquiries.').

[84] Corneal Grafting Act 1952, s. 1(2).

seems preferable. But it may be questioned whether in practice any choice is necessary. It is difficult to envisage a situation in which at least some enquiry is not both reasonable and practicable. Extensive enquiries would clearly be impracticable in the case of an accident victim who was brought into hospital dead, and whose kidneys had to be removed within a very short time if they were to be of use for transplantation.[85] However, at the very least, it would always be both reasonable and practicable to enquire whether the deceased was carrying on his person any indication that he expressed an objection to the proposed use of his body. To ask whether there are any relatives or friends of the deceased who could be contacted is itself an enquiry.

The person lawfully in possession of the body cannot authorize the removal of parts unless he has 'no reason to believe' that there is a relevant objection. He may sometimes have reason to believe that there is a relevant objection even though it is not reasonable or practicable to make a particular enquiry.[86] For example, if he was aware that both the deceased and the surviving spouse were committed members of a religious sect, which was opposed to any use of corpses in the circumstances in question, he would have reason to believe that there was a relevant objection. The fact that it was unreasonable or impracticable to contact the surviving spouse, or any relatives or friends of the deceased, would be irrelevant. He would not be free to authorize the removal.

The person lawfully in possession of the body (or a person designated under section 1(7)) need not seek to contact the deceased's spouse, or relatives, or acquaintances, himself. It would be sufficient if his enquiry of the doctor dealing with the case reveals that such reasonable enquiry as may be

---

[85] Cf. Beattie J., op. cit. n. 53, 37 ('If it proves impossible to locate any person who can validly help, it is thought that the person lawfully in possession will be safe in giving his authority . . . [The Act] only requires reasonable inquiry to be made and does not assert that the spouse or surviving relative must in fact be found.').

[86] The person lawfully in possession of the body will not be precluded from authorizing the removal simply because he is aware that it is statistically likely that if a genealogist and private detective traced all the relatives of the deceased, at least one of them would object. Such an interpretation would render s. 1(2) inoperable. One way of avoiding it would be to adopt the narrow interpretation of 'objects', discussed in n. 62, above.

practicable has already been made, and there is no reason to believe that there is any relevant objection. This would itself be a reasonable enquiry on his part.

C FURTHER CONDITIONS

The removal and use of parts of the body is not lawful by virtue of the Human Tissue Act, simply because it is done in accordance with authority validly given by the person lawfully in possession of the body.[87] The removal must be effected by a 'fully registered medical practitioner'.[88] If he has reason to believe that a coronial inquiry may be required, he may not effect the removal without the consent of the coroner.[89] And before effecting the removal, he must have 'satisfied himself by personal examination of the body that life is extinct'.[90]

II THE MAINTENANCE AND USE OF
WHOLE CORPSES

Even where the deceased left a written request 'that his body . . . be used after his death for therapeutic purposes' the Human Tissue Act only empowers the person lawfully in possession of the body to authorize 'the removal from the body of any part . . . for use in accordance with the request'.[91] It does not deal with the retention and maintenance of corpses prior to the removal of parts for therapeutic purposes. And it does not empower the person lawfully in possession of the body to authorize the use of a whole corpse for therapeutic purposes.

[87] See s. 1(3).

[88] S. 1(4); *R.* v. *Lennox-Wright* [1973] *Crim. L.R.* 529, *Daily Telegraph*, 22 May 1973, p. 7. The stipulation 'No such removal shall be effected except by a fully registered medical practitioner' contrasts with s. 2(2) of the Human Tissue Act, which states that 'No post-mortem examination shall be carried out otherwise than by or in accordance with the instructions of a fully registered practitioner.' Cf. Abortion Act 1967, s. 1(1) ('when a pregnancy is terminated by a registered medical practitioner'), discussed in *Royal College of Nursing* v. *Department of Health and Social Security* [1981] A.C. 800. As to who is 'fully registered', for the purpose of s. 1(4), see generally Medical Act 1956, ss. 7, 18, and see also ibid. ss. 17(3), 25(4), 54(1) (as amended by para. 49 of Schedule 6 of the Medical Act 1978); Medical Act 1978, ss. 21(5), 22(13); *Halsbury*, vol. xxx, para. 3.

[89] S. 1(5).   [90] S. 1(4).   [91] See s. 1(1).

It is frequently desirable to maintain a body on a ventilator, after death has been established, in order to prevent ischaemic damage to the organs before their removal for transplantation.[92] In addition to continued ventilation, this often necessitates the administration of drugs to maintain the condition of the organs.[93] There has been comparatively little use of whole 'functioning' corpses'[94] for therapeutic purposes, or for the purpose of medical education or research.[95] One reason for this is that, as yet, it is rarely possible to maintain heartbeat for more than a few days once there has been a permanent cessation of brain-stem function.[96] Nevertheless, corpses maintained on ventilators have been used to provide cross-circulation for patients with acute hepatic failure.[97]

Although the Human Tissue Act does not provide for the maintenance and treatment of corpses prior to the removal of parts for therapeutic purposes, and although it does not provide for the use of whole corpses for therapeutic purposes,[98] it does not follow that such practices are unlawful. Section 1(8) of the Human Tissue Act states that:

Nothing in this section shall be construed as rendering unlawful any dealing with, or with any part of, the body of a deceased person which is lawful apart from this Act.

There is the possibility that a prior request of the deceased, or the consent of persons with the right to possession of the

[92] Code of Practice, para. 30.
[93] Ibid., para. 31. See generally A. R. Luksza, 'Brain-dead Kidney Donor: Selection, Care, and Administration' [1979] 1 *Br. Med. J.* 1316–19; R. A. Sells, 'Live Organs from Dead People' (1979) 72 *J. Roy. Soc. Med.* 109, 115.
[94] Such corpses will be 'functioning' because artificial ventilation has been provided.
[95] Whole, but 'non-functioning', corpses have long been used for the purpose of medical education and research (see e.g. p. 254, n. 7).
[96] If patients who have sustained 'cognitive death' (see ch. 9, esp. pp. 210–23) were regarded as dead, there would be great potential for the use of whole functioning corpses.
[97] See e.g. R. W. Summers *et al.*, 'Acute Hepatic Coma Treated by Cross Circulation With Irreversibly Comatose Donor' (1970) 214 *J.A.M.A.* 2297–301. ('The donor developed pneumonia, and ultimately, septicemia.')
[98] But authorization can be given for bodies to be used for the practice of anatomy, under the Anatomy Act 1832 (see esp. ss. 7, 8); and s. 2 of the Human Tissue Act 1961 provides for the authorization of post-mortem examinations to establish or confirm the causes of death, or to investigate the existence or nature of abnormal conditions.

body, could authorize what would otherwise be an unlawful interference with a corpse.[99] But, quite apart from this, the maintenance and use of a whole corpse would by no means always amount to any crime or tort. Certain people are said to be under a 'duty' to dispose of the body,[1] but the law does not specify the time within which this must be done. Furthermore, failure to arrange for the disposal of the body would rarely lead to liability being incurred, unless the corpse was left in a place, or in circumstances, which constituted a public nuisance.[2]

The maintenance and use of a whole corpse for a day or two, for therapeutic purposes, would not amount to any offence of preventing the disposal of the body[3]—at least where the person with the right to possession of the body acquiesced in what was done. Provided there was no obstruction of coronial[4] or police[5] inquiries, or of the course of public justice,[6] those responsible would not be committing any criminal offence.[7] A refusal to make the body available to a person who had a right to possession of the body could

---

[99] See P. D. G. Skegg, 'Authorization of the Removal of Cadaveric Transplant Material at Common Law' (1978) 18 *Med. Sci. Law* 90-2.

[1] See pp. 233-5, esp. n. 16.

[2] On the preservation of unburied corpses, see *Doodeward* v. *Spence* (1908) 6 C.L.R. 406, esp. 413-14, and see also e.g. *R.* v. *Price* (1884) 12 Q.B.D. 247, 251; *R.* v. *Noboi-Bosai* [1971-72] P. & N.G.L.R. 271, 279; *Report of the Committee on Death Certification and Coroners* (Cmnd. 4810; 1971), para. 25.01.

[3] As to which, see *R.* v. *Hunter* [1974] Q.B. 95. See also *R.* v. *Roberts* (1980) 20 *Med. Sci. Law* 68; *A.-G.'s Reference (No. 4 of 1980)* [1981] 1 W.L.R. 705, 707F.

[4] See *R.* v. *Purcy* (1933) 24 Cr. App. R. 70; *R.* v. *Pearson* (1954), unreported, noted in *Jervis on the Office and Duties of Coroners* (9th edn., 1957, edd. W. B. Purchase and H. W. Wollaston), 57, n. (*l*).

[5] See Police Act 1964, s. 51(3); *Betts* v. *Stevens* [1910] 1 K.B. 1; *Hinchliffe* v. *Sheldon* [1955] 3 All E.R. 406.

[6] For three cases dealing specifically with interferences with corpses, see *R.* v. *Russell* (1839) 1 Legge 110 (N.S.W.); *R.* v. *Davis* (1942) 42 S.R. (N.S.W.) 263, 265; *R.* v. *Hefferman* (1951) 69 W.N. (N.S.W.) 125. See generally *Offences relating to the Administration of Justice* (Law Commission Working Paper No. 62, 1975), 6-8.

[7] There is reason to believe that the practice of anatomy was itself perfectly lawful at common law: see Anatomy Act 1832, Preamble; *R.* v. *Price* (1884) 12 Q.B.D. 247, 251-2. See also *R.* v. *Feist* (1858) Dears. & Bell 590, 594-5, *in arguendo*. Cf. *Doodeward* v. *Spence* (1908) 6 C.L.R. 406, 415. R. G. Glenn, *Manual of the Laws affecting Medical Men* (1871), 244-5, gives details of the statutory and other arrangements going back to 1540, whereby the bodies of executed criminals were made available for the practice of anatomy.

result in liability to pay damages.[8] However, if anyone with a right to possession had consented to what was done, civil liability would not normally be incurred.[9]

Thus the maintenance and treatment of whole corpses prior to the removal of parts for therapeutic purposes, and the use of whole 'functioning' corpses for therapeutic purposes, will often be lawful.

[8] *Edmonds* v. *Armstrong Funeral Home Ltd.* [1931] 1 D.L.R. 676, discussed in the articles cited in the next note.

[9] On liability for the unauthorized use of corpses for medical purposes, see generally P. D. G. Skegg, 'Liability for the Unauthorized Removal of Cadaveric Transplant Material' (1974) 14 *Med. Sci. Law* 53-7; I. M. Kennedy, 'Further Thoughts on Liability for Non-observance of the Provisions of the Human Tissue Act 1961' (1976) 16 *Med. Sci. Law* 49-55; P. D. G. Skegg, 'Liability for the Unauthorized Removal of Cadaveric Transplant Material: Some Further Comments' (1977) 17 *Med. Sci. Law* 123-6.

POSTSCRIPT

This note has been prepared to alert readers to the more important developments in English law which relate to topics discussed in this book, and which occurred between May 1983 (when the book was completed) and February 1988 (when this note was prepared).

Chapter 1: Lawful Abortion and the Protection of Life

In *C.* v. *S.* [1987] 2 W.L.R. 1108 the Court of Appeal held that a fetus of 18 to 21 weeks' gestation which, even if delivered by hysterotomy, would be 'incapable ever of breathing either naturally or with the aid of a ventilator', was not a 'child capable of being born alive' within the meaning of the Infant Life (Preservation) Act 1929. Unlike Heilbron J. at first instance, the brief judgment of the Court of Appeal did not refer to the term 'viable'. But it would seem to follow from the judgment that a child who is not viable is not a child capable of being born alive, for the purpose of the 1929 Act. (This was the view expressed on pages 8–12 of this book.)

Chapter 2: General Capacity to Consent to Medical Procedures

Section 1 of the Prohibition of Female Circumcision Act 1985 makes it a statutory offence to excise, infibulate, or otherwise mutilate the whole or any part of the labia majora or labia minora or clitoris of another person (s. 1(1)(a)), or to aid, abet, counsel, or procure the performance by another person of any of those acts on that other person's own body (s. 1(1)(b)). Section 2(1) provides that:

> Subsection (1)(a) of section 1 shall not render unlawful the performance of a surgical operation if that operation—

(a) is necessary for the physical or mental health of the person on whom it is performed and is performed by a registered medical practitioner; or

(b) is performed on a person who is in any stage of labour or has just given birth and is so performed for purposes connected with that labour or birth by—

(i) a registered medical practitioner or a registered midwife; or

(ii) a person undergoing a course of training with a view to becoming a registered medical practitioner or a registered midwife.

In determining, for the purpose of section 2(1)(a), whether an operation is necessary for the mental health of a person, no account is to be taken of the effect on that person of any belief on the part of that or any other person that the operation is required as a matter of custom or ritual (s. 2(2)).

Chapter 3: Individual Capacity to Consent to Medical Procedures

In *Gillick* v. *West Norfolk and Wisbech Area Health Authority* [1986] A.C. 112 the House of Lords adopted the view (favoured in the discussion on pages 51—6 of this book) that at common law minors are not incapable by reason of their age alone of consenting to medical procedures. The case concerned the provision of contraceptive advice and treatment for girls under the age of sixteen (as to which, see esp. 172C, 174C—F, 189C—E), but considered views were expressed on the capacity of minors to consent to medical treatment generally. Lord Fraser said (at 169):

It seems to me verging on the absurd to suggest that a girl or a boy aged 15 could not effectively consent, for example, to have a medical examination of some trivial injury to his body or even to have a broken arm set. Of course the consent of the parents should normally be asked, but they may not be immediately available. Provided the patient, whether a boy or a girl, is capable of understanding what is proposed, and of expressing his or her own wishes, I see no good reason for holding that he or she lacks the capacity to express them validly and effectively and to authorise the medical man to make the examination or give the treatment which he advises.

Lord Scarman, like Lord Fraser, quoted with apparent approval a passage from the speech of Lord Brandon in *R.* v. *D.* [1984] A.C. 778, 806. When dealing with the question whether the consent of a child to being taken away by a stranger would be a good defence to a charge of kidnapping, Lord Brandon had said:

In the case of a very young child, it would not have the understanding or the intelligence to give its consent, so that absence of consent would be a necessary inference from its age. In the case of an older child, however, it must, I think be a question of fact for a jury whether the child concerned has sufficient understanding and intelligence to give its consent . . .

Lord Scarman went on to say (at 188—9) that he would hold that:

as a matter of law the parental right to determine whether or not their minor child below the age of 16 will have medical treatment terminates if and when the child achieves a sufficient understanding and intelligence to enable him or her to understand fully what is proposed. It will be a question of fact whether a child seeking advice has sufficient understanding of what is involved to give a consent valid in law.

Lord Bridge expressed full agreement with the reasons of Lord Fraser and Lord Scarman for rejecting the proposition that no girl below the age of 16 is capable of giving a valid consent to 'contraceptive treatment', and Lord Templeman, who dissented, nevertheless accepted (at 201) that:

The effect of the consent of the infant depends on the nature of the treatment and the age and understanding of the infant. For example, a doctor with the consent of an intelligent boy or girl of 15 could in my opinion safely remove tonsils or a troublesome appendix.

Re B (A Minor) (Wardship: Sterilisation) [1987] 2 All E.R. 206 (F.D. and C.A.), [1987] 2 W.L.R. 1213 (H.L.) is an example of a mentally handicapped minor being made a ward of court and leave then being given for a sterilization operation to be carried out. The eight judges who heard the case on appeal, in the Court of Appeal and the House of Lords, were all also of the view that sterilization was appropriate in the circumstances, as being in the ward's interest. The question whether some residual parens patriae jurisdiction remained in the High Court after majority was raised in the House of Lords in *Re B*, but not determined. Subsequently, in *T.* v. *T.* [1988] 2 W.L.R. 189, it was accepted that the High Court does not have this jurisdiction, but that doctors will sometimes be justified in proceeding without consent or court authorization.

Chapter 4: Consent to Medical Procedures

Sidaway v. *Board of Governors of the Bethlem Royal Hospital and the Maudsley Hospital* [1985] A.C. 871 is now the leading case on the test to be applied in determining whether a doctor is in breach of his or her duty of care in advising, or omitting to advise, a patient about the risks of a proposed procedure. (This issue was discussed on pages 82–6 of this book.) In *Maynard* v. *West Midlands Regional Health Authority* [1984] 1 W.L.R. 634, 639 Lord Scarman, with whom the other members of the House of Lords agreed, had said that '*in the realm of diagnosis and treatment* negligence is not established by preferring one respectable body of professional opinion to another' (emphasis added). He had quoted with approval the words of Lord President Clyde in *Hunter* v. *Hanley* 1955 S.L.T. 213, 217, where the Lord President had said:

In the realm of diagnosis and treatment there is ample scope for genuine difference of opinion and one man clearly is not negligent merely because his conclusion differs from that of other professional men . . . The true test for establishing negligence in diagnosis or treatment on the part of a doctor is whether he has been proved to be guilty of such failure as no doctor of ordinary skill would be guilty of if acting with ordinary care . . .

This passage had been cited in *Bolam* v. *Friern Hospital Management Committee* [1957] 1 W.L.R. 582,587, the case which has been taken to lay down the principle that a doctor is not negligent if he or she acts in accordance with a practice accepted at the time as proper by a responsible body of medical opinion (although see p. 83 n. 39 of this book). Before *Sidaway* the House of Lords had accepted that the '*Bolam* test' was applicable to treatment (*Whitehouse* v. *Jordan* [1981] 1 W.L.R. 246) and to diagnosis (*Maynard* v. *West Midlands Regional Health Authority*, above).

In *Sidaway* the House of Lords had the opportunity to rule on whether the *Bolam* test was equally applicable to advice, and in particular the extent to which a doctor should inform a patient about the risks of a recommended procedure. Only Lord Scarman favoured the substitution of an entirely different test for the *Bolam* test, but the other four Law Lords did not all favour the unqualified application of the *Bolam* test in this context. Lord Diplock alone came close to doing so. He stressed that in *Sidaway* the House was concerned with 'volunteering unsought information about risks', and said (at 895):

To decide what risks of the existence of which a patient should be voluntarily warned and the terms in which such warning, if any, should be given, having regard to the effect that the warning may have, is as much an exercise of professional skill and judgment as any other part of the doctor's comprehensive duty of care to the individual patient, and expert medical evidence on this matter should be treated in just the same way. The *Bolam* test should be applied.

However, there was some indication, in the preceding passage in his speech, that he might have taken a different view if the patient had requested information about the risks.

Lord Bridge, with whose speech Lord Keith expressed agreement, did not favour the unqualified acceptance of the *Bolam* test. He accepted that the issue whether non-disclosure was in a particular case to be condemned as a breach of the doctor's duty of care was 'to be decided primarily on the basis of expert medical evidence, applying the *Bolam* test'. But he went on to say (at 900) that:

even in a case where, as here, no expert witness in the relevant medical field condemns the non-disclosure as being in conflict with accepted and responsible medical practice, I am of opinion that the judge might in certain circumstances come to the conclusion that disclosure of a particular risk was so obviously necessary to an informed choice on the part of the patient that no reasonably prudent medical man would fail to make it.

He also said (at 898) that:

when questioned specifically by a patient of apparently sound mind about risks involved in a particular treatment proposed, the doctor's duty must, in my opinion, be to answer both truthfully and as fully as the questioner requires.

Lord Templeman did not mention *Bolam,* or any other English case, but several passages in his speech implied that evidence of medical practice was not conclusive, and that there were circumstances in which a court could decide that a doctor was negligent in failing to inform a patient about risks, even if it was not common practice to do so.

Following *Sidaway,* evidence of medical practice and opinion need not always be treated as conclusive when it comes to determining whether a doctor was in breach of his or her duty in omitting to inform a patient about the risks of a proposed procedure.

In *Blyth* v. *Bloomsbury Health Authority* (reported, very briefly, in *The Times,* 11 February 1987) Kerr L.J. said (at LEXIS transcript, 30−1):

> The question of what a [patient] should be told in answer to a general enquiry cannot be divorced from the *Bolam* test, any more than when no such enquiry is made. In both cases the answer must depend upon the circumstances, the nature of the enquiry, the nature of the information which is available, its reliability, relevance, the condition of the patient, and so forth. Any medical evidence directed to what would be the proper answer in the light of responsible medical opinion and practice—that is to say, the *Bolam* test—must in my view equally be *placed in the balance* in cases where the patient makes some enquiry, in order to decide whether the response was negligent or not. [Emphasis added.]

He went on to say:

> I am not convinced that the *Bolam* test is irrelevant even in relation to the question of what answers are properly to be given to specific enquiries . . . However, on the evidence in the present case this point does not arise, since no specific enquiry was found to have been made.

Neill L.J. (at LEXIS transcript, 45) rejected the suggestion that in *Sidaway* either Lord Diplock or Lord Bridge

> were laying down any rule of law to the effect [that] where questions are asked by a patient, or doubts are expressed, a doctor is under an obligation to put the patient in possession of all the information on the subject which may . . . be available in the files of a consultant, who may have made a special study of the subject.

He said that the amount of information to be given 'must

depend upon the circumstances, and *as a general proposition*, it is governed by what is called the *Bolam* test' (emphasis added).

In *Gold* v. *Haringey Health Authority, The Times,* 17 June 1986 (Q.B.D.), [1987] 3 W.L.R. 649 (C.A.) the trial judge distinguished between advice or warning given in a therapeutic context and advice or warning given in a contraceptive (or 'non-therapeutic') context—where, in his view, the *Bolam* test did not apply. The Court of Appeal rejected this distinction. Lloyd L.J. said (at 656—7):

The fact (if it be the fact) that giving contraceptive advice involves a different sort of skill and competence from carrying out a surgical operation does not mean that the *Bolam* test ceases to be applicable.

(Extraordinarily, Lloyd L.J. and Stephen Brown L.J. relied on the speech of Lord Diplock in *Sidaway*, and appeared unaware of the fact that Lord Diplock's views were not representative of those expressed by the other Law Lords in that case.)

In *Freeman* v. *Home Office (No.2)* [1984] Q.B. 524 the Court of Appeal rejected a submission that the pressures of prison life and discipline were such that a life prisoner could never give a 'valid free and voluntary consent' to medical treatment administered or prescribed by a medical officer of that prison. But Sir John Donaldson M.R. accepted that where, in a prison setting, a doctor has power to influence a prisoner's situation and prospects, a court must 'be alive to the risk that what may appear, on the face of it, to be a real consent is not in fact so'.

Chapter 5: Medical Procedures Performed without Consent

The Mental Health Act 1983 permits some patients to be treated for their mental disorder without consent in certain circumstances (see Pt. IV, esp. ss. 56, 63), but the Act does not regulate the treatment of other medical conditions.

T. v. *T.* [1988] 2 W.L.R. 189 clarified the law on medical procedures performed without consent or statutory authorization. The case concerned a severely mentally handicapped 19-year-old who had become pregnant. Wood J. said (at 203-4; see also 199) that he was content to rely upon

the principle that in these exceptional circumstances where there is no provision in law for consent to be given and therefore there is no one who can give the consent, and where the patient is suffering from such mental abnormality as never to be able to give such consent, a medical adviser is justified in taking such steps as good medical practice 'demands' . . .

The term 'demands' was used to confine the principle to situations 'where based upon good medical practice there are really no two views' of what course of action is in the best interests of the patient's health. Wood J. was of the view that in the case before him good medical practice demanded that an abortion and sterilization be performed, and he made a declaration that to effect a termination of the pregnancy and the sterilization of the woman 'would not in any such case amount to an unlawful assault' by reason only of the absence of the woman's consent. (The 'principle' enunciated by Wood J. is similar to that suggested on page 105, lines 18–22, of this book.)

There are other recent cases in which judges have declared that, in the circumstances, an adult patient's incapacity to consent is no bar to an abortion being performed: see *Anon., The Times,* 28 May 1987, p. 1 (news report) (Latey J.), and *Re X, The Times,* 4 June 1987 (Reeve J.). The women in question had Down's syndrome. In several other cases it has been accepted in passing that a doctor can sometimes proceed without consent or statutory authorization: see e.g. *Sidaway* v. *Board of Governors of the Bethlem Royal Hospital and the Maudsley Hospital* [1985] A.C. 871, 882 D; *Gillick* v. *West Norfolk and Wisbech Area Health Authority* [1986] A.C. 112, 181H–182A, 200G–H; *Wilson* v. *Pringle* [1987] Q.B. 237, 252E–F.

Chapter 6: Drugs Hastening Death

The fault element for murder has been narrowed by *R.* v. *Moloney* [1985] A.C. 905 and *R.* v. *Hancock and Shankland* [1986] A.C. 455. There is now even less likelihood of the law of murder applying to the administration of pain-killing drugs which may have the incidental effect of hastening death (cf. the discussion of the former leading case of *R.* v *Hyam* [1975] A.C. 55, at pages 123–6, 132–3, of this book).

Chapter 7: Allowing to Die

Chapter 8: The Termination of Artificial Ventilation

Chapter 9: Death

There have been no significant developments in English medical law that have affected the matters discussed in these three chapters.

Chapter 10: The Use of Corpses for Therapeutic Purposes

The Corneal Tissue Act 1986 provides for the removal of eyes and parts of eyes for therapeutic and other purposes by persons who are not registered medical practitioners (cf. page 252 of this book). It substitutes two subsections in place of the former section 1(4) of the Human Tissue Act 1961. The new section 1(4) is the same as the old one, except for the fact that it does not apply to the removal of eyes or parts of eyes. Such removals are dealt with in the new section 1 (4A), which provides:

No such removal of an eye or part of an eye shall be effected except by—
(a) a registered medical practitioner, who must have satisfied himself by personal examination of the body that life is extinct; or
(b) a person in the employment of a health authority acting on the instructions of a registered medical practitioner who must, before giving those instructions, be satisfied that the person in question is sufficiently qualified and trained to perform the removal competently and must also either—
(i) have satisfied himself by personal examination of the body that life is extinct, or
(ii) be satisfied that life is extinct on the basis of a statement to that effect by a registered medical practitioner who has satisfied himself by personal examination of the body that life is extinct.

The Anatomy Act 1984 replaced the Anatomy Acts 1832 and

1871. (It also repealed sections 2(1) and 3 of the Human Tissue Act 1961, neither of which provisions affected the use of corpses for therapeutic purposes.) Section 1(5) of the Anatomy Act 1984 provides:

If part of a body is authorised under section 1 of the Human Tissue Act 1961 to be removed for purposes of medical education or research, that section (and not this Act) applies to the removal and use of the part, even if the education or research consists of or involves anatomical examination; but the preceding provisions of this subsection do not prevent this Act applying as regards the body after such removal or where no such removal is made.

Like section 1 of the Human Tissue Act 1961, the Anatomy Act 1984 contains references to 'the person lawfully in possession' of the body (ss. 4(2), (3), 6(2), (3)) and to 'such reasonable enquiry as may be practicable' (ss. 4(3), 6(3)), but does not provide a definition of either term.

TABLE OF STATUTES

TABLE OF CASES

INDEX